The NEW Official Rules

Books by Paul Dickson

Family Words

Dickson's Baseball Dictionary

Think Tanks

The Great American Ice Cream Book

The Future of the Workplace

The Electronic Battlefield

The Mature Person's Guide to Kites, Yoyos, Frisbees
and Other Childlike Diversions

Out of This World: American Space Photography

The Future File

Chow: A Cook's Tour of Military Food

The Official Rules

The Official Explanations

Toasts

Words

There Are Alligators in the Sewers
and Other American Credos

Jokes

Names

On Our Own: A Declaration of Independence
for the Self-Employed

The Library in America

The NEW Official Rules

Maxims for Muddling Through to the Twenty-first Century

Paul Dickson

Addison-Wesley Publishing Company, Inc.

Reading, Massachusetts   Menlo Park, California   New York
Don Mills, Ontario   Wokingham, England   Amsterdam   Bonn
Sydney   Singapore   Tokyo   Madrid   San Juan

Library of Congress Cataloging-in-Publication Data

The New official rules: maxims for muddling through to the 21st century / [compiled by] Paul Dickson.
 p. cm.
Includes index.
ISBN 0-201-17276-3
1. American wit and humor. I. Dickson, Paul.
PN6162.N39   1989
817'.54'08 — dc19   88-37324

Cover design by Steve Snider
Text design by Joyce C. Weston
Set in 11-point Egyptian by Compset, Inc., Beverly, MA

BCDEFGHIJ-DO-89
Second Printing, September 1989

To the fellows — old and new — of the Murphy Center

CALAMITAS NECESSARIA EST

INTRODUCTION

If you know a good story, publish it from time to
time.
> —advice from an editor to
> Charles Poole,
> quoted by the late Bennett Cerf

1. On the Thirteenth Anniversary of
an American Institution

On a fateful night in late 1976 yours truly picked up a
cardboard shoe box and a set of alphabetical dividers and
began filing slips of paper on which he had been collecting
odd mock-scientific rules and laws that helped to describe
our flawed universe. The box was given the imposing title
of the "Murphy Center for the Codification of Human and
Organizational Law."

The prime motive in the creation of the Center was, of
course, altruisitic: advancing human knowledge, the search
for truth, and so on. There was a secondary motive however,
which was to take the frustrations of everyday life — both
mine and other people's — and turn them into something. If
I was to be pecked to death by ducks, I figured to slurp a
little duck soup along the way. *Boston Globe* columnist Leigh
Montville wrote in 1987, "Only a columnist could turn personal disgrace, disaster, and discomfort into a marketable
product." This obtains for the self-appointed director of the
Murphy Center as well, — also known as the director-for-life
— and the Center's many fellows.

This point is driven home all the time. An example oc-
curred on the eve of the director's last birthday, when he felt
burdened by the fact that the word *ancient* kept flashing

across his mind. The aphoristic enzyme started pumping, and this was the result:

Rule of 49. The great comfort of turning 49 is the realization that you are now too old to die young.

In the thirteen years following its founding, the collection has grown to fill ten metal file drawers that have been used to create two books (three if you include the one now in your hands), a dozen posters, a line of wordy coffee mugs, a calendar, and several score magazine and newspaper articles.

Meanwhile the Center has taken on a life of its own as a repository for the cerebral oddments of thousands of people. It still averages four or five letters a day and is listed in several directories of research institutions (in the same books as Brookings and the Rand Corporation). Many have assumed that it is more than a stack of beat-up garage sale file boxes and written to the Center asking for jobs, advice on starting a research institute, and financial grants for research.

Now it has come time to mark the thirteenth anniversary. It is a date of note because people hardly ever mark odd anniversaries, especially the thirteenth. The Murphy Center has chosen to do this because (1) its director has been twice involved with groups that have celebrated tenth anniversaries only to discover at the last moment that it was actually either the ninth or the eleventh, and (2) given that the Center was named for Murphy's Law, the thirteenth seems oddly appropriate.

It might be a good idea to celebrate this anniversary with a special bonus. Without further ado, here are the nine best and most important laws that have ever come into the Center. I say these are the best for the simple reason that they are truly useful guides to persons stumbling around in the last years of the twentieth century.

──────────── SPECIAL BONUS ────────────

Agnes Allen's Law. Almost anything is easier to get into than out of.
— Agnes Allen

Allen's Motto. I'd rather have a free bottle in front of me than a prefrontal lobotomy.
— Fred Allen

Barnes's Law of Probability. There's a 50 percent chance of anything — either it happens or it doesn't.
— Michael R. Barnes

Bax's Rule. You should make a point of trying every experience once — except incest and folk dancing.
— Arnold Bax

Cloninger's Law. In a country as large as the United States it is possible to find at least fifty people who will believe, buy, try, or practice anything.
— Dale O. Cloninger

Hellmann's Principle. Keep cool, but do not freeze.
— discovered by A. Peter Hollis on the side of a jar of mayo

Hovancik's Wait till Tomorrow Principle. Today is the last day of the first part of your life.
— John Hovancik

Lansburgh's Observation. There is no column on the score-card headed "remarks."
— Sidney Lansburgh, Jr.

Olsen's Necktie Law. The only way to prevent getting food on your necktie is to put it in the refrigerator.
— anonymous

The great benefit that has accrued to the director of the Murphy Center has been the sublime thrill of opening the Center's mail every morning. It gets Christmas cards, wedding announcements, family photos, job applications, and long essays on the behavior of the wheels of supermarket shopping carts. In the past four years alone the Murphy Center has received more than three thousand separate envelopes from as far afield as Kathmandu and Saskatoon. They have contained, among other things:

- Hideous fortune cookie messages (e.g., "Don't blame failures on others. You just didn't work hard enough.")
- Ominous unsigned lines often written with great effort on lined notebook paper ("Air Force One is haunted," "Never try to be nice to a man with a tattoo on his face.")
- Elaborate letters from people who have discovered universal truth (replete with diagrams), religious tracts, and chain letters implying that the Murphy Center will come to an untimely demise if the chain is broken. The Center also has a file of letters written in languages the director did not study in high school (Danish, Greek, Portuguese, and so on).
- Unusual objects, including a "perfect mousetrap." Unusual advice, including that from a Californian suggesting that one should not bathe for several days before seeing one's doctor. "This is a potent tool to keep the doctor from asking you to return," she writes, adding, "I've kept good health and good bank accounts with this simple device." Unusual postcard messages, including this one with a Hagerstown, Maryland, postmark, which begins:

Dear Earthling,

Hi! I am a bisexual creature from outer space. I have transformed myself into this postal card. Right now, I am having sex with your fingers. I know you like it because you are smiling. Please pass me on to someone else . . .

- Requests for legal advice — a Dalton, Georgia, woman wrote the Center in July 1988 to ask: "Have you any info on a law in Georgia that it's against the law to slap a man on the back? I have heard this all my life and would like to know if it is true." (The Center's courteous reply was that if it wasn't against the law, it should be.)
- Bizarre news clippings with headlines like WHILE BEING TESTED, ROBOT RUNS AMOK AND SELF-DESTRUCTS, MAN WHO SAYS HE WED MOTHER NEGOTIATING TV MOVIE DEAL, and "BOMB" ON JET A SOILED DIAPER.
- Some have relied on the Center as an archive for the absurdities of the age. For instance, a St. Louis man, Mark Lord, sent a letter along with a Fudgsicle wrapper advertising a soccer ball that could be had for $9.95 cash or 3,475 wrappers. Lord wrote, "My eleven-year-old figures that one Fudgsicle bar a day for nine and one-half years will get him his 3,475 wrappers. But the postage on 3,475 wrappers could be $9.95." Others write small dissertations on such topics as airline food, traffic lights, and the fact that the universe is expanding.
- Several have written to the Center expressing an interest in taking part in its research projects (obviously, people who have never seen *The Bride of Frankenstein*), and there was also one letter from a perplexed member of the species who wanted to know if these laws and rules were the result of the work of some legislative body. The letters have ranged in length from a single line to a handwritten letter of 125 pages containing the major lessons of life learned by an elderly gent from the state of Washington.

Before moving to a rich and all-new sampling from the Center's files, it is worth noting that the latest crop of laws and observations tends to be increasingly precise and scientific and contains little of the generalized negativism of the original Murphy's Law ("If anything can go wrong, it will"). For instance, the last few years have seen several fellows report the verifiable fact that any given dashboard will cause any given car clock to stop working — apparently this is a law of physics as immutable as the one that holds that the force of driving a "for sale" sign into a front yard will cause the hot water tank to explode.

2. Hard News from the World's Smallest, Worst-Funded, but Easiest-to-Understand Think Tank

There is news here from the Murphy Center for the Codification of Human and Organizational Law. Big news.

But first, a little background:

In all the earlier reports from the Center, it has been assumed that Murphy's Law was the prime operational scheme at work in understanding the latter half of the twentieth century. The Center itself, in fact, was named in honor of that law, which says, *"If anything can go wrong, it will."* It dutifully collected restatements of and corollaries to the basic law up to and including this recent example from Gerald Manning of Cork, Ireland:

Gerald's Meta-Murphic Law. Murphy's Law does not apply to Murphy's Law. **Corollary.** If Murphy's Law could go wrong, it would, but it can't so it doesn't.

This caused the Center's director to pause and think. When stated in this manner, the law begins to have problems. There is, at the very least, a crack in a law that does not obey itself. It would be like allowing the Law of Gravity to apply to all but Isaac Newton.*

Here, then, is the news. Increasing evidence is mounting that Murphy's Law is not infallible. This was first put into words by one of the Center's far-flung fellows, "Cleve" Bishop of Littleton, Colorado, who wrote to report:

Bishop's Revision. When you count on Murphy's Law — it doesn't work.

This radical revision had been suggested some months earlier in the form of

Law of Murphy's Law's Self-Application. If Murphy's Law can go wrong, it will, and it will do so exactly when you want to show its accuracy.
— from Onesimo T. Almeida, Brown University

and

Gayer's Amendment to Murphy's Law. Anything that can go wrong will go wrong, except at the repair shop, where it will magically, mysteriously (and temporarily) repair itself. (Once outside the repair shop again, see Murphy's Law.)

Or, as German fellow Gisela Herzfeld of Hannover discovered,

All you *want* to go wrong does *not*. [Alles, was schiefgehen <u>soll</u>, geht <u>nicht</u> schief.]

The positive corollary of this is

---

*Fellow Gene F. Hoffnagle of Staatsburg, N.Y., suggests that this crack in the law can be useful:

Hoffnagle's Quandary or Anticipatory Paradox. Just when Murphy's Law is certain to apply, it doesn't — thus confirming Murphy's Law.

Osgood's Exception. Whatever can go right, might!

This was stated by radio commentator Charles Osgood after telling the story of a family that had unwittingly stored four bottles of nitroglycerin on a shelf in their basement for forty-one years without incident. When the bottles were discovered and destroyed by a police bomb squad, it was estimated that there was enough power in them to have destroyed several city blocks.

But there is more to this. What we are witnessing is not an exception or two but a serious flaw: Murphy's Law applies to Murphy's Law. Another Murphy fellow, D. Park Teter of Hazelhurst, Wisconsin, expressed this as

Murphy's Flaw. If anything *can't* go wrong [i.e., Murphy's Law], it will.

Halley's Comet is a good case in point. If Murphy's Law had been at work, it would have slammed into the earth or, at the very least, created widespread panic. Instead it made itself all but invisible. Typical was a *Washington Post* editorial bidding farewell to the biggest celestial flop since Comet Kohoutek made itself all but invisible. It noted that "despite the Halley's Comet dolls, the Halley's Comet guidebooks, and the Halley's Comet star maps published daily in the newspaper, not a single person in the metropolitan area actually got an eyeful."

The law in effect for the Comet Halley was, in fact,

Fetridge's Law. Important things that are supposed to happen do not happen, especially when people are looking.

The little-known law was named by and for Claude Fetridge, an engineer working for NBC Radio, who in 1936 came up with the idea of a live broadcast to report on the departure of the swallows from their roost at Mission San

Juan Capistrano on St. John's Day, October 23. Fetridge's equipment-laden crew arrived to find that the swallows had left a day early. The law was all but forgotten until H. Allen Smith wrote of it in a 1963 essay in an attempt to explain why a toothache that strikes suddenly on Sunday on the golf course disappears while walking up the stairs to the dentist's office on Monday.

Fellows of the Murphy Center have reported a number of Fetridgean events. Here is one that appeared in a 1984 letter to the Center from William G. Downs of Omaha:

> I was once privileged to attend an outstanding proof of the absolute truth of Fetridge's law. . . . It was in Sioux City, Iowa, the occasion was the opening of a new channel of the Floyd River, which was being diverted to avoid a repetition of a disastrous flood in the fifties. The corp of engineers had spent millions on levees, bank riprap, etc. The Mayor, City Council, chief of the engineers, and a representative of the Iowa Governor's Office gathered to see the great event. The diversion dam had been mined so that a charge would open and send the water down the new channel. All set: TV cameras ready, telephoto lenses on newspaper [cameras]. Down the plunger on the charge box and a little, feeble poof — a puff of smoke. Dam intact.

Put another way: if Murphy's Law worked, we would never board an airplane; but Fetridge's, Bishops', *et al.* allow us to get on a plane with full knowledge that we will spend time "holding" on the runway and in the air and that inflight service will always start at the other end of the cabin.

Fetridge may, in fact, get us to the year 2000. For years we have been listening to a parade of witnesses before congressional hearings warning us of all sorts of potential Murphetic disasters. They stack up like so much cordwood, and there are now doomsday scenarios that are hot (the greenhouse effect) and cold (your new ice age and nuclear winter), while others foretell a disastrous population explosion and still others portray a population decimated by disease and toxic waste. Murphy's Law would have the polar ice cap melt way ahead of the scenario; Fetridge's Law allows planeloads of experts to return from the Poles to allow sheepishly that Pittsburgh will not become the next Atlantic City — that it may be getting warmer, but not that warm.

Even at this late date, Fetridge deserves to be honored for his discovery. Perhaps they could name a posited environmental disaster for him (the dreaded Fetridge effect) or, better yet, how about Comet Fetridge?

Finally, there is the case of the Murphy Center itself, which so far has been exempt from the law. Without a dime in federal or philanthropic grant money, it has forged ahead without a major or minor disaster. (To its everlasting credit, it was once preemptorily turned down for a grant from a philanthropic foundation which it had not asked for in the first place.)

It has never spent $435 on a hammer or $7,662 on a coffeepot, assembled 2,700 pairs of shoes, put its petty cash in a faltering savings and loan, or been visited by a crew from "60 Minutes." It has no policies and tolerates no meetings, and there is no organizational chart. At one point the director considered dividing the Center's work into two divisions — the Division of Human Imperfectibility and the Institute for the Study of the Perverse Nature of Inanimate Objects (for wobbly shopping-cart wheels, mean-spirited zippers, and the like — but this was finally rejected as too bureaucratic.

On the contrary, the Center has continued to attract followers who freely offer it their prized discoveries and observations. They hail from all fifty states, all but one of the Canadian Provinces, and thirty other countries, from Australia to Zimbabwe.

Here, then, is proof of the Center's riches in the form of the latest crop of rules, laws, and observations collected between 1979 and 1988. Not all of these are new (one of the A entries is actually two hundred years old), but they all apply. They are published in strict accordance with a discovery reported by Charles Einstein in the *New York Times* of September 7, 1986:

DiGiovanni's Law. The number of laws expands only to fill the publishing space available.

If you have half as much fun reading this as we had assembling it, then we had twice as much fun as you.
> — The Director and the Fellows of the Murphy Center (who borrowed the sentiment from Monty Python.)

A

Abley's Explanation. Marriage is the only union that cannot be organized. Both sides think they are management.
— William J. Abley, Kamloops, British Columbia, Canada

Abrey's Law. The motive for motiveless crimes is that the wrongdoers wish to demonstrate their own rottenness.
— John Abrey, Cleveland, England

Accounting, The Four Laws of. (1) Trial balances don't. (2) Working capital doesn't. (3) Liquidity tends to run out. (4) Return on investments never will.
— anonymous

Achilles' Biological Findings. (1) If a child looks like his father, that's heredity. If he looks like a neighbor, that's environment. (2) A lot of time has been wasted arguing over who came first — the chicken or the egg. It was undoubtedly the rooster.
— The late Ambassador Theodore C. Achilles, Washington, D.C.

Ackley's Law. Every recovery is hailed by an incumbent president as the result of his own wise policies, while every

recession is condemned by him as the result of the mistaken policies of his predecessor.
— Gardner Ackley, chairman of the Council of Economic Advisors under President Lyndon B. Johnson, who revealed his law upon his recent retirement as professor of economics at the University of Michigan; from Neal Wilgus, Albuquerque, N.M.

Ackley's Second Axiom. Familiarity breeds attempt. **Third Law of Roller Skating.** Everyone spends at least SOME time on the floor (or sidewalk).
— Bob Ackley, Plattsmouth, Neb.

ACW's Theorems of Practical Physics. (1) When reading a magazine story, it is always continued on an unnumbered page — usually in the middle of the special advertising section. (2) The value of an object is inversely proportional to the security of its packaging (compare a $.25 package of faucet washers with the velvet-lined box containing a $6,000 diamond ring). (3) The volume times the frequency of the neighboring dog's bark is inversely proportional to the intelligence of its owner.
— Ashley C. Worsley, Baton Rouge, La.

Adams's Law. (1) Women don't know what they want; they don't like what they have got. (2) Men know very well what they want; having got it, they begin to lose interest.
— A. W. Adams, Magdalen College, Oxford, England

Addis's Admonitions. (1) If it don't fit in a pigeonhole, maybe it ain't a pigeon. (2) Never play cat-and-mouse games if you're a mouse. (3) Ambiguity is the first refuge of the wrong. (4) The shadow of your goalpost is better than no shade at all. (5) There's no cure for the common scold. (6) The weak shall inhibit the earth. (7) You will never see a cat obedience school.
— Don Addis, St. Petersburg, Fla.

Adkins's Rule of Milk and Other Precious Commodities. The less you have, the more you spill.
— Betsy Adkins, Gardiner, Me.

Adler's Distinction. Language is all that separates us from the lower animals, and from the bureaucrats.
— Jerry Adler, *Newsweek,* December 15, 1980; from Robert D. Specht

Advertising Admonition. In writing a patent medicine advertisement, first convince the reader that he has the disease he is reading about, secondly, that it is curable.
— R. F. Fenno, 1908

Advice to Officers of the British Army. (1) Ignorance of your profession is likewise best concealed by solemnity and silence, which pass for profound knowledge upon the generality of mankind. A proper attention to these, together with extreme severity, particularly in trifles, will soon procure you the character of a good officer. (2) As you probably did not rise to your present distinguished rank by your own merit, it cannot be reasonably be expected that you should promote others on that score. (3) Be sure to give out a number of orders. . . . The more trifling they are, the more it shews (sic) your attention to the service; and should your orders contradict one another, it will give you an opportunity of altering them, and find subject for fresh regulations.
— discovered by Stuart G. Vogt of Clarkesville, Tenn. who has a copy of the sixth edition of the small book entitled *Advice to the Officers of the British Army*, published in 1783

Agel's Law of Tennis Doubles in which a Husband and Wife Are on the Same Side. Whenever the husband poaches on his wife's side of the court and shouts, "I've got it, I've got it," you can safely bet that he doesn't.
— Jerome Agel, *New York Times*, July 30, 1980

Air Force Inertia Axiom. Consistency is always easier to defend than correctness.
— anonymous; from Russell Fillers, Bethel, Conn.

Airline Food Facts. Believe it or not, there are only two things wrong with airline food — One, the food. Two, the way it's prepared.
— in an ad for Midway Metrolink, *New York Times,* June 7, 1983; from Joseph C. Goulden, Washington, D.C.

Mrs. Albert's Law. If the house is neat, it doesn't have to be clean.
— forwarded by Dr. Bernard L. Albert, Scarsdale, N.Y.

Albrecht's Analogy. I have a vacuum-tube mind in a solid-state world.
— George Albrecht, Bethesda, Md.

Albrecht's Epistolary Effort. Troublesome correspondence that is postponed long enough will eventually become irrelevant.
— Mark Albrecht; from Brooks Alexander, Berkeley, Calif.

Alcoholic Axiom. The effort and energy an intoxicated person spends trying to prove he is sober is directly proportionate to how intoxicated he is.
— Randall L. Koch, Kenosha, Wisc.

Alden's Laws. (1) Giving away baby clothes and furniture is a major cause of pregnancy. (2) Always be backlit. (3) Sit down whenever possible.
— Nancy Alden, Drexel Hill, Pa.

Alex's Iron Axiom. Life is the ultimate I.Q. test.
— Alex Fraser, Washington, D.C.

Alice's Conclusion. A genius is never housebroken, and if a writer, he is always too much in the house, with his overflowing books and papers that must not be touched, and his odd visitors, and his superhuman need of quiet — or of immediate comforting companionship.

> — Jacques Barzun, on Alice Gibbens's understanding of Henry James, in *A Stroll with William James*; from Fred Dyer

Alice's Law of Compensatory Cash Flow. Any money not spent on a luxury one considered even briefly is the equivalent of windfall income and should be spent accordingly.

> — Alice Trillin, quoted by her husband, Calvin, in *Alice, Let's Eat*; from John R. Labadie, Seattle, Wash.

Alicia's Discovery. When you move something to a more logical place, you only can remember where it used to be and your decision to move it.

> — Alicia K. Dustira, New Haven, Conn.

Alida's Rule. The larger the house, the more likely the addition.

> — Alida Kane, Washington, D.C.

Alinsky's Sword. Favors granted always become defined as rights.

> — Saul Alinsky, 1960s community organizer; from Stu Goldstein, M.D.; who adds, "Cuts both ways: to the 'ins', as a warning, to the 'outs' as a device. 'Can't we just this once, as a special favor [have a variance from the code; stay up late; etc.]?

Alkula's Observation. A library will be most busy on Thursday. Everyone remembers Thursday that they have something due on Friday, hence the rush. Corporate/R&D/Techical libraries will be the most busy 11–2 Thursdays be-

cause everyone decides to "do a little research on my lunch hour."
— Joan C. Alkula, Fort Jackson, S.C.

Allcock's Law of Communication. The time that passes before you hear about an event is in direct proportion to the extent to which it affects you.
— John Allcock, University of Bradford, Bradford West Yorkshire, England

Allen's Formula. If you want to be a success in life, just show up 80 percent of the time.
— writer/actor/director Woody Allen, quoted in Chuck Conconi's column, *Washington Post*, November 30, 1984

Allen's Lament. Everybody wants to be waited on.
— Mary Allen, McLean, Va.

Allen's Law of Popularity. The more popular something is, the more likely it is that a religious personage will object to it.
— Stephen Allen, Essex Junction, Vt.

Allen's Reassurance. He's got more talent in his whole body than you've got in your little finger.
— Gracie Allen, heard on the rebroadcast of an old radio show, WAMU

Allen's Rule of Universal Constancy. The only thing constant in the Navy is the varying rate of change.
— from Daniel K. Snyder, Pearl City, Hawaii, who attributes it to Bob Allen and adds, "Codified at the Fleet Ballistic Missile Training Center in Charleston, South Carolina, in early 1977, but since that time found to be applicable not only to the Navy, but to the world in general"

Allen's Tenet. The strength of one's opinion on any matter in controversy is inversely proportional to the amount of knowledge that the person has on that subject.
— Patrick J. Allen, Chicago, Ill.

Almeida's Law of Book Reviews. No book is as good or as bad as its reviewer says. **Corollary.** If the reviewer says its neither, it definitely is not that either.
— Onesimo T. Almeida, Brown University

Alt's Axiom. A parent will always worry about the wrong child. **Scholl's Corollary.** A child will always worry about the wrong parent.
— Don Alt and Marilyn Alt Scholl, Deerfield, Ill., from the latter

Aman's Discovery. Management is always trying to fine-tune the solution before it defines the problem.
— Wayne Aman, Burnsville, Minn.

Ames's Working Hypothesis. The self-employed person is uniquely in a position to define success however he pleases.
— Mary E. Ames, *Washington Post,* March 6, 1983

Amis's Admonition. You can't believe anyone but yourself, and don't trust yourself too completely. **Amis's Advice.** Go ahead and be different — if you think you can stand the beating you'll get. **Amis's Discovery.** There are a lot more cowboy boots than there are cowboys. **Amis's Famous Saying.** Obesity looks best on fat people.
— Jim Amis, Springfield, Mo.

Amos's Law. All my ideas are good, it's only the people who put them into practice that aren't.
— the character Amos Brearly, British "Emmerdale Farm" TV series, from Peter Scott, Portsmouth, England

Amundsen's Discovery. Victory awaits those who have everything in order. People call this luck.
— polar explorer Roald Amundsen; from Marshall L. Smith

Ancient Volkswagen Proverb. Anything adjustable will sooner or later need adjustment.
— newspaper ad, *California Aggie,* November 23, 1983

Andersen's Answer. It's all the same.[Submitted with this notation: "Five or six years ago, after twenty-one years of fruitlessly searching for my own personal ticket to immortality, I was approaching a state of abject despair. On my twenty-second birthday, in what might be loosely described as a beatific visitation, I was provided with **Andersen's Answer.** . . . Anyway, I was afraid that I might lose track of this indispensable truth, so I went and had it tattooed onto my right arm." A photo of the tattoo was enclosed.]
— Lance Andersen, Anchorage, Alaska

Andersen's Discovery. It matters not so much whether you do something well or badly, but how you get out of doing it honestly.
— Kurt Andersen, *The Real Thing*

Anderson's Distinction. My grandfather believed there are two kinds of people — those who know how the world fits together and those who think they know. The former work in hardware stores, the latter in politics.
— Josef Anderson, *Los Angeles Times,* October 5, 1980; from Robert D. Specht

Andrea's Admonition. Never bestow profanity upon a driver who has wronged you in some way. If you think his window is closed and he can't hear you, it isn't and he can.
— Margo-Rita Andrea Kissell, Toledo, Ohio

Andrea's Law of Diminishing Returns. The time it takes to return from someplace is always shorter than the time it took to get there. This is because you've been there already.
— Andrea L. Miller, Downey, Calif.

Anjard's Teen Theorem. Their mouths grow disproportionate to their height.
— Dr. Ron Anjard, Kokomo, Ind.

Ann's Law of Inevitability. You never meet that terrific person until the day before your vacation ends.
— Ann L. Moore, Exeter, N.H.

Anonymity, Superior Credibility of. People are more likely to believe a quote if it is anonymous.
— Steve Stine, Skokie, Ill., who adds, "I have noted that people believe a quote 'author unknown' so much better that sometimes known attributions are deleted." An example follows:

Anon's Contribution to the National Security Debate. The difference between the military and the Boy Scouts of America is the Boy Scouts are allowed to carry knives and they have adult leadership.
— found by Lt. Col. N. E. Kass, Fort Walton Beach, Fla.

Armitage's Finding. Anything put off this morning will reach critical mass during lunch break.
— R. Armitage, Scunthorpe, England

Armstrong's Collection Law. If the check is truly in the mail, it is surely made out to someone else.
— James S. Armstrong, San Francisco, Calif.

Asa's Law. Every author hopes that at least one of his epigrams will grow up to be a cliché.
— Asa Wilgus, *Sparks from the Scissor Grinder,* 1950; from distant relative Neal Wilgus

Austin's Law. If there is no legitimate objection to progress, an illegitimate one will be found.
— E. H. Austin; from James Honig, Cocoa, Fla.

"Automatic" Defined. If something is automatic, that simply means that you can't repair it yourself.
— unknown, radio call-in, KDKA

Avery's Razor. Show me a man that doesn't like Cadillacs and I'll show you a man of violent opinions. All of them wrong.
— the late H. Allen Smith, from his fictional neighbor, Avery; from David Ennes, Sequim, Wash.

Babbitt's Evolutionary Discovery. Evan Mecham proves that Darwin was wrong.
— Senator Bruce Babbitt, former governor of Arizona, on the then-governor, quoted in *Newsweek,* November 16, 1987

Backhouse's Law. Salary is inversely proportional to the amount of time spent serving the public.
— Roger Backhouse, Ilford, Essex, England

Badger's Indiana State Police Rule. Few motorists have a clean enough conscience to pass a police car on the highway even when it is traveling below the speed limit.
— Joseph E. Badger, Santa Claus, Ind.

Bagdikian's Observation. Trying to be a first-rate reporter on the average American newspaper is like trying to play Bach's *Saint Matthew Passion* on a ukulele. . . .
— Ben Bagdikian, *The Effete Conspiracy*; from Robert D. Specht

Bailey's Law of the Kinked Helix. A telephone cord hangs freely with no kinks only in television shows. **Bailey's Law of the Disappearing Signature.** An ink pen will run dry in the middle of a flourishing signature on a very important letter that has just been retyped for the fifth time.
— Kent Bailey, Vienna, Va.

Bailey's Revised Conclusion. We certainly got the evil of two lessers.
— Lansing Bailey, letter to *Newsweek,* December 1, 1980; from Robert D. Specht

Baird's Law. Sex, like money, is an inexhaustible commodity. The problem is getting others to part with it. **Corollary 1.** Getting others to part with it is exhausting. **Corollary 2.** The other person will become exhausted second.
— J. Stacey Baird, Hanover Park, Ill.

Bakalar's Three Laws of Publishing. (1) Whenever you show an author the cover of his book before publication, he hates it. (2) Whenever an author cites a specific clause of his contract, he cites it incorrectly and the error is in his favor. (3) Whenever anyone in the world of publishing — author, editor, publisher, anyone — says, "It's not the money, it's the principle," it's . . .well, you know what it is.
— Nicholas Bakalar, New York, N.Y.

Baker's First Law of Federal Geometry. A block grant is a solid mass of money surrounded on all sides by governors.
— Ross K. Baker, *American Demographics,* January 1982

Baker's Law of Economics. You do not want the one you can afford.
— Scott R. Baker, Cleveland, Ohio

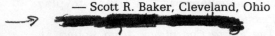

Balliew's Laws for Switchboard Operators. (1) The phone rings least when you have nothing else to do. (2) When a person asks to be put on hold, he will not be there when you get back to him, no matter how fast you do it. (3) People who are away from the office get the most calls. (4) Callers give very long messages only when at least two other calls are coming. (5) Employees change extension numbers only if you have just revised the list of extension numbers. (6) Callers who address you by name always call you by the name of the person who worked there before you. (7) Callers give their area code only when it's the same as yours. (8) Callers are least likely to believe someone is out of the office when the person is out of the office. (9) The most persistent callers are the ones with the least important business. (10) The phone will not ring for the first fifteen minutes of the day unless you're late. If you're late, it will ring continuously until you arrive. (11) Personal calls always come when you are away from your desk or very busy. (12) Callers will ask for extension numbers instead of names only when the person they want is away from his usual extension. (13) The most important calls always have the worse connections. (14) The call you make the greatest effort to answer will be a wrong number.
— William Luther Balliew IV, San Francisco, Calif.

Banacek's Eighteenth and Nineteenth Polish Proverbs. (18) The hippo has no sting, but the wise man would rather be

sat upon by the bee. (19) If the butterfly had the teeth of the tiger, it would never make it out of the hangar.
— the old TV show "Banacek"; from Leslie Nelson, Santa Ana, Calif.

Bang!'s Laws. (1) The ability to concentrate on what's being said varies inversely with its importance. (2) Church sermons have an unsettling habit of relating to your questionable behavior of the previous week. (3) The people who cheat at games are the ones who complain the loudest when a clever player exploits an unusual (but perfectly legitimate) strategy to win.
— TV critic Derrick Bang! (who added the exclamation point to his name); from Tom Gill

Bank's Law of Misplaced Objects. You always find something in the last place you look for it.
— Jim Banks, Bozeman, Mont.

Banks's Revision. If at first you do succeed — try to hide your astonishment.
— Harry F. Banks

Barbara's Fashion Observation. Permanent press isn't. **Barbara's Law of Exploitation.** You can't be treated like a doormat if you don't lie down. **Barbara's Rule of Bitter Experience.** (1) When you empty a drawer for his clothes and a shelf for his toiletries, the relationship ends. (2) When you finally buy pretty stationery to continue the correspondence, he stops writing.
— Barbara K. Mehlman, Great Neck, N.Y.

Barbour's Law of Television. In TV, you have six weeks to make history or be history.
— John Barbour, host of the TV show "That's Incredible"; from Steve Stine

Barker's Proof. Proofreading is more effective AFTER publication.
— Phil Barker, Selly Park, Birmingham, England

Barnes Industrial Admonition. Dueling with forklifts will be discontinued immediately.
— E. E. Barnes, *Design News*, May, 5, 1975

Bars, Rules for. (1) Never try to pick up a woman who is wearing a Super Bowl ring. (2) Never order a drink where you get to keep the glass.
— the first by comedian Garry Shandling, the second by columnist Roger Simon; from Steve Stine.

The Bartlesville Argument for the Abolition of Foreign Language Classes. If English was good enough for Jesus, it's good enough for us.
— from Joshua M. Bear of Ankara, Turkey, who points out that this argument was used by a group in Bartlesville, Okla., opposing the teaching of foreign languages in the schools

Bartol's Observations. (1) If the bottom falls out, you can rest assured that the sides will tumble down on top of you. (2) Whatever kind of sandwich you order, the guy next to you will have one that is bigger and juicier and smells better.
— Karen Marie Bartol, Silver Spring, Md.

Basham's Law of Debugging Recursive Programs. It's always harder than you expect to debug a recursive program, even after taking Basham's Law into account.
— *Open Apple* newsletter, February 1986; from Shel Kagan

Bastl's Laws. (1) If there are two parts to anything, you will always miss the first part. (2) Through many years of dili-

gence, perseverance, and hard work, one can successfully maintain one's position at the bottom of one's profession.
— James F. Bastl, Westchester, Ill. (Originally published in the *Chicago Tribune*, November 20, 1983)

Batt's Laws. (1) The piece you pick out of a mixed box of chocolates will always be the kind you can't eat. (2) Once you overcome your fear of public speaking, you'll never be asked to speak again. (3) The long-winded person will always answer your long distance calls.
— Al Batt, Hartland, Minn.

BB's Group Dynamics Dictum. In a group, the unknowing will try to teach the lesser skilled or knowing; for example, a poor bridge player will coach a new player in bidding even though some of the advice will be wrong. **BB's Poker Theorems.** (1) Poker and sleep do not mix. (2) A poker player always will feel that s/he will get even on the very next hand — two at the most.
— Bruce "BB" Brown, Mar Vista, Calif.

Bear's Observation on Belaborers of the Obvious. Some people seem to think that the expression is "to make a short story long."
— Joshua M. Bear, Ankara, Turkey

Beck's Political Laws. (1) A politician's gestures increase in direct proportion to the number of his media consultants. (2) Campaign expenses always rise to exceed contributions. (3) In politics, an ounce of image is worth a pound of good ideas. **Corollary.** A good slogan beats a good solution. (4) Flubs get more news coverage than facts.
— Joan Beck, *Chicago Tribune*, January 23, 1984; from Steve Stine

Beichman's Law. Whenever an intellectual says "we" or "our" — as, for example, "we are overfed" or "our guilt," — and the subsequent sentences are highly derogatory to the pronominal antecedent, the intellectual absolves himself and his immediate audience from any of the psychopathological symptoms he is describing, and, consequently, from any responsibility for what is happening or is about to happen.
— Arnold Beichman, *Nine Lives About America,* 1972; from Joseph C. Goulden

Belcher's Law. Traffic increases to fill the road space available.
— J. R. Belcher, London, England

Benchley's Discovery. It took me fifteen years to discover I had no talent for writing, but I couldn't give it up because by that time I was too famous. **Benchley's Lesson.** A dog teaches a boy fidelity, perseverance, and to turn around three times before lying down. **Benchley's Therapy.** Tell us your phobias and we will tell you what you are afraid of.
— Robert Benchley

Bennett's Laws of Horticulture. (1) Houses are for people to live in. (2) Gardens are for plants to live in. (3) There is no such thing as a houseplant. **Bennett's Law of the Do-It-Yourself Movement.** Every job you tackle turns out to be seven (7) times more bloody awkward than it ought to be.
— H. Bennett, West Midlands, England

Ben's Highway Rule. If you see one Army truck, you'll see a hundred more.
— six-year-old Ben Brown, Chicago, Ill.

Bentov's Law. One's level of ignorance increases exponentially with accumulated knowledge. For example, when one

acquires a bit of new information, there are many new questions that are generated by it, and each new piece of information breeds five or ten new questions. These questions pile up at a much faster rate than does the accumulated information. The more one knows, therefore, the greater his level of ignorance.
> — Itsahak Bentov, *Stalking the Wild Pendulum,* 1977; from Neal Wilgus

Berla's Version. If you file it, you'll never need it. If you need it, you never file it.
> — Michael Berla, Columbia, Md.

Bernstein's Laws for Presenting Science to a Lay Audience. (1) Do not try to make things more visual than they are. (2) Do not speak more clearly than you think. (3) Don't overplay your hand.
> — Jeremy Bernstein, in commenting on Public Broadcasting Service TV science shows in *Natural History,* February 1986; from Steve Stine

Berra's Clarification. It's déjà vu all over again.
> — Yogi Berra, quoted on WTOP, January 22, 1986

Beste's "Rose by Any Other Name" Principle. The more the name of a product promises, the less it delivers. (For example, cheap stereo equipment often has the word "super" in its name, while the best equipment is usually named like a consulting firm.)
> — Ian Beste, Berkley, Calif.

Beton's Discovery. Expressways aren't.
> — John A. Beton, Chicago, Ill.

Bettman's Revision. History does not repeat itself; historians simply repeat each other.
> — Otto Bettman, *New York Times,* October 18, 1981; from Shel Kagan

Beville's Rule of Secrecy in Business. Secrecy is the enemy of efficiency, but don't let anyone know it.
> — Richard Beville, London.

Bianculli's Fourth, Seventh, and Tenth Laws of TV. Fourth. All TV heroes can find parking spaces whenever and wherever they find them. **Seventh.** Any motor-driven vehicle that becomes temporarily airborne is required to fly, and land, in slow motion. **Tenth.** Few people on TV have TV sets in their living rooms, and almost no one on TV watches TV.
> — David Bianculli, Knight-Ridder Newspaper TV column, January 3, 1986

Bierman's Law of Contracts. (1) In any given document, you can't cover all the "what ifs." (2) Lawyers stay in business resolving all the unresolved "what ifs." (3) Every resolved "what if" creates two unresolved "what ifs."
> — Melvin Bierman, APO, Miami, Fla.

Bill's Briefing on Annoying Events. One time is an accident. Two times is a coincidence. Three times is an enemy action.
> — anonymous, from Arlen Wilson, San Francisco, Calif.

Bishop's Basketball Rule. If the player isn't sure of making a free throw, do not have him make the sign of the cross.
> — Unknown, from a Frank Deford article in *Sports Illustrated*; from Mel Loftus

Bishop's Law. The less you know about an opportunity, the more attractive it is.
> — Unknown, from Sidney Gross, Seattle, Wash.

Bishop's Query. If "sense" is so common, how come we don't see more of it around?
— C. B. "Cleve" Bishop, Littleton, Colo.

Black's Discovery. He who laughs first laughs last . . . if nobody laughs in the middle.
— from Barney C. Black, Alexandria, Va., who discovered this on a bathroom wall in 1966

Blackwell's Impossibilities. (1) You cannot tighten one shoelace without tightening the other one (2) A true gardener cannot pull just one weed.
— Alexander W. Blackwell, Pebble Beach, Calif.

Blake's Lament. If I'd known I was gonna live this long, I'd have taken better care of myself.
— Jazzman Eubie Blake on his 100th birthday, February 1983

Blake's Law. Anything that can change, is.
— Kathleen Blake, Dallas, Tex.; from F. D. McSpiritt

Blay's Discovery. Long-playing recordings scratch, pop, click, wobble, and warp in direct proportion to the value placed on them by their owner. Hated recordings have built-in damage inhibitors that only self-destruct when the record is passed on to a loving recipient.
— Robert E. Blay, Rutland, Vt.

Bloom's Seventh Law of Litigation. The judge's jokes are always funny. **Bloom's Theorem of Reduced Expectations.** Less is less. **Bloom's Law of Chocoholism.** Anything tastes better if it's made with chocolate.
— Judith Ilene Bloom, Los Angeles, Calif.

Blount's Law of Bluffing. You can never appear to be cleverer than you are if you never fake anything.
— Roy Blount, Jr., quoted in the *Atlantic Monthly*; September 1984; from Steve Stine

Blutarsky's Axiom. Nothing is impossible for the man who will not listen to reason.
— the character Blutarsky, played by John Belushi, in the movie *Animal House*

Bob's Rule of Grammar. Double negatives are a no-no.
— Bob Johnston, Richmond Hill, Ontario, Canada

Bodine's Law. In self-service stores one usually has a fool for a clerk.
— Walt Bodine, "The Walt Bodine Show," November 9, 1979

Boehm's Entropic Addendum. Matter cannot be created or destroyed, nor can it be returned without a receipt.
— John Michael Boehm, *New York Times*

Bokum's Advice. You can't be happy with a woman who pronounces both d's in Wednesday.
— "Dog" Bokum, from Bob Specht's *Expectation of Days,* 1982 (Bokum is a character in Peter De Vries's *Sauce for the Goose,* 1981.)

Boliska's Realization. Do you realize that if it weren't for Edison we'd be watching TV by candlelight?
— Ed Boliska, quoted in Jack Smith's column, *Los Angeles Times,* February 11, 1981; from Robert D. Specht

Bombeck's Law. The more absurd the item, the more likely you are to need it the day after you throw it away.
— Erma Bombeck, *Chicago Sun-Times,* January 7, 1987; from Steve Stine

Bonham's Educational Proposal. Deans of education schools should insist that no doctoral candidate be allowed to get by without presenting a dissertation that can be read and understood by the first ten intelligent passersby at the school's front door.
— George W. Bonham, *Change,* April 1978; from Robert D. Specht

Boren's Presidential Motto. I've got what it takes to take what you've got.
— humorist James Boren's 1984 presidential platform

Borkon's Rule. The farther a seat is from the aisle in a theater or concert hall, the later the patron arrives.
— Bernard B. Borkon, D.M.D., San Francisco, Calif.

Born Loser's Sixty-seventh Law. Ask some people what time it is, and they'll tell you how to make a watch.
— *Born Loser* comic strip, December 15, 1985; from Tom Gill

Boston's Discovery. Cash flow is an oxymoron.
— Bruce Boston, Fairfax, Va.

Boswell's MPG Rule. Nothing gives a used car more miles per gallon than the salesman.
— Billy Boswell of Gaithersburg, Md., quoted in Bob Levey's column, *Washington Post,* November 7, 1985

Boucher's Observations. (1) He who blows his own horn always plays the music several octaves higher than originally written. (2) You can't have the ocean except at sea level.
— Sharon Boucher, Placerville, Calif.

Bowers's Law. Hubris always boomerangs.
— Dr. John Bowers; from Jo Rozanski, Normal, Ill.

Boxmeyll's First Law of Nicknames. If it fits, it sticks.
— Don Boxmeyll, *Washington Post,* January 3, 1980

Boyd's Managerial Survival Law #1. When faced with a crisis, take the inevitable and turn it around to make it look like a conscious decision.
— Richard D. Boyd, Ukiah, Calif.

Boyle's (Latest) Laws. (1) The first pull on the cord will always send the drapes the wrong way. (2) Your career will unfold as a series of miscalculations, not all yours. (3) There are people you cannot trust with your money; so with your emotions. (4) Your future will depend on having the courage of your miscalculations. (5) If they discover your standards, they will use them against you. (6) If you gain the doctorate, you will lose your first name. (7) Today's disaster is tomorrow's archaeology. (8) It is possible to make the right mistake. (9) Anything sore will be bumped more often. (10) No one will grow who is not stretched. (11) Every life is a solo flight. (12) The ears have walls.
— Charles P. Boyle, Annapolis, Md.

Brabender's Law. The most inactive player during the World Series will be the most active during the clubhouse follies.
— named for Gene Brabender of the Baltimore Orioles, who first demonstrated the law in the 1966 World Series, by George Vecsey of the *New York Times.*

Brady's First Law of Problem Solving. When confronted by a seemingly difficult problem, it is easier solved by reducing it to the question "How would the Lone Ranger have handled this?"
— Karyn Brady, Phoenix, Ariz.

Brady's Law of Reporting. Sources always return phone calls as you're leaving the office for home.
— the late Dave Brady, sportswriter for the *Washington Post,*

quoted shortly after his death by Ken Denlinger in that
newspaper, April 12, 1988; from Joseph C. Goulden

Branstadt's Dilemma. It's very difficult to cope if you haven't
anything to cope with.
— Wayne Brandstadt, Chicago, Ill.

Brattman's Rules. Unpleasant Physical Work. When co-
workers want to prove that they are macho, let them. It's
better than doing the work yourself. **Used Textbooks.** Only
use the underlinings of an A student. **Elementary School
Fights.** The one who tells the teacher first is generally believed. Be first. **Periodicals.** Magazines always come in faster
than you can read them. **Hobby Spending.** After you have
purchased the most expensive piece of equipment your
hobby requires, you will soon tire of the whole thing.
— Steven Ronald Brattman, Los Angeles, Calif.

Brecht's Reminder. As a grown man you should know better
than to go around advising people.
— Bertolt Brecht; from Bernard L. Albert

Bremner's Qualification. You must have a dirty mind to be a
successful copy editor.
— journalism professor John B. Bremner, quoted in the *Wall
Street Journal,* along with some examples of headlines
that passed clean-minded copy editors: "Textron Inc.
Makes Offer to Screw Co. Stockholders" and "Uranus
Rings Gaseous"

Brenner's Location Is Everything Rule. If you want to run
with the big dogs, you've got to go potty in the tall grass.
— TV sports anchor Glenn Brenner, Washington, D.C.,
quoted in the *Washington Post,* March 15, 1986

Breslin's Rule. Don't trust a brilliant idea unless it survives the hangover.
> — Jimmy Breslin, on the TV show "Saturday Night Live," May 18, 1986

Brewster's Observation on Chicken. No other meat looks so much like what it used to.
> — Christopher R. Brewster, Alexandria, Va.

Brian's Law. The longer you wait to write a thank-you note, the longer it must be.
> — Unknown, from Jean Pike, Modesto, Calif.

Briggs's Physics. A spilled drink flows in the direction of the most expensive object. **Briggs' Inevitabilities.** (1) There is no such thing as a flattering snapshot of oneself. (2) A pimple will attract more attention at a party than a facelift. (3) If the alarm really doesn't go off, it is still a fake-sounding excuse for being late to work. (4) If it's not on the shelf, then there is none in the back of the store either. (5) If the doctor (or dentist) says the procedure will produce "a little discomfort," it will hurt like medieval torture.
> — Judye Briggs, Dallas, Tex.

Briggs's Restaurant Rule. The seafood is always fresh, even in Arizona.
> — Thomas E. Briggs, Jacksonville, Fla.

Brinnick's Rule. Fixident, don't.
> — Ken Brinnick, North Windham, Me.

Brock's Advice. Always wear well-made, good-fitting, expensive shoes and keep them clean, no matter how poor you are.
> — D. R. Brock, Dayton, Ohio

Brodersen's Never, Never Land. (1) Never shake hands with a man holding a chain saw. (2) Never try to put on a pullover while eating a carmel apple. (3) Never kiss the hand of a lady after she's been to the self-service gas station. (4) Never try to adjust your clothing in a crowded elevator. (5) Never use a felt-tipped marker to clean your ears. (6) Never ask the highway commissioner if he plays bridge. (7) Never wave to your friends at an auction.
— William E. Broadersen, Northfield, Minn.

Broder's Warning. When "everybody" in the nation's capital agrees on something, it is prudent to be skeptical.
— David S. Broder, in his *Washington Post* column, May 22, 1988

Brogan's Constant. People tend to congregate in the back of the church and the front of the bus.
— John C. Brogan, Merion, Pa.

Bronfman's Rule. To turn $100 into $110 is work. To turn $100 million into $110 million is inevitable.
— Edgar Bronfman, Chairman, Seagram Company, quoted in *Newsweek*, December 2, 1985

Brooks's Catch-22 of Conservation and Renewable Energy. (1) If savings from a proposed conservation measure are small, the measure is not considered worth the government's time; however, if savings are large, the measure is said to be too disruptive of the economy. (2) If the measure depends on voluntary compliance, the objection is that it will not work; however, if it depends on mandatory compliance, it cannot be countenanced by the government. (3) If the measure is cost-effective, it is asked why the government should give people money to do something they should do by themselves anyway; if it is not cost-effective, it is asked why the government should give people money to do something that will not pay off. (4) And finally, the measure can be quashed completely by declaring the matter a provincial responsibility.

— David Brooks, former Director, Office of Energy Conservation, Canada; from Steven Woodbury

Brooks's Observation. If it's not the same thing, it's the same thing.

— Wally Brooks; from E. C. Pesterfield, Summit, N.J.

Broome's Revision. Cast your bread upon the waters and you will be accused of polluting the environment.

— Jon Broome, Vienna, Va.

Brother Roy Smith's Observation. At banquets the microphone is always too short for tall people and too tall for short people. Also, the microphone whistles and hums louder the closer it is to the time for the main speaker to address the audience.

— Brother Roy Smith, C.S.C., Notre Dame, Ind.

Brotman's Discoveries. (1) The reason that there are more obnoxious New Yorkers and Texans is because there are more New Yorkers and Texans. (2) College is a fountain of knowledge where students have come to drink.

— Sol G. Brotman, Baltimore, Md.

Brown's Third Aphorism. Nothing worth learning is learned quickly except parachuting. **Brown's Postulate.** No matter how low your own self-esteem, there are probably others who think less of you. **Brown's Point.** One of the virtues of propaganda is that it is easy to understand. **Brown's Revision.** Man does not breed by love alone.

— Professor David S. Brown, Washington, D.C.

Buchwald's Theorem. Tax reform is when you take the taxes off things that have been taxed in the past and put taxes on things that haven't been taxed before.
— Art Buchwald, quoted in *Forbes,* April 26, 1982

Buffett's Poker Principle. If you've been in the game thirty minutes and you don't know who the patsy is, *you're* the patsy.
— Warren E. Buffett, Chairman, Berkshire Hathaway, Inc., quoted in the *New York Times,* April 5, 1988; from Joseph C. Goulden

Bunker's Conclusion. You cannot buy beer, you can only rent it.
— the character Archie Bunker, on the TV show "All in the Family"

Bunn's Discoveries. (1) A drunk will never spill a drink on another drunk. (2) Half the world doesn't know how. The other half lives. (3) If a person is stubborn and wins, he's got guts. If he's stubborn and loses, he's dumb.
— Dean Bunn, Minneapolis, Minn.

Bureau Termination, Law of. When a government bureau is scheduled to be phased out, the number of employees in that bureau will double within twelve months after that decision is made.
— James A. Cassidy, Philadelphia, Pa.

Burgy's Definition of Statistics. A bunch of numbers running around looking for an argument.
— George Burgy, Rockville, Md., quoted by Bob Levey in his column, *Washington Post,* November 16, 1984

Burma Shave Certainty. Within this vale . . . of toil . . . and sin . . . your head grows bald . . . but not your chin.
— set of sequential signs advertising Burma Shave, ca. 1946

Burns's Autobiographical Explanation. I got paid. If they give me some more money, I may even read it.
— comedian George Burns on his new book, *USA Today,* October 17, 1984

Burns's Flaws. (1) You always discover you're out of toothpaste the morning of your dental appointment. (2) Your sons will remember to put the toilet seat lid down only in public restrooms. (3) Children acquire an ear for good music only after they have suffered a hearing loss at rock concerts. (4) A child will forget to change his socks only when you take him shopping for new shoes. (5) A teenager will only return your car with a full tank of gas when he's had a fender bender.
— Catherine Burns, Winslow, Me.

Butler's Conclusion. A hen is only an egg's way of making another egg.
— Samuel Butler; from Robert D. Specht

Buxbaum's Rule. Nothing stimulates interest in foreign affairs like having a son of military age.
— Martin Buxbaum, quoted in Bill Gold's column, *Washington Post,* May 6, 1981

Byars's Bylaws. (1) Never work for a boss who opens the company mail. (2) The customer is always right . . . and ignored.
— Betty Joe Byars, High Point, N.C.

Byrd's Last Law of Politics. Potholes know no party.
— Senate Majority Leader Robert Byrd, during the 1987 debate on the president's veto of the highway bill

Byron's Tart Caveat to the Voyager. Wives in their husband's absences grow subtler, and daughters sometimes run off with the butler.
— Don Widener, in his biography of Jack Lemmon, *Lemmon*; from Barry Hugh Yeakle, North Manchester, Ind.

Cagle's Law of Interest. The more interesting the activity you are engaged in, the more urgent will be the situation that eventually takes you away from it. **Cagle's Law of Janitorial Blindness.** Full garbage cans exude a certain substance that causes them to become invisible to the janitors. Empty and nearly empty cans do not have this quality.
— David B. Cagle, Santa Monica, Calif.

Callen's Correlation. The I.Q. of a group is inversely proportional to the additive total of that of the individuals in the group.
— Thomas H. Callen II, Burke, Va.

Callie's Law of Dinner Preparedness. When the smoke alarm goes off, dinner is served.
— Caroline Curtis, Falls Church, Va.

Campbell's Finding. If you accidentally put the carbon paper in backwards, you will type a perfect letter.
— Gardner Campbell, Jr., Scarborough, Me.

Campbell's Law. A sinner can reform, but stupid is forever.
— Lt. Col. William P. Campbell III, USAF, Eglin Air Force Base, Fla.

Campbell's Law of Criticism. When you hear person A criticizing person B, you learn more about person A than about person B.
— James G. Campbell, Toorak, Victoria, Australia

Camus's Graffiti. Sisyphus was basically a happy man.
— Albert Camus

Canfield's Corollary to the "You Can't Win 'em All Rule". You can't even *fight* 'em all.
— Monte Canfield, formerly of the General Accounting Office; from Sharon Lynn, Washington, D.C.

The Canine Culinary Distinction. EVERYONE ON THE PREMISES IS A VEGETARIAN EXCEPT THE DOG.,
— sign in front of a Loudoun County, Va., home and reported in Bob Levey's column, *Washington Post,* April 17, 1987

Cannon's Law of Arena Seating. No matter how small the arena there will alway be someone on the top row.
— Phil Cannon, Cordova, Tenn.

Captain Airways Eighth Law. The longer the title, the lousier the movie.
— John Carmody, *Washington Post,* February 20, 1980, invoked in discussing *Those Magnificent Men in Their Flying Machines*; from Joseph C. Goulden

Carlin's Law. If you nail together two things that have never been nailed together before, some schmuck will buy it from you.
— George Carlin, "Class Clown" album; from Richard Manning

Carmel's Construct. When the traffic congestion in a city becomes so serious that getting around the city is difficult, that

city will then begin excavating for a subway system, with
the result that moving around the city becomes virtually
impossible.
> — Ann Carmel, Phoenix, Ariz., who was in Washington, D.C.,
> when work began on the Metro system

Carlisle's Rule. To find the I.Q. of any committee or commission, first determine the I.Q. of the most stupid member and
then divide that result by the number of members.
> — Carlisle Madson, Hopkins, Minn.

Carl's Quip. Driveways are always longer in the winter.
> — Carl Mattson, Winfield, Ill.

Caroline's First Law of Housekeeping. Every flat surface is
a table.
> — Caroline Laudig-Herschel, Mountain View, Calif.

Caron's Suggestions. The pessimist thinks the old days were
better, the optimist thinks things will get better. Both are
wrong.
> — Don Caron, Knoxville, Tenn.

Carrington's Train Laws. (1) The delay of time of your train
is directly proportional to the importance of your arriving on
time. (2) The size of the crowd in a train is in direct proportion to the amount of work to be done before arrival.
> — Simon Carrington, Buckinghamshire, England

Carson's Observation on Footwear. If the shoe fits, buy the
other one too. **Carson's Political Advice.** Only lie about the
future.
> — Johnny Carson, on "The Tonight Show"

Carver's Law. The trouble with radicals is that they read only radical literature, and the trouble with conservatives is that they don't read anything.
> — Professor Thomas Nixon Carter of Harvard, quoted in *The New Republic,* March 28, 1970, and identified as a conservative monument of half a century ago; from Joseph C. Goulden

Carvlin's Commentaries. (1) In marriage, a warm heart seldom compensates for cold hands. (2) The risk in a business-venture should not seriously outweigh the prospective reward, as, for example, in picking a policeman's pocket.
> — Tom Carvlin, Dolton, Ill.

Cassandra's Law of Predicted Atmospheric Disasters. The first forecasts are usually the worst.
> — Patrick Michaels, Va. State Climatologist, in an article on the greenhouse effect, *Washington Post,* June 15, 1986

Cavanagh's Laws of Bureaucratic Management. (1) The process is the substance. (2) The staff is the line.
> — Richard E. Cavanagh, Washington, D.C.

Cavalry Journal Discovery. A staff study is a record of the tortuous thought processes between a set of invalid assumptions and a foregone conclusion.
> — in a mid-1930s issue of that journal; from Jerry Cowan

Celine's Laws. (1) National security is the chief cause of national insecurity. (2) Accurate communication is possible only in a nonpunishing situation. (3) An honest politician is a national calamity.
> — Hagbard Celine, in Robert Anton Wilson's *Illuminati Papers*; from Neal Wilgus

Cerf's Law of Knowledge. You don't have to be in **Who's Who** to know what's what.
— Bennett Cerf; from Steve Stine

Chaipis's Conclusion. The majority of people are people.
— Tom Chaipis, owner of Magoo's Cafe, New York, quoted in the *New York Times,* April 4, 1978; from Robert D. Specht

Chamfort's Unassailable Observation. Bachelor's wives and old maid's children are always perfect.
— Don Widener, in his biography of Jack Lemmon, *Lemmon*; from Barry Hugh Yeakle

Chandler's Typification. They are what human beings turn into when they trade life for existence and ambition for security.
— Raymond Chandler, *The Little Sisters*; from Joseph F. Walsh, Jr.

Chaplin's Rules. (1) The smaller the democracy, the more complicated its political system. (2) The newer the democracy, the longer its national anthem.
— Stephen M. Chaplin, McLean, Va.

Chapman's First Law of Journalism. The amount of attention devoted to a subject is inversely proportional to its substantive content.
— Stephen Chapman, in his column, *Chicago Tribune,* July 17, 1985; from Steve Stine

In an earlier column Chapman presented **Chapman's Theorem of Justice.** The courts are the last refuge of the unpersuasive.

Chavarria-Aguilar's Warning. Beware of learning another man's language: neither of you may really want to know what the other has to say.
— O. L. Chavarria-Aguilar, San José, Costa Rica

Chensky's Truisms. (1) A carpenter always writes on a board. (2) A fool and his money are soon audited.
— Ed Chensky, Riverside, Ill.

Cher's Matrimonial Analogy. Husbands are like fires. They go out when unattended.
— actress Cher, quoted in the *National Enquirer,* August 22, 1983; from Bernard L. Albert

Chesterton's Point. "My country, right or wrong" is a thing that no patriot would think of saying, except in a desperate case. It is like saying, "My mother, drunk or sober."
— G. K. Chesterton, in Johnathan Green's *The Cynic's Lexicon*

Chism's Law of Completion. The amount of time required to complete a government project is precisely equal to the amount of time already spent on it.
— Shelby Chism, Overland Park, Kans.

Christmas Paradox. If God had wanted us to worship Christ at Christmas, he would never have given us money.
— from Judie Wayman, Mayfield Heights, Ohio, who heard it from a friend

Chuck's Conclusion. No member of society is completely useless — they can always be used as a horrible example.
— a man named Chuck, who sent his finding to the Center on the stationery of the Alberta Vocational Centre, Lac La Biche, Alberta, Canada

Chuck's Law of Contract Negotiations. Travesty is a constant — no matter which side of the table you sit on.
— Anon. From Gerald Lee Steese, Long Beach, Calif.

Churchill's Marital Admission. My wife and I tried two or three times in the last forty years to have breakfast together, but it was so disagreeable we had to stop.
— Winston Churchill, quoted in *Forbes,* June 30, 1986

C.J.'s Law. Philosophy doesn't get the washing-up done.
— the character C.J. in the British TV series "The Rise and Fall of Reginald Perrin"; from Shel Kagan

Clarke's Law. Improving something is admirable, but inevitably five times zero is still zero.
— Dean Travis Clarke, Glen Cove, N.Y.

Clark's Clamor.
Where are they?

How many were they?
Which way were they going?
I must find them.
I am their leader.
— from Bob Kerr, Amarillo, Tex., who spotted this sign on the office wall of Hugh Clark

Clark's Conclusion. In order not to be boring, generalizations must be slightly risky.
— Sir Kenneth Clark

Clark's Tool-of-the-Trade Law. Th k y always go s on Saturday night.
— John Clark, San Francisco, Calif.

Claudia's Assurance. When writing a personal letter, as soon as you begin a new sheet of paper, you will run out of things to say.
— Claudia Costello, Manassas, Va.

Clay's Conclusion. If you ever saw a cat and a dog eating out of the same plate, you can bet your ass it was the cat's food.
— Representative William Clay (D.-Mo.), in commenting on the suggestion that public employee unions form a coalition with Jimmy Carter in 1980; from Marshall L. Smith

Clifton's Advice. Don't give up high ground 'til you know you're over the pass.
— Kelly H. Clifton, Hiroshima, Japan, who says that it was derived from backpacking but seems to have wider application. Also:

Clifton's Conclusion. Anything designed to do more than one thing does no thing very well. **Corollary.** Don't buy a car that flies.

Clovis's Consideration of an Atmospheric Anomaly. The perversity of nature is nowhere better demonstrated than by the fact that, when exposed to the same atmosphere, bread becomes hard while crackers become soft.
— E. Robert Clovis; from Stephen Bishop

Cochran's Definition of Health Insurance. A system of reimbursement that pays many thousands of dollars for treatments that never cure hospital patients but will not pay for a shot of penicillin to cure double pneumonia in the office.
— Paul W. Cochran, M.D., Topeka, Kans.

Cockrell's Law of Pizza Kinetics. All mushrooms on any given pizza will gravitate to the slice or slices of the one who

dislikes them the most, and leaving none to those who like them.
— Reed Cockrell, Darlington, Wisc.

Cohen's Law. There is no bottom to worse.
— Robert V. Cohen, M.D., Abington, Pa.; who learned it from his grandfather

Cohen's Law of Chronic Illness. The spouse of the chronic patient dies first.

Cohn's Law on the Thickness of a Southern Girl's Southern Accent. The thickness increases by the square of the distance she travels north of the Mason-Dixon line.
— essayist David Cohn, quoted by James J. Kilpatrick; from Tom Gill

Colburn's Comment on Professional Meetings. There is more collected stupidity in a professional meeting of educators than in any other gathering of equal size.
— John W. Colburn, who adds, "I have been informed that the name of any other profession may be sustituted for 'educators' and the comment will still be valid"

Collins's Laws of Discontinuity. (1) Objects that start out sequential break sequence by the time you get them. **Corollary.** The volume numbers actually present in a multivolume work start with the sequence 1, 2, 4, 4, 7. **Corollary.** Any deck of cards contains fifty-one cards at the end of the first hand. (2) Normal distribution isn't. **Corollaries.** The number of television sets required to satisfy the viewing needs of a family on any one night is 0 or 4. The number of passengers on your plane is 7 or 386. The length of warning of the visit of the chief executive is 3.2 minutes or 47 days. The actual

amount of food prepared for a party as a percentage of guest's requirements is 86 percent or 192 percent.
— D. S. Collins, Harpenden, England

Col's Conclusion. Cash in the hand means a bill in the mail.
— Colin Hewitt, Gosford, New South Wales, Australia

Comer's Law. Never mistake asthma for passion and vice versa.
— A.J. Comer, Huntington Valley, Pa.

Condon's Laws. Business Eating. (1) The cost of an expense account lunch is always inversely proportional to the amount of business done. (2) Executive meetings always conclude in time for lunch. (3) Executive lunches never conclude in time to return to the office. **Responsibility.** (1) The Chief Executive is always abroad when the manure hits the fan. (2) The Chief Executive is always available to make an easy decision. (3) The Deputy Chief Executive is always seen to make the lousy decision. (4) The thickness of the Chief Executive's carpet is in direct proportion to the amount of buck-passing carried out. **Return.** The size of the car in which a past pupil arrives for the college reunion is in inverse proportion to the size of the brain of that pupil.
— John Condon, Dublin, Ireland

Confusion, First Law of. If the boss calls, get his name.
— James Warren, Las Cruces, N.M.

Connolly's Rules of Travel. (1) Take double the money. (2) Take half the luggage. (3) Make sure you can carry all luggage at least half a mile by yourself. (4) Do your washing. (5) Take a pair of pliers and a screw driver.
— Mike Connolly, New South Wales, Australia

Conway's Law. In any organization there will always be one person who knows what is going on. That person must be fired.
> — letters column, *New York Times,* May 15, 1980; from Robert W. Sallen

Cooper's Discovery. Life isn't fair, but neither is death.
> — Ed Cooper; from M. Kottmeyer

Cooper's Law for Practicing Politicians. Principles become modified in practice by facts.
> — quoted by James J. Kilpatrick in his column, April 3, 1981; from Steve Woodbury

Cooper's Truths. (1) The number of postal clerks is inversely proportional to the number of patrons (this can be proven by visiting any Washington, D.C., post office). (2) The amount of hair removed by a barber is inversely proportional to the cost of the haircut. (The hair stylist at the mall will charge you $15 to rearrange your hair, while the small-town barber on Broad Street will make you look like a Parris Island recruit for $2.)
> — Bob Cooper, Bethany, Okla.

Corporate Morality, Maxim of. Morality moves down the corporate ladder, but seldom up.
> — *The 59 Second Employee*; from R. Stevan Jonas

Corrales's Conclusions. (1) Sophistication is knowing enough to keep out of the crack of the theater seat in front of you. (2) A rut is a grave with both ends kicked out. (3) Toes are what keep your feet from fraying at the ends. (4) A millennium is something like a centennial — only it has more legs. (5) How is it that George Washington slept in so many places and yet never told a lie? (6) Fortunately, the wheel was in-

vented before the car, otherwise the scraping noise would be terrible.
— Marsha J. Corrales, San Antonio, Tex.

Corvin's Rule of Rules. If you screw the rules, they will multiply.
— G. F. Corvin, Nairobi, Kenya

Cosgrave's Law. People will often sell their friends down the river in order to impress those they do not like.
— sentiment expressed by former Irish Prime Minister Liam Cosgrave, who noted that the British were noted for selling their friends down the river to appease their enemies; from Peter Robinson, Paris

Cosnow's Reflection While Attempting to Rodent-Proof a Bird Feeder.
The Guru sat on a mountain high
Above the worldly rush.
His hair had felt no VO 5
His teeth had known no brush.

When I asked him to enlighten me
He spoke these words of truth:
NOTHING IS ALL-PURPOSE
AND NOTHING'S SQUIRREL-PROOF.
— Allen Cosnow, Glen Coe, Ill.

Cotter's Laundromat Mystery. Why is it that when there's an attendant to make change, the change machine works, and when there isn't, it doesn't?
— John Cotter, *Washington Post,* December 6, 1987

Coucheron-Aamot's Distinction. Foreigners often ask what is the difference between American political parties? It is really very simple. With the Republicans, you worry that

they have not found solutions to the nation's problems. With the Democrats, you are afraid that they might think of something.
— H. Coucheron-Aamot, Albuquerque, N.M.

Couch's Probabilities. (1) With all the discounts, incentives, and cash-back payments, a new car will cost far more than you had planned. (2) An agenda becomes a list of subjects there wasn't time to discuss.
— W. Roy Couch, Saco, Me.

Cooper's Discovery. That any liquid accidentally spilt automatically doubles in volume.
— Lady Curzon Cooper, London, England

Covert Conversation Rule. If you don't want your children to hear what you are saying, pretend you're talking to them.
— anonymous

Cowan's Revelation. When a person says, "I'm as good as you are!," it means that he thinks he's better.
— Jerry Cowan, St. Croix, Virgin Islands

Cox's Conclusion. Self-sealing envelopes don't — except when you have accidentally left the letter out.
— Geoff Cox, Harpenden, Herts, England

Cozgriff's First Principle for Dealing with Potentially Life Threatening Situations. Relax — otherwise you might die all tensed up.
— Cadet Ralph Cozgriff; from David Little

Craig's Antique Dealer's Rules. (1) Five percent of the collectors account for 95 percent of your sales in 10 percent of your time; 95 percent of the collectors take up the other 90

percent of your time. (2) If I had a nickel for everyone who looked at my merchandise and said "I'll be back," I could retire to the south of France. (3) I am a very wealthy man, but it's all tied up in inventory. (4) The rarity of any item you possess is directly proportional to the number of stupid questions people ask you about it.
— antique dealer John S. Craig, Torrington, Conn.

Cranston's Explanation. Inflation is not all bad. After all, it has allowed every American to live in a more expensive neighborhood without moving.
— Senator Alan Cranston, quoted in the *Atlantic Monthly*, January 1981

Crenna's Discovery. Futurism is passé. **Crenna's Law of Political Accountability.** If you are the first to know about something bad, you are going to be held responsible for acting on it, regardless of your formal duties.
— policy advisor C. D. Crenna, Ottawa, Canada

Crescimbeni's Rule on Air Travel. Don't be afraid of flying; be afraid of crashing! **Crescimbeni's Rule on Working.** Don't worry about people not working at their jobs in the afternoons. It is in the morning when they don't work. In the afternoons they don't come in.
— Joseph Crescimbeni, Lake City, Fla.

Crinklaw's Observation. (1) Nowadays the order of life is reversed: sex is first enjoyed, marriage follows, and after marriage comes virginity. (2) Nice guys may not always finish last, but the bad guys do start with certain advantages.
— Don Crinklaw, St. Louis, Mo.

Critchfield's Certitude. If, while driving and attempting a turn, a driver spots a pedestrian anywhere within the horizon, that pedestrian will be in a position to block said turn

for the maximum inconvenience of the driver. **Critchfield's Staple Surmise.** (1) All staplers are empty. (2) Any stapler that isn't empty is broken. (3) Staple supplies may be found only when one is really looking for scissors.
— Donald Critchfield, Washington, D.C.

Crock's Law. No matter how large an area you are in, if a fly is present, it will land on you.
— Terry L. Crock, Massillon, Ohio

The Cronkites' Contrary Views of Death. *Walter Cronkite:* "When I go, I'd like to go like Errol Flynn — on the deck of my 70-foot yacht with a 16-year-old mistress." *Betty Cronkite:* "You're going to go on a 16-foot boat with your 70-year-old mistress."
— in *USA Today*'s compilation of 1986's Unforgettable Quotes

Cross's Conclusion. Had the Edsel been an academic department, it would be with us yet.
— K. Patricia Cross, quoted in *Change,* June 1974; from Robert D. Specht.

Crowell's Undeniable Law of Fate. Whatever will be, will be, whether or not it ever occurs.
— Donald K. Crowell, San Bernadino, Calif.

Crudup's Law. Mediocrity always succeeds over originality.
— anonymous; from Nigel Stapley

Culkin's Conclusions. (1) A lot of things have happened in this century, and most of them plug into walls. (2) We don't know who discovered water, but we're pretty sure it wasn't a fish.
— Father John Culkin, Fordham University; from Robert D. Specht and Stephen J. Chant

Cuomo's Aphorisms. (1) When in doubt, mull. (2) Let them eat polenta. (3) If it's a free press, why do newspapers use coin boxes? (4) In government, a dollar saved is a dollar overlooked.
— New York Governor Mario Cuomo, who attributes them to the fictional A. J. Parkinson, according to the *New York Times,* May 22, 1984; from Joseph C. Goulden

Cummings's First Law of Human Behavior. Something not worth doing at all is not worth doing well.
— Dr. Nick Cummings, San Francisco, Calif.; from Joseph Zmuda

Cynthia's Verities. (1) The spare has gone flat too. (2) Divorce may be final, but it is not terminal.
— Cynthia MacGregor, New York, N.Y.

 D

Dabney's Prime Axiom of Washington Thought. All ideas are merely the weapons of political struggle. **Corollaries.** (1) There is no such thing as truth. (2) Anyone who deals in general ideas is merely pushing the interests of his class, or of whoever's paying. (3) There is no such thing as right and wrong. (4) No one is capable of speaking to the general good.
— Dick Dabney, *Washington Post,* October 16, 1979

Dale's Dictum. People don't make the same mistake twice; they make it three times, four times, or five times.
— Michael Dale

Daniel's Delight. If it is ironic, it is probably true.
— D. Park Teter, Hazelhurst, Wisc.

Dart's Dictum. Talking to politicians is fine, but with a little money they hear you better.
— Justin Dart, Chairman, Dart Industries, quoted by Mark Green in *The New Republic,* December 13, 1982

Data Processing Laws (Assorted). (1) On a clear disk you can seek forever. (2) Programs seek to expand themselves beyond available memory. (3) Compatible tapes aren't. (4) The volume of data to be keypunched determines the number of keypunch operators who will call in sick. (5) Profanity is the one language data-processing people know best.
— from Virginia Beckwith, Arkansas Social Services, who collected them

The Data Processor's Rule of Thumb. The usefulness of a computer printout is inversely proportional to its weight.
— Timothy Snyder, Chicago, Ill.; letter to *Business Week,* November 23, 1987

Daugherty's List of Things a Person Should Never Say. (1) "That's impossible!" (2) "You can't do that to me!" (3) "I'll love you forever." (4) "And that's my final offer!" (5) "I'll never hurt you." (6) "This hurts me more than it hurts you." (7) "It'll be a cold day in hell before I'll ever do that!"
— William J. Daugherty, Washington, D.C.

David's Law of Habits. Any bad habit is easier than the corresponding good habit.
— David McKay, Havertown, Pa.

Davidson's Law of Weather Variance. The arrival of spring always trails expectations. The arrival of summer always precedes expectations. Autumn arrives on time. Winter arrives when it wants to.
— Jeff Davidson, Falls Church, Va.

Davison's Law. One allows to come to rest any sizable object — laundry basket, grocery bag, shoes, etc. — in that exact location to impede as many foot traffic paths as possible.
— W. Harper Girvin, Charlottesville, Va.

Davis's Discovery. If you want to start a bug collection, paint your lawn furniture.
— Lee A. Davis, Wilmington, Del.

Davis's Law of Surviving a Hostile Press. If you hear your name mentioned on the radio, turn it off. If you encounter it in the *Congressional Record*, stop reading. Similarly if in a column.
— Chester Davis, who held various New Deal positions, quoted by John Kenneth Galbraith in *A Life in Our Times;* from Joseph C. Goulden

Davis's Law of Traffic Density. The density of rush-hour traffic is directly proportional to 1.5 times the amount of extra time you allow to arrive on time.
— Norman M. Davis, Chicago, Ill.

Davis's Warning. Always be suspicious of a politician who says that something can never happen.
— Dr. M. I. M. Davis, Surrey, England

Dawn's Judgment. The judgment of any group varies inversely as the square of the number of persons in the group. (If 1 person has x judgment, 2 persons will have 1/4x judgment, 10 will have 1/100x judgment, etc.)
— Dawn Barry, St. Charles, Ill.

The Dean-Boyd Law. Stupidity is intelligence cleverly disguised. **The Beeton Contradiction to the Dean-Boyd Law.** Maybe it's the other way around.
— Kevin A. H. Dean, Don Mills, Ontario, Canada, with Jeff Boyd and Carolyn Beeton

Dean's Law of the Balance of Nature. The balance of nature must be maintained, therefore fate will act in opposition to desire. **Corollary.** If you are in a hurry to get somewhere, nature will not be in a hurry to get you there.
— Kevin A. H. Dean, Don Mills, Ontario, Canada

December Constant. During Christmas, all worthwhile social events will occur on the same evening.
— Anonymous

De-Evolutionary Observation. God made man, but he used a monkey to do it.
— in the song "Jocko Homo," by Devo; from Nigel Stapley

DeLaney's Laws for Predicting Picnic Weather. (1) If the forecast is 10 percent chance of showers, you'll get the whole 10 percent. (2) The sun will shine brightly at the rejected alternative location.
— Robert L. DeLaney, Johnson City, N. Y.

Denham's Dictum. In a given organization, job performance, whether excellent or incompetent, is overlooked providing you conform.
— Ron Denham, Park Ridge, Ill.

Density Characteristics of Executives Rising in an Organization. Cream rises and sewage floats.
— Anonymous

Depuy's Dictates. (1) In any magazine the number of pages lacking pagination numbers is directly proportional to the number of advertisements. (2) Most unnumbered pages occur in those parts of the magazine to which the reader is directed for article continuations. **Penmanship.** The greater one's efforts to write an impressive signature, the more awkward are the results, except when signing insignificant documents such as parcel delivery receipts. **Vision.** When a

person who normally wears eyeglasses appears before you without them, you cannot see him as clearly.
— Raymond H. Depuy, Chambersberg, Pa.

deQuoy's Observation. Some of the world's best work has been done by people who didn't feel very well that day.
— Glenna deQuoy, New York, N.Y.

DeRock's Law of Dullness. Dullness is directly proportional to the number of brown suits in a crowd.
— Doug DeRock, Western Springs, Ill.

DeVault's Razor. There are only two laws: (1) Someday you will die. (2) If you are reading this you are not dead yet.
— Yvonne G. T. DeVault, Redwood City, Calif.

DeViney's Axiom. You should always try to become boss because otherwise they'll give it to some other dumbbell.
— G. H. DeViney, Palatine, Ill.

DeVries's Cosmic Observation. The universe is like a safe to which there is a combination. Unfortunately, the combination is locked up inside the safe.
— Peter DeVries, *Let Me Count the Ways*; from Arnold Harris

Diana's Law of Diminishing Enthusiasm. There are more entries in the first half of the alphabet.
— Diana VerNooy, Teaneck, N.J.

Diane's Secretary's Axiom. The more you want done, and the faster you want it done, the longer it will take to get it done, and the greater the chance of errors being made because of too much to do in too little time.
— Diane K. Stanley, Fremont, Neb.

Dick's Dilemma. If you live in California, your factory authorized sales representative lives in New Jersey. If you live in New Jersey, your factory authorized sales representative lives in White Rock, South Dakota. If you need further assistance, please feel free to contact our home office in Hong Kong.
— John A. Mattsen, Finlayson, Minn.

Dickson's Definition. A pessimist is a person who mourns the future.
— Isabelle C. Dickson, Ardsley-on-Hudson, N.Y.

Dickson's Discoveries. (1) Golf, sex, and child-rearing prove that practice does not make perfect. (2) No two hotel/motel shower faucets work the same way. (3) When weeding, the best way to make sure what you are pulling is a weed and not a valuable plant is to pull on it. If it comes out of the ground easily, it is a valuable plant. (4) Everytime you think that you've "paid your dues," you get a renewal notice. (5) You don't know it yet, but your name is on somebody else's list of "things to do today." That person will wait to call you until he or she has plenty of time. Meanwhile, you will put someone else's name on your list of "things to do today." You will wait to call until you have plenty of time to talk.
— Paul Dickson, Director, Murphy Center

The Dieter's Discoveries. (1) The calorie isn't a unit of energy. It's a unit of taste. (2) If it isn't the calories that make it taste good, it's the cholesterol.
— Gail White, New Orleans, La.

Dillon's Rule. The soup de jour is always cream of broccoli.
— Janet Dillon, Walnut Creek, Calif.; from Tom Gill

Diminishing Appreciation, the Law of. The more secure it is, the less you appreciate it.
— Neal Wilgus, Albuquerque, N.M.

Dines's Reminder. If you hear that everybody is buying a certain stock, ask who is selling.
> — James Dines, quoted in the *Baltimore Sun*, November 9, 1983

Distin's Discovery. Cat hair is attracted to and will adhere to anything except the cat.
> — Mary Distin, Monmouth, Ill.

Dixon's Law of Manhattan Movement. Everyone in New York is in a hurry except the person walking in front of you.
> — Mike Dixon, New York, N.Y.

Dobson's Dilemma. (1) Following the rules won't get the job done. (2) Getting the job done is no excuse for not following the rules.
> — from Bob Vopacke, Sacramento, Calif.

Dr. J's Distinction.

If they say they love you,
    trust their behavior.
If they say they don't love you,
    trust their words.
> — John H. Dickey, Ph.D., Aurora, Colo.

Doctor Orbit's Laws. (1) **The Unexpected.** Don't count your chickens before they cross the road. (2) **Discretion.** If one observes shit congregating in the vicinity of a fan, it is prudent to unplug the fan. (3) **Computer Systems.** The relative importance of a computer system is inversely proportional to the contrivedness of its acronym.
> — Charles A. Belov, West Hartford, Conn.

Documentation, Five Laws of. (1) What is convenient for the documentor will be inconvenient for the user. (2) All manuals are out of date. (3) All distribution lists are inaccurate.

(4) Each supplement doubles the number of versions. (5) Clean documentation cannot improve a messy system.
> — Edmund H. Weiss, *Structured Documentation;* from Steve Stine.

Doherty's Dictum on Juvenile Work Productivity. One boy, one boy; two boys, half a boy; three boys, no boy.
> — Indianapolis grocer Patrick Doherty; from Bob Einbinder

Dolan's First Law. Bad times make good stories. **First Corollary.** Good times make dull stories.
> — Michael Dolan, Washington, D.C.

Dolan's Law. If a person has had any connection with Harvard University or the state of Texas, he will find a way to make that known to you during the first ten minutes of your first conversation.
> — Marty Dolan; from Joseph M. McCabe (The law might be amended to include the U.S. Marine Corps)

Doolittle's Definition. A bore is a person who monopolizes the conversation talking about himself when you want to talk about yourself.
> — in *Doolittle, A Biography,* by Lowell Thomas and Edward Jablonski; from Stephen J. Chant

Doris's Law of Looks. No matter what you wear, you will not look good if you look cold.
> — Doris Brown; from her son, Joe Eddy Brown, Glen Ellyn, Ill.

Dorothea's Comforting Thought for the Day. I've broken so many mirrors in my life, if I live long enough to have all that bad luck, I'll be lucky.
> — Dorothea Gildar, Washington, D.C.

Dottie's Law. Any attempt to simplify creates more complications.
— Dorothy Turcotte, Grimsby, Ontario, Canada

Douskey's Rule Concerning the Odds of Capitalizing on Previous Success. Sequels never equal.
— Franz Douskey, Mount Carmel, Conn.

Draftee's Discovery. Cleanliness is next to godliness except in the Army, where it is next to impossible.
— Martin Russell, Yonkers, N.Y.

Drakenberg's Discovery. If you can't seem to find your glasses, it's probably because you don't have them on.
— Delores Drakenberg, Willmar, Minn.

Driscoll's Discovery. The higher one is in a hierarchy the more befuddled one becomes when one attempts to operate the photocopy machine.
— Robert S. Driscoll, Staten Island, N.Y.

DuBow's Laws of Attorney Fee Compensation. (1) Never accept a check from a man accused of passing bad ones. (2) Never accept cash from a man accused of counterfeiting. (3) If your client is a good-looking woman and wants a divorce, get your fee in advance.
— Myron DuBow, Sherman Oaks, Calif.

Dugger's Law of Texas Politics. Possession is the first nine tenths of the law, and politics is the tenth.
— Ronnie Dugger, *The Politician*; from Joseph C. Goulden

Duke Kahanomoku's Treatise. For free, take; for buy, waste time.
— Duke Kahanomoku, who was often quoted by Arthur Godfrey on the radio; from Paul C. Hewett

Dull's Advice. If you can use it, pull it.
— Joan Dull; from David Finger, Wilmington, Del., who points out that it was created by Ms. Dull as a reference to pulling strings to get a job, but that it has broader applications

Dunning's Law. No more than 50 percent of the blow dryers in men's restrooms will work at any given time.
— Bob Dunning, *Davis* (Calif.) *Enterprise,* December 19, 1985; from Tom Gill

Dunn's Dally on Doing. Never do now what must be done or you may not find anything to do when you are looking for something to do later. **Dunn's Observation.** If all the telephone calls from firms claiming that they are in the neighborhood installing siding, solar heat, roofing, carpeting, basement waterproofing, insulation, kitchen cabinets, patios, storm windows, rec rooms, bathroom tile, etc., were true, the city would need massive around the clock traffic control on my street so they could get another car down the street to give me my free estimate "as long as they are in the neighborhood."
— Russell J. Dunn, Sr., Lakewood, Ohio

Dunstan's Dilemma. Logic is like cricket — it is admirable as long as you are playing according to the rules. But what happens to your game of cricket when someone suddenly decides to bowl with a football or bat with a hockey stick? Because that is what is continually happening in life.
— Dunstan Ramsay, in *The Manticore,* by Robertson Davies; from Catherine Pfeifer, Milwaukee, Wisc.

Durocher's Edict. You don't save a pitcher for tomorrow; tomorrow it may rain.
— Leo Durocher; from R. H. Roth, Lamboing, Switzerland

Duverger's Law. The simple-majority single-ballot system favors the two-party system.
— French political scientist Maurice Duverger, *Political Parties: Their Organization and Activity in the Modern State;* from Charles D. Poe

Dwyer's Law of Pins. If you unwrap a new article of clothing that is secured by *n* pins, you will remove *n* − 1 pins. And that pin will pierce you in a place that hurts.
— Edward J. Dwyer, Cherry Hill, N.J.

Dykema's Laws. One-on-One Law. Your house makes strange noises only when you are alone. **Good News for Pencil Rules.** The pen never wears out at the end of a sentence.
— Denise Dykema, Morrison, Ill.

Ebert's Box Rule. If a printed ad for a movie features a row of boxes at the bottom, with the stars in those boxes, the movie is not worth watching.
— film critic Roger Ebert, paraphrased from his article, *Chicago Sun-Times*, June 23, 1985; from Steve Stine.

Eddie's Law of Location. All football is played on the other side of the field.*
— Euan F. Eddie, Folkestone, Kent, England

Ehre's Law of Double Doors. In approaching an entrance that has two doors; YOU WILL (1) always enter the locked side; (2) always push when you should have pulled (or vice versa); (3) always, even when the door says to push or pull, do the opposite 90 percent of the time.
— Victor T. Ehre, Jr., Edwardsville, Ill.

Electronic Elegy. Beware of buying anything when the manuals are bigger than the equipment.
— B. V. D. Smith, Downers Grove, Ill.

Eling's Observation. During radio or TV programs, any word you fail to hear will also go unheard by anyone else present.
— Stan Eling, Smethwick Warley, West Midlands, England

Ellenson's Miscellaneous Natural Laws. Interesting Food. "Interesting" food is that which lies somewhere between palatable and ptui. **Inevitable Boo-boos.** In the course of every endeavor there lurks a mistake not made. **Accountability.** Accountability measures the ability to *account*, not the ability to do the job. **Corollary 1**: If one insists on accountability, that is what one will get. **Corollary 2**: If accountability is paramount, that is *all* one will get. **Reductionist Law of Gottas and Shoulds.** There is only one gotta and one should in life: You *gotta* live with the consequences of your actions, and you *should* remember that. **Causal Loci.** Blame for any given condition or occurrence will automatically shift until it settles on the least influenceable variable (e.g., crime may be blamed on social structure, the failure of a business on national economic conditions, etc.).
— Gerald S. Ellenson, Huntington Beach, Calif.

Elliot's Law. Ice cream cones always fall scoop-down.
— Kandis Edward Elliot, *Journal of Irreproducible Results*, November-December 1985; from Neal Wilgus

Elliott Household Rules. (1) No matter when you start, bedtime happens at 11:30 P.M. (2) There's no such thing as a "long winter evening," since none of the chores saved for a long winter evening ever gets done. (3) All clocks in the house conspire to display totally different readings. (4) The cat never goes out the door the first time you open it.
— Owen Elliott, Ridgefield, Conn.

Ellison's Conclusion. The two most common things in the universe are hydrogen and stupidity.
— Harlan Ellison, *Omni*, February 1987; from Catherine Pfeifer, who noted that it appeared in the context of comments on censorship: "These would-be censors are monsters. And they will always be with us because the two most common things in the universe are hydrogen and stupidity."

Ellison's Law. In this society . . . what happens to blacks will eventually happen to whites.
— author Ralph Ellison

Ellis's Reciprocal. An unwatched pot boils immediately. **Corollary.** The speed with which boiling milk rises from the bottom of the pan to any point beyond the top is greater than the speed at which the human brain and hand can combine to snatch the wretched thing off.
— H. F. Ellis, "Men in Aprons," *Punch*; from Ross Reader.

Ellis's Rule of the Road. In freeway driving, slow drivers always need left lane exits, fast ones right lane exits.
— Andy Ellis, KCBS, San Francisco, Calif.

Ellstrand's Law of Dietary Discretion. If it fits on your plate, it fits in your stomach!
— Beverly Ellstrand, Park Ridge, Ill.

Elsner's Observations. (1) Calories are delicious. (2) Smokers can't read. (3) When you come in late for work, everybody notices; when you work late, nobody notices.
— Raymond F. Elsner, Littleton, Colo.

Elway's Response. *Q* (to John Elway during the week before Super Bowl XXI): What's the stupidest question you've been asked this week? *A:* That's it.
— *Washington Post*, January 25, 1987

Emmanuel's Law of Customer Satisfaction. Customer satisfaction is directly proportional to employee satisfaction.
— Daniel Emmanuel, Dallas, Tex.

Emerson's Rule. Never read a book that is not a year old.
— Ralph Waldo Emerson, who, it is noted by the director of the book-dependent Murphy Center, did not say anything about *buying* books before they are a year old

Emery's Theory of Relativity. Are you talking fence posts or towns?
— Emery Warren; from John A. Staedler, Merced, Calif., who explains, "Two fence posts a mile apart are quite far, but two towns a mile apart are quite close."

Ensminger's Theory of Multiplicity. Trees always drop more leaves than they bear.
— Jim Ensminger; from John Schaefer

Epps's Elevator Law. A crowded elevator smells different to a short person.
— Buddy Epps; from Don Schofield, Charleston, S.C.

Evans's Law. The cars with the dead battery will have all the other vehicles pinned in the garage.
— George Evans, Greeley, Colo.

Evans's Laws. (1) Nothing is ever simply black and white; and just as often it's not gray either. (2) **Everything** is the fault of a repressed Catholic childhood — especially if you didn't have one. (3) I think; but I'm still not convinced I am.
— Gareth J. Evans, Loughborough, Leics, England

Evans's Second, Third, and Fourth Laws. (2) Everyone succeeds 100 percent of the time — at what they're really up to. (3) That man or woman you see who is so beautiful, rich,

talented and charming that you would literally die for them — remember somewhere out there is a person who is sick and tired of them. (4) People and projects, like arrows, tend to hit the ground at the same angle they took off. **Evans's Eternal Question.** The Eternal Question is not "What is Truth?" or "What is the Meaning of Life?" The question asked by more people since the beginning of time is 'Why do I keep doing this stuff to myself?" **Evans On Creation.** It is ironic that the most sophisticated eye in all of nature's creation was given to the common housefly — so that it may better sit on your potato salad.
— James T. Evans, Houston, Tex.

Evelyn's Law. A woman is like a teabag — you never know her strength until she gets into hot water.
— woman named Evelyn, radio call-in show, WRC, Washington, D.C. The same show yielded the following:

Exxon's Law of Energy Costs. We've upped ours, now up yours.

Eyberg's Romantic Reminder. Regardless of how good we are *in* bed, our relationship is entirely dependent on how good we are *out* of bed.
— John E. Eyberg, Columbia, Mo.

* This law was presented with a considerable amount of research, including Eddie's observations at one-sided Rugby football contests. He reports, "I noticed that in a match in which, for example, team A beat team B by 80 points to 4, when I moved to an observation point behind team B's goal line, which they had been gallantly but ineffectively defending, the time of my arrival coincided exactly with their one and only score of the match at the other end of the field."

Farbinger's Rule. Brown-nosing a professor is best accomplished by asking a pointless question related to his or her own specific academic specialty, and then nodding one's head and uttering "uh-huh" every so often as the professor gives an answer. This will give the appearance of being truly interested and therefore deserving of attention, consideration, and better grades.
— Warren Farbinger, Berkeley, Calif.; from Ian Beste

Farkus's Law. There will always be a closer parking space than the one you found. **Goodman's Commentary on Farkus's Law.** But if you go looking for it, someone else will already have taken it.
— Lee Goodman, Prairie Village, Kans.

Farmer's Law. The easiest crops to grow are weeds and pests.
— heard at the University of California, Davis; from Tom Gill.

Fassett's Law. The first elevator to arrive is going in the wrong direction.
— Lloyd A Fassett, M.D.

The Fast Lunch Rule. The rich can make you famous, but the poor can make you a hero.
— Anonymous; from Dr. Joseph A. Horton

Federal Emergency Advisory. In case of fire, flee with the same reckless abandon that occurs each day at quitting time.
— from Bob Levey's column, *Washington Post*, September 10, 1985, in which he quotes this line from a government bulletin board

Feldman's Revisions. (1) For every actor, there's a reactor. (2) As ye sew, so shall ye rip. (3) A snitch in time saves nine.
— Monroe Feldman, Silver Spring, Md.

Fenster's Law. One man's confusion is another man's Ph.D thesis.
— Bob Fenster, *Sacramento Bee,* February 23, 1986; from Tom Gill

Fenster's Movie Food Maxims (a selection). (1) Never read labels. There is nothing good for you inside a candy bar, so forget it. That's why they keep it dark in movie theaters. (2) Never get serious at a candy counter and order a hot dog because you're hungry. Bad movie hot dogs are a fact of life. Resist the temptation to think you can find nourishment in a theater.
— Bob Fenster, quoted in the *Washington Post*

Fenwick's Rule. You may never reach a solution, but you're never absolved from the responsibility of trying.
— former Representative Millicent Fenwick, N.J., quoted in the *Washington Post,* November 22, 1979

Ferguson's Office Rules of Thumb. (1) When the boss is out always answer his line second. He is probably on the other line. (Or, the boss never calls on his own line.) (2) The size and severity of the buck passed is inversely proportional to the size of your paycheck. (3) If all the phone lines ring at once, put them all on hold until they hang up. (4) Never answer a person who says, "May I ask a stupid question?" (5) When callers begin with "I have a problem . . . ," they usually do. When they say, "I have a small problem," it is usually too big for you to handle.
— Eve M. Ferguson, Washington, D.C.

Ferreire's Pentgon Parking Lot Theory of World Affairs. The state of the world can be accurately gauged by the number of cars in the Pentagon parking lot on any given midnight.
— Larrie Ferreire, Alexandria, Va.

Fields's Advice. Start off every day with a smile and get it over with.
— W. C. Fields

Findsen's First Law. The coffee cup is always emptied just as the waitress goes on break.
— art critic Owen Findsen, *Cincinnati Enquirer*

The First Sergeant's Response. "I'd rather be wrong than look the goddamn thing up."
— from Brian M. Foley, Wake Island, Mid-Pacific, who recalled this immortal reply from his "top kick" during his days as a soldier. "I can still remember his voice as it boomed across the company area," writes Foley.

Fitzloff's Fact. Organizational consolidation is invariably followed by a minimum increase in administrators of one third.
— John F. Fitzloff, Chicago, Ill.

Flashman's Law of Frontier Diplomacy. There is some natural law that ensures that whenever civilization talks to the heathen, it is through the person of the most obstinate, short-sighted, arrogant, tactless clown available.
— the character Sir Harry Flashman in George MacDonald Fraser's *Flashman and the Redskins*; from Bob Einbinder

Flory's Laws. (1) The more crap you put up with, the more crap you are going to get. (2) Whenever you put out a trough full of public money, you are going to find some pigs with all four feet in it. (3) As time goes on, everything gets heavier.
Mrs. Flory's Addition to the Third Law. . . . and further.
— K. C. Flory, Oconomowoc, Wisc.

Foley's Dicta. (1) People are generally down on things they ain't up on. (2) If the count goes two strikes against you, cancel the meeting.
— Joe Foley, Kensington, Md., quoted in the *Montgomery Journal,* November 5, 1981

Formal Attire Rule. Wearing a rented tuxedo causes a flat tire.
— anonymous; from Tom Gill

Fortner's Law. It takes less time to avoid it than to explain it.
— George A. Fortner, Cincinnati, Ohio

Fortune Cookie Message. Don't blame failures on others. You just didn't work hard enough.
— found by James Thorpe III

Foster's Laws. (1) Children will always have to go to the bathroom as soon as you sit down in a restaurant. (2) The person who says, "It is only money," is most likely to want to cheat you.
— Marguerite H. Foster, Palo Alto, Calif.

Foster's Revelation. For every axiom there is an equal and opposite reaxiom.
— Nicholas Foster, Bernardsville, N.J.

Fowler's Constant. No matter where you sit on an airplane, when deplaning, the person in front of you will be unable to locate his/her suit bag in the forward coat closet.
— Professor Don D. Fowler, University of Nevada, Reno

Fowler's Rule. A book is never finished, it's abandoned.
— Gene Fowler, quoted in H. Allen Smith's *The Life and Legend of Gene Fowler;* from Alan G. Lewis

Fraknoi's Lament. Wherever you are, the eclipse is visible somewhere else.
> — Andrew Fraknoi, Astronomical Society of the Pacific; from Tom Gill

Frand's Eighth and Ninth Laws of Product Development. (8) The amount of time necessary to develop a new product is always one unit of time longer than you think it should be. A one-month project will take one quarter, a two-quarter project will take two years ,etc. (9) There is no such thing as a conservative market projection.
> — Erwin A. Frand, *Industrial Research and Development,* January 1983; from Mack Earle

Fran's Olfactory Observation. Dirty hands make your nose itch.
> — from Mary Ann Mrazek, Lombard, Ill.

Fraraccio's Law. It's not *what* you know, it's how fast you can find it out.
> — John C. Fraraccio, Brick Town, N.J.

Fraser's Additions. (1) Almost all emotional wounds are self-inflicted. (2) The longer the cruise, the older the passengers. (3) Life is like chess . . . all the mistakes are there, waiting to be made. (4) Love is like snow: you don't know when it will come or how long it will last or how much you'll get.
> — Alex Fraser, Washington, D.C.

Fresco's Query. Why is it when liberals win elections it is called polarization? Yet when conservatives are victorious it is labeled a mandate.
> — Victor Fresco, letter to the *Los Angeles Times,* June 25, 1981; from Robert D. Specht

Friedman's Comment on Presenting Averages Without Their Components. That is like assuring the nonswimmer that he can safely walk across a river because its average depth is only four feet.
— economist Milton Friedman, *Newsweek*, January 10, 1972; from Don Nilsen

Fuchs's Fact. If your name can be spelled wrong, it will be.
— Monika Fuchs, Stockholm, Sweden

Fullner's Laws of Menial Employment. The more menial a job an individual has, the higher the probability of meeting friends, relatives, and acquaintances while at work. (Discovered working at a filling station.) **Public Telephones**: A public telephone is never being used except when you want to use it. **Bad Examples**: A bad example is more readily followed than a good one.
— Randall L. Fullner, San Jose, Calif.

Dr. Futch's Finding. The longer the patient lives, the greater his chances of recovery.
— William D. Futch, St. Petersburg, Fla., who points out that it "has been a great comfort to many patients' families"

Galbraith's Laws. 1st. Modesty is a vastly overrated virtue. **Junkets.** A junket is any business trip which, if taken by anyone but yourself, would be considered unnecessary. **Congressional Testimony.** A lie at a congressional hearing gets you by for the moment at the cost of trouble later on.
— John Kenneth Galbraith; from Joseph C. Goulden

Gallagher's Law. People like crowds. The bigger the crowd, the more people show up. Small crowd, hardly anybody shows up.
— comic Leo Gallagher; from Jim Dawson, Los Angeles, Calif.

Gallagher's Rule. Never apologize for your terrible friends. We are all *somebody's* terrible friends.
— the late Jack Gallagher, sometime Dean of Trinity, quoted in Bernard Levin's column, *Times* (London), July 9, 1980

Gallup's Theological Assertion. I could prove God statistically.
— George Gallup; from Don Nilsen

Gannon's Theory of Relativity. Grandchildren grow quicker than children.
— William P. Gannon, Glenolden, Pa.

Garreau's Second Law of Publishing. The less the readers know about how a publication is put together by its editors, the happier they are.
— Joel R. Garreau, *Washington Post*

Gayer's Amendment to Murphy's Law. Anything that can go wrong will go wrong, except at the repair shop, where it will magically, mysteriously (and temporarily) repair itself. (Once outside the repair shop again, see Murphy's Law.)
— Dixon Gayer, quoted in Jack Smith's column, *Los Angeles Times*, June 27, 1985; from Carol T. Stewart, Arlington, Va.

Geist's Basic Rule for Travel with Kids. Never in the same direction.
— William E. Geist, *New York Times*, October 10, 1982

General Electric Razor. The next time you're in a meeting, look around and identify the yesbutters, the notnowers, and the whynotters. Whynotters move companies.
— in a 1984 General Electric advertisement

Gene's Guidance. Grovel, it works.
— Colonel Eugene C. Habisher; from Bob Ackley, Plattsmouth, Neb.

George's Postulate. It is difficult to explain something to someone who has infinite wisdom.
— George E. Waggoner, Jr., Dearborn Heights, Mich.

Giachini's Law. Every man catches himself in the zipper of his fly once, and only once during his lifetime.
— Walt Giachini, Novato, Calif.

Gibson's Bermuda Law. If the grass is greener on the other side of the fence, your neighbor has an elephant for a pet.
— Ron Gibson, Germantown, Tenn.

Gilbert's Discovery. Any attempts to use any of the new super glues results in the two pieces sticking to your thumb and index finger rather than each other.
— Mike Gilbert, Santa Ana, Calif.

Gilbert's Observation. The surest sign of a crisis is that when you have a major problem, no one tries to tell you how to do your job.
— Anonymous; from Steve Masse, Concord, Mass.

Gill's Corollary to Fraknoi's Lament [q.v.]. Don't worry. If you are in the right place to see the eclipse, it will be foggy or overcast anyway.

Gill's Law of Agriculture. The easiest crops to grow are weeds and bugs.

Gill's Strapping Tape Conundrum. The package you receive in the mail will be either so insecurely wrapped that the post office has mangled it beyond recognition or wrapped so tightly that King Kong couldn't pry it open.
— Tom Gill, Davis, Calif.

Gilmore's Warning. The worse the society, the more law there will be. In Hell there will be nothing but law, and due process will be meticulously observed.
— Grant Gilmore, *New York Times,* February 23, 1977; from Don Nilsen

Godsey's Bookselling Laws. (1) You will invariably be sent twenty copies of a particularly bad book and only two copies of a bestseller. (2) If an author has appeared on television promoting his book within the last week, you and the warehouse will be out of stock. (3) The second book in a trilogy will be out of stock. (4) Air conditioning will leak only over books ranging in price from $11.95 and up. (5) No matter how much of an eye you keep on the adult magazines, they will always turn up in the religious section in the back of the store. (6) Two fingers and a typewriter can do a world of damage. (7) The week after you buy a much-wanted book in hardcover, the paperback version will appear; the month after that the hardcover will go on the bargain table as a remainder.
— Joyce Godsey and the staff of Waldenbooks #617, Methuen, Mass.

Gold's Law. There are two four-letter sources for ninety percent of all human troubles: S-E-X-X and M-U-N-Y.
— Herbert Resnicow, *The Gold Solution,* 1983; from Charles D. Poe

Goldthwait's Law of Animals. Animals are our friends, but they won't pick you up at the airport.
— comedian Bob "Bobcat" Goldthwait; from Steve Stine

Gomme's Law. A backscratcher will always find new itches.
— Andor Gomme, Stoke-on-Trent, England

Gongola's Electrical Paradox. The amount of zortch received from contact with a live wire on an aluminum ladder is not incumbent upon a nuclear or coal producing generating plant.
— Frank J. Gongola, Chicago, Ill.

Gooden's Rule. A woman's opinion of a man's sexual attraction is always in inverse ratio to her own sexual attraction.
— B. B. W. Gooden, Twickenham, Middlesex, England

Goodhardt's Forecasting Rule. Forecasting is never difficult; if it is not easy it is impossible.
— Professor Goodhardt; from James Rothman

Gordon's Laws of Motion. (1) The fastest way of getting some place is being there. (2) Go before you leave — this will prevent sudden stops. (3) Don't leave if you have to go. (4) It won't move if you don't fix it.
— Dr. Kurtis J. Gordon, Pleasant Grove, Utah

Goulden's Rule of Citations. The higher the rank of the author of a military memoir, the lesser the chance of a subordinate officer to be cited in the text, unless he is a batman or the subject of a court-martial (i.e., corps commanders ignore division chiefs of staff, and regimental commanders leave anonymous company and platoon commanders). Conversely, every rifleman in the First Marine Division "fought

with General Oliver Smith (or Colonel Chesty Puller) in Korea."
— Joseph C. Goulden, Washington, D.C.

Grabel's Temporary and Freelance Workers' Dilemma. There is always plenty of work when you can't and not enough work when you can.
— Steven M. Grabel, San Francisco, Calif.

Gramm's Laws. (1) It's crowded at the bottom. (2) The early worm gets the bird. (3) You're always on the wrong end of the train.
— Eugene Gramm, New York, N.Y.

Granger's Advice. Don't say you've paid your dues until you're at least 40.
— Bill Granger, *Chicago Tribune*, May 27, 1984; from Steve Stine

Grant's Axiom. If, in any quantity of chicken salad, there exists a single knob of chicken gristle, then it will find its way into the teeth of he who can least stand chicken gristle.
— Michael Grant, *San Diego Union*

Gray's Law of Maximum Knowledge. People reach their point of broadest education on the night before they take their Ph.D. prelims. **Gray's Law of the End of Learning.** University faculty learn nothing outside their narrow field of specialization once they have passed the preliminary examination for the Ph.D.
— Paul Gray, Claremont, Calif.

Graziano's Discoveries. (1) No solution is better than any solution. (2) Money can't buy happiness. Poverty can't buy happiness.
— Cindy Graziano, Chicago, Ill.

Green's Dictum. The bottom line is only the tip of the iceberg.
— Jay Green, Las Cruces, N.M.

Greene's Hotel Razor. The best measure of whether a hotel cares about you or not can be found in your room lamps. If the hotel cares about you, the button to turn the lamp on and off will be found on the base of the lamp, within easy reach. If the hotel does not care, the button will be found somewhere up beneath the shade, or on a little plastic clicker attached to the cord — where you have to search to locate it.
— Bob Greene "Rules of the Road," *Esquire,* August 1983.
    He adds that the other measure of whether a hotel cares
    about you is whether or not it has installed a red message
    light on your telephone.

Greene's Commentary on Life. The chief enemy of good is better.
— Dr. Milton Greene; from Dr. Bradford Walters, Detroit,
    Mich.

Greene's Law. Life is a do-it-yourself project.
— Bill Greene, from Joseph M. McCabe

Greenfield's Observation. Too many liberal Democrats have come, over the years, to worship . . . the state and to see it as the natural agent of the Lord's will, even though you can't reach it by telephone much after 4:30 in the afternoon.
— Meg Greenfield, *Newsweek,* December 15, 1980; from
    Robert Specht

The Gregory Productivity Axiom. Any discussion of increasing productivity refers to that of others.
— Walter Gregory, Milford, Conn., who explains: "Through-
    out years of participation in management meetings, a re-
    curring topic was the increasing of productivity. Never

once did one of the participants ever submit that his or her own productivity might be increased."

Gren's Law of Public Speaking. It's the hometown audience that expects the most and appreciates you the least.
— Jack Gren, Fort Wayne, Ind.

Gretchen's Defense. They said today that we should stock up on canned goods. So I went out and bought a case of beer.
— Galveston carpenter John Gretchen III, preparing for a hurricane, quoted in *Forbes,* October 8, 1984

Grice's Historical Perspective. We live on the point of the Arrow of Time — and have to look *back* for the shaft. **Grice's Law of Yellowed Lecture Notes.** Teaching is like prostitution — you got it, you sell it, and you still got it!
— John C. Grice, Greensboro, N.C.

Grissom's Law. The smallest hole will eventually empty the largest container, unless it is made intentionally for drainage, in which case it will clog.
— Dave Grissom, Coronado, Calif.

Grollinger's Observation on Opera. Only in opera can 300-pound sopranos die from consumption. **Grollinger's Axiom on Accountants and Auditors.** Old accountants/auditors never die — they just lose their balance. **Grollinger's Intimation on Immortality.** Death is usually incurable, except in Transylvania. **Grollinger's Maxim on Manufacturing.** If it's manufactured in America, it was probably assembled in Mexico or Taiwan. **Corollary.** The converse is also true.
— Stephen J. Grollinger, Westmont, Ill.

Gross's Laws. (1) Good work and mediocre work pay about the same. (2) In the search for the guilty, he who gave the warnings will be remembered. (3) There is always money

for the task force. (4) It is better to wear out than rust out. (5) Nothing is worse than a nervous boss, especially when you are the one who is making him nervous.
— Sidney Gross, Seattle, Wash.

Grubnick's Process for Effecting Action via Paperwork Within the Bureaucracy. (1) Blitz it with paperwork. (2) Say as little as possible, in as many ways as possible, as verbosely as possible. (3) Always try to tell them what they want to hear. (4) And never, never, never let the facts interfere with your story.
— David S. Grubnick, Fairbanks, Alaska

Gudeman's Paradox. Anyone I know who might qualify for MENSA has brains enough not to.
— Al Gudeman, Des Plaines, Ill.

Guitry's Distinction. You can pretend to be serious; you can't pretend to be witty.
— Sacha Guitry, quoted in the *Chicago Tribune*, July 27, 1986; from Steve Stine

Gunn's Law. An egalitarian society is one that has only two classes of people — those who are equal and those who keep them that way.
— Ben W. Gunn, Herts, England

Gunter's Airborne Discovery. (1) Upon being served a meal aboard an aircraft, the aircraft will encounter turbulence. (2) The strength of the turbulence encountered aboard an aircraft is directly proportional to the temperature of your coffee.
— Tony J. Gunter, Fort Jackson, S.C.

Gurney's Album Observation. If you get up to fix a skip on a record, the skip will fix itself just before you get to the

turntable. **Corollary.** After you fix a skip on a record, the next skip will not occur until after you are comfortably seated again.
— Spencer Gurney, Hanover, N.H.

Gustafson's Advice. Anything you look for in the Yellow Pages will not be listed in the category you first try to find it under. Start with the second.
— John W. Gustafson, San Francisco, Calif.

Gustafson's Observation. There is no virtue in consistency if you are consistently wrong.
— Art Gustafson; from Lloyd W. Vanderman, Oxon Hill, Md.

Guthery's Observation. In an evolving man-machine system, the man will get dumber faster than the machine will get smarter.
— Scott B. Guthery, Austin, Tex

Guy's Law. If a person puts a for sale sign on the lawn, the water heater blows up.
— caller named Guy, call-in radio show, Grand Rapids, Mich.

Haas's Rule. Everybody's vacations are a nuisance, except one's own.
— Timothy Haas, Woldingham, Surrey, England

Hackett's Rules. (1) Prophets of doom usually find it. (2) Expeditions cause rain. (3) Short-range planning always supersedes long-range planning.
— David K. Hackett, Knoxville, Tenn.

Hagan's Law of Tool Placement. It's in the other room.
— Jim Hagan; from W. E. McKean II

Hagman's Conclusion. Television is the opium of the last part of the twentieth century.
— actor Larry Hagman, on the TV show "Donahue"; from Steve Feinfrock

Haldane's Rule. Any legislation that does not purport to apply, and is not actually applied (a very different thing), to all social classes alike, will probably be unjustly applied to the poor.
— J. B. S. Haldane, quoted in *The New Yorker,* October 22, 1984; From Steven R. Woodbury

Hale's Black Hole Rule. Every messy desk contains a black hole, in which papers placed on one side disappear for three months, and then reappear on the other side. **Hale's Mail Rule.** When you are ready to reply to a letter, you will lack at least one of the following: (1) a pen (or pencil or typewriter), (2) stationery, (3) postage stamp, or (4) the letter you are answering. **Hale's Vacation Rule.** More happens in the two weeks you are away from the office on vacation than in the fifty weeks you are there. **Nonvacation Corollary.** More happens in the one hour you are at lunch than in the seven you are in the office.
— Irving Hale, Denver, Colo.

Hallen's Credo.

If you bend like the willow
you will never break your back
but you may find your nose on the ground.
— Walter Scott Hallen, Evanston, Ill.

Hall's Laws. Common Sense. The lower one's intelligence, the more likely one is to believe that intelligence and common sense are inversely related. **Vehicular Noise.** There is

an inverse relationship between the intelligence of the driver and the noise made by the driver's vehicle. **Radio.** The worse the music, the better the reception. **Strapping Things to Cars.** When a group of people finish strapping an unwieldy object to a car, someone in the group will say, "That's not going anywhere!"
— Donald M. Hall, Radford, Va.

Hall's Laws of Politics. (1) The voters always want less taxes and more spending. (2) Citizens want honest politicians until they want something fixed. (3) Constituency drives out consistency (i.e., liberals defend military spending and conservatives social spending in their own districts).
— Robert A. Hall, Minority Whip, Mass. Senate

Halperin's Laundry Rule. All lingerie put in the washer inside out comes out of the washer inside out. All lingerie put in the washer right side out — comes out inside out.
— Judith Halperin, Chicago, Ill.

Hammer's Rule of Reality. Official and Genuine never are.
— Ed Hammer; from Don Schaefer, Park Ridge, Ill.

Hancock's Law of the Pizza. The one who pays for the pizza gets the last slice.
— jazzman Herbie Hancock, in a Pizza Hut commercial, late 1985; From Steve Stine

Hanlon's Classification of Airline Passenger Seats. (1) All window seats are over the wing. (2) All aisle seats are opposite the galley. (3) All "Smoking" seats are opposite the lavatory. (4) All "Non-Smoking" seats are where you can't see the movie. (5) All seats where you can see the movie are next to the window seats whose occupants refuse to pull the shades down.
— Alfred Hanlon, Alexandria, Va.

Hansen's Law. If your new car is parked close enough to another car so that its driver can ding you with his door, he will ding you with his door.
— Louis S. Hansen, San Francisco, Calif.

Hanson's Treatment of Time. There are never enough hours in a day, but always too many days before Saturday. **Hanson's Observation of Conventions.** The most interesting moment at a convention is when you walk in late and everyone watches you. The most irritating moment at a convention is when someone else walks in late and interrupts your thought.
— Gary W. Hanson, Sioux Falls, S.D.

Harber's Rule of Photography. Open the lens two stops to compensate for the lens cap.
— Dick Harber, University of Southern California Department of Cinema, ca. 1973; from Richard Manning

Hardie's Two-Sided Sword. Enthusiasm often masks a great deal of incompetence. **Hardie's License Plate Observation.** Autos with women's names on the plates are usually driven by men.
— James Hardie, Phoenix, Ariz.

Hardy's Observation. Though a good deal is too strange to be believed, nothing is too strange to have happened.
— Thomas Hardy; from Stephen J. Chant

Harkness's Discovery. The harder it is to stay awake on the drive home, the harder it will be to fall asleep when you get there.
— R. J. Harkness, Ruth, Calif.

Harlan's Advice to Hecklers. Don't start an argument with somebody who has a microphone when you don't; they'll make you look like chopped liver.
— Harlan Ellison, in a speech at the University of New Mexico, ca. 1980; as recalled by Steve Stine

Harmer's Observation. You spend most of your university career avoiding the people you met during Fresher's Week.
— unknown; from Gareth J. Evans

Harrel's Collection of "Worst Questions I Have Been Asked". (1) Where did you lose it? (2) Have I kept you waiting? (3) You asleep? (4) Will you promise not to get mad if I ask you something? (5) You don't remember me, do you?

Harrel's Discoveries. (1) When a part of your anatomy is hurting, every friend you meet will hit you in that spot. (2) You can always judge a man's character by his activities when he is away from home.
— C. Jack Harrel, Superintendent, Kingfisher Public Schools, Kingfisher, Okla.

Harriet's Dining Observation. In every restaurant, the hardness of the butter pats increase in direct proportion to the softness of the bread being served.
— Harriet Markman; from Steve Markman, Pasedena, Calif.

Harris's Rule of Perennial News. Whatever other news stories may or may not occur from year to year, there will always be (1) a collision or oil spill involving a Liberian freighter, (2) a man, who after slaughtering at least five people with a gun or knife, will be described by his neighbors as a "decent, quiet, family man," (3) on a monthly basis, at least two substances in common, everyday use that some scientists will claim are cancer-related.
— Arnold Harris, Miami, Fla.

Harrison's Teaching Inequities. Young inexperienced teachers get (1) the worst disciplined classes, (2) the largest classes, (3) the least academic classes, (4) the greatest pupil/teacher contact time, (5) the least financial reward, and (6) the least time for preparation.
— R. C. Harrison, teacher, Garden City, England

Hart's Thirteenth Law of Political Economics. Financial markets will tolerate a Republican deficit but will run screaming in panic from a Democratic deficit a fraction its size.
— Senator Gary Hart, *Houston Chronicle,* July 21, 1988; from Charles D. Poe

Harvey's Reminder. In times like these, it is helpful to remember that there have always been times like these.
— Paul Harvey; from B. L. Albert

Harwitz's Finding. A top-secret government study indicates that we wouldn't be any worse off if we let the economists predict the weather and the meteorologists predict the economy.
— Paul Harwitz, *Wall Street Journal,* March 19, 1980; from Robert D. Specht

Dr. Haslam's Medical Rules. (1) The patients who thank you are the ones for which you have done the least. (2) The nicest people always have the worst illnesses. (3) The patient who begins a consultation with the words "Now you know I don't come to the doctor for every little thing . . ." is the one who does. (4) When explaining illness to patients, the only way to avoid being misunderstood is never to say anything. (5) Whatever day you tell a patient to start taking the contraceptive pill, her period will be due on her wedding day.
— David Haslam, M.D., Cambridgeshire, England, submitted with the full list, which first appeared in *World Medicine,* July 28, 1979

Hassell's Modified Maxim. Hard work never hurt anyone, but then neither did a whole lot of good rest.
— Richard Arthur Hassell, quoted in the *Journal of Irreproducible Results,* a 1984 issue

Hassinger's Rules. (1) Nothing is as simple as you thought it was going to be. (2) Nothing goes as quickly as you expected it to go. (3) Nothing ends up costing what you expected to spend.
— Herman Hassinger, Moorestown, N.J.

Hass's Revision of Lord Acton. Power over oneself is a good thing, the more absolute the better. It is power over *others* that corrupts, because the more power one has over others, the less power the others have over themselves.
— N. Sally Hass, Sleepy Hollow, Ill., responding to **Acton's Law** (Power corrupts. Absolute power corrupts absolutely.)

Hastings's Boogie Axiom. The single most requested item in the library is the most likely to grow legs and walk. **Corollary.** As the number of requests for the *Rand McNally Road Atlas* increases, so does the probability of its being stolen.
— Carole Marie Hastings, *Reference Librarian,* a 1983 issue

Haught's Query for Spouses with a Motorcycle. Why don't you get a mistress instead? Nobody ever got killed falling off a mistress.
— Jim Haught of the *Charleston Gazette* quoting his wife, *Forbes,* February 23, 1987

Hauser's Truths. (1) If you have a garden wedding, the cesspool runs over. (2) The only time you get dealt a royal flush is when you are down to your last five dollars.
— Georgia Hauser, Albion, Calif.

Havens's Law. Déjà vu is only a poor memory — you *have* done it before.
— H. Gordon Havens, Kansas City, Mo.

Hazlitt's Conjecture on Consistency. Never say "never" and always avoid "always."
— John M. Hazlitt, South Bend, Ind.

Hawkeye's Conclusions. (1) It's not easy to play the clown when you've got to run the whole circus. (2) The tedium here is relieved only by the boredom.
— the character Hawkeye Pierce in "M*A*S*H"

Hebert's First Law of Highway Engineering. Freeways aren't. **Hebert's First Law of Nonsuccess.** It's lonely at the bottom, too. It's just more crowded.
— John M. Hebert, New Baltimore, Mich.

Hegel's Rules of Order. (1) Before you argue or debate, define the terms. (2) Before that, define "define."
— Gene Hegel, Elgin, Ill.

Heilson's Discovery. Time is nature's way of keeping everything from happening at once.
— Jeffery W. Heileson, Santa Ana, Calif.

Heinemann's Law of Executive Recruitment. The best way to get a good managerial job is to have had a good managerial job, no matter how thoroughly you screwed it up.
— George A. Heinemann, Crystal Lake, Ill.

Heinlein's Economic Given. People who go broke in a big way never miss any meals. It is the poor jerk who is shy a half slug who must tighten his belt.
— novelist Robert Heinlein, quoted in *Forbes*, April 14, 1980

Heisey's Principle of Reference Librarianship. The only patron on a bad night will spend hours in the mystery section, then come to the desk ten minutes before closing and demand *all* available material on atomic energy for a paper due tomorrow morning.
— R. F. Heisey, Arlington, Va.

Helen's Inanimate Object Lessons. (1) The certainty of an object's loss is directly related to the "specialness" of the place you put it. (2) If you buy a new one, the old one will turn up (90 percent probability.) **The Cognitive Corollary.** The more confident you are of remembering, the more likely you are to forget. **The Bonus Intuitive Rule of Object Placement.** Once you finally find an object, put it in the **first** place you thought to look for it, particularly if you returned to that place more than once in your search. Do NOT apply any other rule of logic to this choice. Do NOT choose a place that seems in any way "special."

Helen's Model for Predicting the Behavior of Machinery. All machines are equipped with desperation detectors: The more desperate you are to meet any sort of deadline, the more intractable they become. Operators will note: these detectors are not fooled by superficial acting, or the feigned appearance of calm.
— Helen Fleisher, Silver Spring, Md.

Helen's Rule of the Two-Year-Old. (1) They will *never* tell you that they have to go to the bathroom . . . (2) until after you have dressed them in boots, mittens, coat, snowpants, scarf and hat. (3) By the time you undress them, it's too late. (4) If it's not too late, it was a false alarm. (5) If it was a false alarm the first time, it won't be a false alarm once you get them dressed again.
— from John A. Mattsen, Finlayson, Minn.

Helen's Query. If I dialed the wrong number, why did you answer?
— Helen E. Jolliffe; from her son

Hellinger's Law. Today's cheap trick becomes tomorrow's precedent.
— the character Nick Hellinger in the TV movie "Hellinger's Law," which aired on CBS on March 10, 1981. In his review, critic Tom Shales of the *Washington Post* pointed out that it was also the "First Law of Television"

Helmer's Rule of Self-Enlightened Nonresistance. When dealing with fools, do whatever is necessary to make them happy and get them off your back.
— John (?) Helmer, *Texas Observer,* September 13, 1985; from Joseph C. Goulden

Helms's First Rule for Keeping Secrets. Nothing on paper; paper can be lost or stolen or simply inherited by the wrong people; if you want to keep something secret, don't write it down.
— former CIA Director Richard Helms, quoted in *The Economist,* April 12, 1980; from Joseph C. Goulden

Helprin's Discovery. Marxists are people whose insides are torn up day after day because they want to rule the world and no one will even publish their letter to the editor.
— novelist Mark Helprin, *Winter's Tale*

Hembree's Law. Interaction of industrial, scientific, and political entities always selects the course which makes the most profit for the largest corporations.
— Hugh Hembree, *Mensa Bulletin,* November 1984

Hemingway's Law. The most essential gift for a good writer is a built-in, shock-proof crap detector.
— Ernest Hemingway, *Paris Review*, 1958; from James E. Farmer

Henderson's Rule of Movement. The dogs may yap, but the caravan moves on. **Henderson's Texas A&M Rule.** Once is tacky, twice is tradition.
— Lt. Col. Joe C. Henderson, USAF, Texas A&M University

Henry J's Rule. When your work speaks for itself, don't interrupt.
— automotive pioneer Henry J. Kaiser

Hepburn's Distinction. I don't want to be alone. I want to be left alone.
— Katherine Hepburn, quoted in *TV Guide*, December 15, 1973; from Don Nilsen

Hepler's Laws of Business. (1) You can never tell. (2) It all depends.
— Professor Hal Hepler, Michigan State University; from Robert Nelson

Herburger's Law of Small-Town Lawyers. Where there is only one lawyer in town, the lawyer can't make a living. But when there are two lawyers in town, both of them will make a good living.
— from Calvin E. Deonier, Ritter, Ore.

Herold's Constant. When a politician, particularly on the stump, says that he'll "reconsider," "reevaluate," or "study" something once elected, he's going to kill it.
— R. A. Herold, Ottawa, Ontario, Canada

Hertz's Instructions for the Lost. Having gotten lost while driving, do the following — proceed until you either (1) reach a dead end, or (2) find a more major road. If (1), turn around until you reach (2). Keep this up and you will find yourself on a big enough road that will be recognizable or a big enough town that you can get directions.
— Louis D. Hertz, Margate City, N.J.

Hesting's Law of Inspiration. Any brilliant idea conceived after sunset is doomed not to be acted upon; brilliant ideas lose their appeal overnight.
— Chad Hesting, Columbia City, Ind.

Hewett's Diagnosis. If you are worried about your drinking, you should be. The converse is not true.

Hewett's Observation. The rudeness of a bureaucrat is inversely proportional to his or her position in the governmental hierarchy and to the number of peers similarly engaged. (If there is one window open, it will be staffed by Godzilla's cousin.)
— Paul C. Hewett, Wilmette, Ill.

Hewitt's Laws. (1) If you've got a problem that can be solved with money, you haven't got a problem. (2) When you light a cigarette backwards it will be the last one in the pack. (3) When you think to wind the grandfather clock, one of the hands will be over the keyhole. (4) Babies cry. (5) Old ladies get dizzy. (6) Memos marked Personal and Confidential are neither. (7) If it looks like jive, it probably is.
— John H. Hewitt, M.D., Rockville, Md.

Hiestand's Law. People who forget to turn off their car headlights almost always remember to lock their doors.
— James W. Hiestand, Chattanooga, Tenn.

Higgins's Definition of an Optimist. A man treed by a lion who enjoys the view.
> — the Rev. George Higgins, Briarcliff, N.Y.; from a sign displayed in front of his church

Hilldrup's Genuine Barbecue Law. Anyone who says he can slice barbecue can't.

Hilldrup's Law of Home Improvement. There is no such thing as one termite.
> — Robert P. Hilldrup, Richmond, Va.

Hinshaw's Corollary. Gall will get you further than talent.
Hinshaw's Corollary to one of Kenworthy's Laws [*q.v.*]. To achieve longevity in an organization, be available but not visible.
> — Elton Hinshaw, Secretary-Treasurer, American Economic Association, Nashville, Tenn.

Hinson's Discoveries. (1) Rarely is anything lost on *top* of something. (2) Anytime that one sets down a loaded trash bag, said bag will slowly fall over in the most undesirable direction. (3) Never, never read the fine print. There ain't no way you're gonna like it. . . . Otherwise, it would printed in large print.
> — Archie Edward Hinson, El Cajon, Calif.

Hirabayashi's First Law of Housekeeping. There is no convenient time for the cat to throw up on the carpet.
> — Judy Hirabayashi, Oakland, Calif.

Hitchcock's Staple Principle. The stapler runs out of staples only while you are trying to staple something.
> — Wilbur W. Hitchcock, U.S. Consul, Buenos Aires, Argentina

Hoffer's Discovery. The last grand act of a dying institution is to issue a newly revised, enlarged edition of the policies and procedures manual.
— philosopher Eric Hoffer; from W. J. Vogel

Hoffman's Pothole Law. Any public road having waited a minimum of five years for badly needed paving during which time no underground construction has taken place, except by gophers and moles, will within one week of being resurfaced be torn up by at least five public or private entities to make long-scheduled, not emergency, repairs; such entities will always work consecutively and not conjunctively.
— Agnes Hoffman, Rio Nido, Calif. (originally published in the *San Francisco Chronicle,* May 20, 1985)

Hoffnagle's Key to Time Management. If you have too much time, procrastination will insure that you need even more; and if you have too little time, fear will insure that you need even less.
— Gene F. Hoffnagle, Clinton Hollow, N.Y.

Hoff's Law of Departure. The plane's delayed departure time is directly proportional to the time it took to get to the airport.
— E. P. Hoff, Fremont, Calif.

Hoff's Rule of Responsibility. Dividing 100 percent responsibility between two persons gives 10 percent for each of them.
— Aksel Hoff, Haslev, Denmark

Hofstadter's Law. It always takes longer than you think it will take, even if you take into account Hofstadter's Law.
— Douglas R. Hofstadter, *Scientific American,* January 1982; from Steve Stine

Holben's Law. Everything costs at least $100.
— Stephen Holben, Denver, Colo.

Holberger's Rule. It doesn't matter how hard you work on something; what counts is finishing and having it work.
— quoted in Tracy Kidder's *The Soul of a New Machine;* from Shel Kagan

Holden's Findings. (1) Experience is something you don't get until just after you needed it. (2) When a chamber of commerce brags that its city is halfway between the mountains and the seashore, or equidistant from whatever other attractions, what they're saying is that it's in the middle of nowhere.
— William M. Holden, Fair Oaks, Calif.

Holleran's Recollection. [My father] gave me two pieces of advice: never to save money on shoes, and to treat oneself to a steak dinner now and then.
— Andrew Holleran, *Nights in Aruba*

Holliday's Discoveries. (1) People with coughs always have concert tickets. (2) For every member who works for a volunteer organization there are two others who don't like what he's doing. (3) If lonely, sort laundry, get out the vacuum cleaner, put trash bags inside the door, and company will arrive.
— Phillip Holliday, North Webster, Ind.

Holloway's Rule. You never know until you find out.
— Scott Holloway; from Michael Kehr, York, Pa.

Holmes's Priority Rule. It's better to be a masochist, than not kissed at all.
— Joseph Holmes, Philadelphia, Pa.

Holton's Hypothesis. The length of a presentation is in inverse proportion to its value.
— Richard Holton, Western Springs, Ill.

Honcho's Law of Wind Chimes. Regardless of the velocity of the wind, your wind chimes chime only when you are trying to go to sleep.
— "Honcho" Holland, Encinitas, Calif.

Hoover's Benediction. Blessed are the young for they shall inherit the national debt.
— Herbert Hoover, quoted in *The Executive Quotation Book*, St. Martin's Press

Hoover's Question. If a man tells you that he never tells the truth, can you believe him?
— R. Hoover, Worth, Ill.

Hopkins's Baby Law. Much of what goes in must come out, but not necessarily by the expected route. [Ms. Hopkins insists that this law does not appear in other collections of laws because either it is too obvious or "it results in so much wearisome work that the human mind has evolved a subconscious automatic repression of it to ensure that too prominent an awareness of it does not endanger the wish to propagate the species."]
— C. M. Hopkins, Berkshire, England

Horowitz Collection, A Selection from the. (7) Sowing wild oats is no way to break new ground. (15) Live unrepressed. Don't stifle any yawns. (57) Cultivate a green thumb. Hedge your bets. (59) Lane hoppers never achieve the inside track. (130) Nothing succeeds like recess. (138) Send flowers to funerals of people who have [had] no time to smell the roses.

(163) Marry a slowpoke and the both of you will end up as two peas in a plod. (234) Before getting angry let off some esteem. (259) Being tied up all day is a poor way to get yourself together. (266) People who make mountains out of molehills suffer from piles. (410) A man of many hats is rarely in top form. (434) Cut your losses. The best bargain is flee-bargaining. (435) Hanging around the water cooler can get you into hot water.
> — Stanley Horowitz, Flushing, N.Y., from his unpublished collection of aphorisms, *The Nerd's 500 Peachy-Keen Secrets of Success: An Unlikely Guide to the Top*

Horrigan's Lament. Today, you can get designer pasta, but you can't get your shoes repaired.
> — Patrick Horrigan, quoted in *Newsweek* on his Manhattan neighborhood, April 20, 1987

Horton's Observation on Professionalism. It's better to be lucky than good, but slightly less reliable.
> — Joseph A. Horton, M.D., Morgantown, W. Va.

Hoskins's Truth. He who has not, ain't got.
> — from George Albrecht

Howard's Comparison. Permitting your life to be taken over by another person is like letting the waiter eat your dinner.
> — Vernon Howard; from Bob Heimberg, Las Vegas, Nev.

Hoyle's Hoylerism. Good enough isn't.
> — Betty Hoyle, Orlando, Fla.

Hubbard's Constant. The fellow that brags about how cheaply he heats his home always sees the first robin.
> — Hoosier humorist Kin Hubbard (1859–1915)

Huddleston's Observation. Message importance varies directly with the ignorance of the colleague left in charge of your telephone.
— Dr. Jo H. F. Huddleston, Bracknell, Berkshire, England

Humpert Unhappy Homily. The older you get, the easier it is to resist temptation, but the harder it is to find.
— Joseph H. Humpert, M.D., Ft. Mitchell, Ky.

Humphreys's Rules. (1) Nothing is cheaper than pencils. (2) If they notice the after-shave, you've got too much on. (3) If it needs an exclamation point, it isn't important. (4) It is more helpful to say "no" than to say "I'll think about it." (5) "Why?" is infinitely less important than "What now?" (6) The cost of a fire is never less than the cost of a fire extinguisher. (7) Signatures apart, the more important a person is, the worse his handwriting. (8) Everyone hates the one who cries, "Bingo!" (9) A dog is a dog until he's facing you; then he's Mr. Dog. (10). It is impossible to be famous and private.
— David H. Humphreys, English School, Nicosia, Cyprus

Humphreys's Second Law of Human Behavior. People will use immediate resources to solve immediate problems. **Corollary.** In 80 percent of cases, you will find the solution to a given problem within your arms' reach, if you are willing to improvise or compromise.
— Daniel Humphreys, Cincinnati, Ohio

Hunt's Lament. A billion dollars is not what it used to be.
— Bunker Hunt, after failing to corner the world's silver market, quoted in *Time*, December 29, 1980

Hutber's Law. Improvement means deterioration.
— the late Patrick Hutber, city editor of the *London Daily Telegraph*, who created it in the 1960s. It is still invoked

when an improvement is announced which results in the curtailment of, say, Saturday deliveries; from Russell Ash

Huygen's Theory of Theories. Whenever you explain to a friend a completely new and original theory you have just developed on any political, philosophical, or social subject, you will read your own words the next day in a magazine you know your friend also reads.
— Freddy Huygen, Antwerp, Belgium

Hynes's Advice. When you have a lot of things to do, get your nap out of the way first.
— Jeremiah Hynes; from his daughter Jo Anderson, Deerfield, Ill.

Hynes's Discovery. Dilatoriness is a virtue, and is often rewarded — unlike most of the other virtues.
— Professor Sam Adams Hynes, Princeton University; from James Thorpe III

 **I**

Immutability, Three Rules of. (1) If a tarpaulin can flap, it will. (2) If a small boy can get dirty, he will. (3) If a teenager can go out, he/she will.
— anonymous, in the *Robbins Reader*, a 1980 issue

Industrial Rules. (1) Interchangeable parts won't. (2) High pressure oil lines will spray visiting dignitaries.
— circulated in the early 1960s at the Raytheon Company in Andover, Mass.; from Richard K. Jolliffe, Saskatoon, Saskatchewan, Canada

Indiana Jones's Response to the Next Problem. "I don't know. I'm making it up as I go along."
> — in the movie *Raiders of the Lost Ark;* from Elizabeth Lundren, D.V.M.

Inlander's Theory of Relativity. Everybody has relatives.
> — Charlie Inlander, Philadelphia, Pa.; from Steve Stine

Inskip's Rules. (1) Don't sweat the small stuff. (2) It's all small stuff.
> — Dr. Richard Inskip, Director, American Academy of Family Physicians. This set of rules has also been attributed to University of Nebraska cardiologist Robert Eliot.

The Insurance Catch-22. If you want it, you can't get it, but if you'll never use it, and don't need it, you can buy all you want.
> — Brian McCombie, "My Turn," *Newsweek,* August 11, 1986

Invisible People's Rule of Management. If I tell a man to do what he does not want to do, I am no longer chief.
> — words of the chief of the Invisible People in the movie *The Emerald Forest*

Irving's Laws. (1) Never judge a book by its cover price. (2) Never get into an argument with a recorded message. (3) Don't let the boss know you're a male chauvinist. She may not like it.
> — "Irving," quoted in Ed Cooper's column, *Magazine & Bookseller.*

Issawi on Revolution and Revolutionaries. (1) Those who are continually in revolt become revolting. (2) Revolutions are high jumps, not long jumps. One turns right over and seems to reach the sky, but lands very close to where one took off.

(3) The Revolution is a sweet, innocent maiden, constantly being seduced and as often betrayed.
— Professor of Near Eastern Studies Charles Issawi, **Princeton Alumni Weekly**. He has given us many laws, including these recent discoveries:

Issawi's Saws. On going up and down. What goes up decelerates; what comes down accelerates. **On sex and money.** Sex and money are like tea and coffee — two delicious ingredients which, when mixed together, produce a foul concoction. **On cutting waste from budgets.** Budget cutters cannot cut waste, because waste is not budgeted. **On letters of recommendation.** A professor knows he has reached the peak of his academic career when the letters of recommendation he writes exceeds those he solicits by a ratio of 24 to 1.

Italian Sayings. (1) Every man tries to bring water to his own mill. (2) The world is made of stairs, and there are those who go up and those who go down.
— in Ed McBain's *Eight Black Horses,* 1985; from Charles D. Poe

J's Business Maxim. When perplexed, confused, frustrated and all else has failed, fall back on the truth. **J's Density Characteristics of Executives Rising in an Organization.** Cream Rises and Sewage Floats.
— Anonymous

Jack Frost's Law. If you need statistics to prove it, it probably wasn't true in the first place.
— from Dr. Joel A. Tobias, Medford, Ore., who points out that Frost was his professor of medicine at the University of Pennsylvania

Jacob's Discovery. If a community's name includes the word "center," it's in the suburbs. If it includes the word "city," it's in the country. If its name is Center City, it's two cottages and a gas station.
— Norma Jacob, Kennett Square, Pa.

Jacobs's First Dictum of Computer Operation. Computers are awfully stupid — they do exactly what you tell them to do.
— Lewis G. Jacobs, San Francisco, Calif.

Jacobson's Rules and Laws. Rain. If you want rain for your new garden, just plan a beach vacation. **Money.** If you have no cash in your wallet, you will also have no checks in your checkbook. If you do have a check left in your book, you will not have a suitable I.D. in your wallet.* **Matchmaking.** If you try to sneak your way through a surprise introduction of a co-worker to your best college friend, you will quickly learn they were divorced from one another in 1982. **Law of Promotion, 1967:** Just when you think you've got the promotion in the bag, some new guy will come along and marry the boss's daughter. **Law of Promotion, 1987.** Just when you think you've got the promotion in the bag, some new gal will come along and marry the boss's son.
— Roberta B. Jacobson, APO, N.Y.

---

*This rule prompted a corollary from Carol Schuette Linden of Wilmette, Ill.:
Linden's Extension of Jacobson's Rules of Money. If you have only one check left in your checkbook and a suitable I.D. in your wallet, you will make a mistake when writing the check which will necessitate the check being voided.

James's Lament. The problem with learning to speed read is you run out of funnies too fast.
— Alice James, Mesquite, Tex.

James Research Rule. The topic you seek is never in the index.
— H. L. James, San Jose, Calif.

Janitorial Blindness, Law of. Full garbage cans exude a certain substance that causes them to become invisible to the janitors. Empty and nearly empty cans do not have this quality.
— David B. Cagle, Santa Monica, Calif.

Jan's Law of Sensitivity. If you're not going nuts, you're not paying attention.
— Janis Jones, Sunland, Calif.

Jan's Measure. There's an ounce of truth in every pound of lie.
— Jan Jennier, Bowie, Md.

January's Cruel Lesson. You will not win one of those million dollar magazine sweepstakes that come in the mail. Knowing this, you will spend hours filling them out and in the process will accidentally order a magazine devoted to either subsistence farming, needlepoint, or bow hunting.
— the Director

Jardine's Constant. In a health club, if there is only one other locker occupied, it will be the one above yours.
— Andrew F. Jardine, Philadelphia, Pa.

Jean's Law. Keep your feet close to the ground.
— Jean Pike, Modesto, Calif.

Jeff's Law of the Vanishing Mystique (Male Version). As soon as a ravishing woman actually gets out of a sporty car, she is no longer ravishing. **Jeff's Law of Traffic Lights:** The slowpoke you're stuck behind will always make it through a yellow light, just slow enough so that you can't.
— Jeffrey P. Davidson, Falls Church, Va.

Jensen's Law. When you're hot, you're hot, and when you're not, everybody is watching.
— Lynn Jensen, Littleton, Colo.

Jesson's Law of Office Supply Dynamics. There is never a paper clip on the floor when you need one.
— Dick Jesson, San Francisco, Calif.

Jewell's Rule of Domestic Horticulture. The probability of grass growing in any given spot is inversely proportional to one's desire to have it there.
— History Professor Fred R. Jewell, Harding University, Searcy, Ark. who formulated the rule one day "while pulling sizable outcroppings of grass from the cracks in my driveway and simultaneously noting the bare spots in my lawn just a few feet away"

Jim Nasium's Law. In a large locker room, with hundreds of lockers, the few people using the facility at any one time will all be at their lockers and will be next to each other so that everybody is cramped.
— Gary Neustadter, San Jose, Calif.

Jim's Rule. The rental of any apartment in a major city will guarantee that the building will go condo.
— Unknown, WIND Radio

Joany's Law. The human mind is wonderful thing. It begins working the moment you're born, and doesn't stop until you have to speak in public.
— anonymous, from Tom Gill

Jobson's Law of Sailing. If you can't tie good knots, tie plenty of them.
— in a Dewar's Scotch ad featuring yacht racer Gary Jobson; from Steve Stine

Joe's Discovery. The reliability of any copier is inversely proportional to the number of copies needed.
— Unknown, WIND Radio

Johnson's Culinary Admonitions. Don't spit in the soup. We've all got to eat.
— President Lyndon B. Johnson; from Erwin Knoll

Johnson's Discoveries. (1) At the end of a talk, an average of three people will shake the speaker's hand. (2) Originality is a vain myth. (3) No matter how many of them you collect, there will always be some more.
— Willis Johnson, Jr., Atlanta, Ga.

Johnson's Fingernail Corollary. The difficulty of the task requiring longer fingernails increases in direct proportion to the remaining available, usable amount of fingernail.
— Frank "Louie" Johnson, Bangor, Me.

John's Rules. (1) One size fits all means one size fits nobody. (2) Never step in anything soft. (3) A penny saved is a penny. (4) Early to bed, early to rise, and your girl goes out with other guys.
— Unknown, WRC Radio

John's Understanding. If you do something really dumb once, it's stupid. If you repeat it often, it's philosophy.
— Christopher John, Meadow Valley, Calif.

Jolliffe's Rules for Parents. (1) No article of clothing left behind at school will ever be found in the Lost and Found Box. Exception: If the lost items were a pair, one of them will. (2)

After all have reached agreement, regardless of the bicycle you eventually buy your child, the next-door neighbor's kid will be given the one your child really wanted after all. (3) The amount of time a child plays with a new Christmas toy is always one-fifth of the time it took for the parent to assemble it. (Also known as the Hawaiian rule. According to the man who discovered the rule, "We bought our daughter a huge Barbie doll house in Hawaii, at a big saving, and lugged it all the way back to Canada. I spent several evenings putting it together and assembling all the furniture. She has played with it for a grand total of one hour and seventeen minutes.)

— Richard K. Jolliffe, Saskatoon, Saskatchewan, Canada

Jones's Advice on Surviving Thermonuclear War. Just dig a hole, cover it with a couple of doors, then throw three feet of dirt on top.

— T. K. Jones, The Pentagon, quoted on the *Washington Post 1982 Calendar*

Jones's Anthropological Discovery. There was no profanity in the original languages of the American Indians. But, of course, there was no federal income tax, either.

— Franklin P. Jones, quoted in the *Wall Street Journal*, August 27, 1983

Jones's Law of Inverse Properties. The architectural style of the house is inversely proportional to the personal style of the entertainer. The outre Cher, for example, prefers staid Tudors, while the more reticent Robert Redford lives in a spectacular glass-and-steel aerie perched atop Utah mountains.

— Landon Y. Jones, *Great Expectations*; from Steve Stine

Juall's Law on Losing. You may beat me, but you cannot defeat me. **On Winning**: It doesn't matter if you win or lose, it matters only if you beat the point spread.

— Wally Juall, East Lansing, Mich.

Jump's Discovery. Life is a lot like golf: you drive hard to get to the green and then you end up in the hole. **Jump's Query.** One of the great mysteries of life is how the idiot your daughter married can be the father of the smartest grandchildren in the world. **Jump's Rule of Monthly Meetings.** Monthly meetings always last two hours, regardless of the number and importance of the items on the agenda. This is because if there is little to be discussed, the participants will spend more time discussing each point because there is no pressure to move things along . . . [T]he time available . . . is controlled by the same factor which **limits** meetings to two hours when there is **much** to discuss, which is that when you have reached two hours there are always a few people who are being called by nature, and usually the chairperson is one of them.
— Gary Jump, Bensenville, Ill.

Just's Seventh Law of Traffic Behavior. The more decrepit the vehicle, the more maniacal the driver.
— the Rev. Christian F. Just, Euclid, Ohio

Kachur's Elementary School Teacher Laws. (1) The loudest human voice cannot compete with a pencil sharpener. (2) Parents who show up for conferences or open house are the ones who don't need to. The parents of the problem kids never show up. (3) The students with the worst behavior have the best attendance. (4) If Easter recess comes early, it'll snow; if late, it'll rain. If you decide to vacation in Florida, after you arrive, you'll hear on the radio weather news that it's sunny and mild back home.
— Miriam Kachur, Pennsauken, N.J.

Kagan's Theorem of the Hidden Agenda. There is always more going on than you think. **Corollary.** And it's always worse than you imagine.
— Shel Kagan, Canoga Park, Calif.

Kahn's Laws. (1) Vice presidents never call back. (2) Entrepreneurs always call back.
— Steve Kahn, *Wall Street Journal*, March 21, 1984

Karl's Laws of Bureaucratic Paperflow. (1) Every bureaucracy generates paperwork in a logarithmic fashion. A one-page directive will inevitably lead to five-page guideline, a ten-page procedure, and a twenty-five-page report. (2) Any attempt to clarify the information contained in a directive, guideline, or procedure will increase the amount of paperwork in each of the subsequent steps.
— Ed Karl, Urbana, Ill.

Kass's Plagiarism.
Those who can — do.
Those who cannot — teach.
Those who can do neither — inspect.
— Lt. Col. Nicholas E. Kass (Retired), USAF Fort Walton Beach, Fla.

Kastor's Rule Number One for Speech-Givers. Before lobbing a joke at anyone else, aim one at yourself.
— Elizabeth Kastor, *Washington Post*, February 4, 1985. She followed the rule with this: "'All my life I've wanted to run for president in the worst possible way,' Walter Mondale told a National Press Club audience Saturday night. 'And I did.'"

Katz's Aphorisms. (1) That which cannot be explained in a brief article is never explained in a big book. (2) Few things inhibit the undertaking of a new venture more than the fear of ridicule. (3) The scientist who claims that your research

is not in the mainstream really means that only his is. (4) The mathematician who insists there can be no such thing as non-Newtonian calculus is more often than not the fellow who specializes in non-Euclidean geometry.
— Robert Katz, Archimedes Foundation, Rockport, Mass.

Kazurinsky's Discovery. It is impossible to know if the refrigerator light really goes out when you close the door because you eat the only witnesses.
— Tim Kazurinsky, on the TV show "Saturday Night Live"

Keeleric's Law. Persecution of deviants (for a doctrine) is inversely proportional to the deviation.
— George Keeleric, Galway, Ireland

Kelleher's Explanation. The Congress is constitutionally empowered to launch programs the scope, impact, consequences and workability of which are largely unknown, at least to the Congress, at the time of enactment; the federal bureaucracy is legally permitted to execute the congressional mandate with a high degree of befuddlement as long as it acts no more befuddled than the Congress must reasonably have anticipated.
— U.S. District Court Judge Robert Kelleher, Central District, Calif., *American Petroleum Institute* v. *Knecht,* August 31, 1978; from Steven R. Woodbury

Kelley's Law of Bladder Capacity. The bladder capacity of a spectator at a public event (football game, concert, etc.) is inversely proportional to his or her distance from the aisle.
— John R. Kelley, Jr., Alexandria, Va.

Kelly's Counsel on Hiring Counsel. On any given day, 50 percent of the lawyers in American courtrooms are losers.
— Thomas W. Kelly, Washington, D.C.

Kempley's Equine Cinematic Rule. When a horse is on the screen (unless of course it's the famous Mr. Ed), the Kleenexes on the floor should outnumber the Milk Dud boxes.
— film critic Rita Kempley, *Washington Post,* October 12, 1984

Kennedy's Market Theorem. Given enough inside information and unlimited credit, you've got to go broke.
— Joseph P. Kennedy; from Lawrence Gutter

Kennevan's Conundrum. Why is it that when a professor says, "That's a good question," he never has a good answer?
— Walter J. Kennevan, Professor Emeritus, American University, Bethesda, Md.

Kenworthy's Laws of the Bureaucracy. (a selection). **Competency.** The competency of any executive level official of government is inversely proportional to the number of his or her "special" or "executive" assistants. **Assistants.** The arrogance of any "special" or "executive" assistant to a secretarial level official is inversely proportional to the age and experience thereof. **Career Bureaucrats.** The influence of any Government Service career bureaucrat is inversely proportional to the age of the furnishings of his or her office.

Values in the Bureaucracy. (1) In government, influence is most admired; longevity is most respected; but anonymity is most prized. (2) Respect is what is earned from one's supervisors instead of a promotion or raise. (3) The deeper the carpet you're called upon, the deeper the trouble you're in.

Cabinet Law. A cabinet officer's most efficient activity is foreign travel; his or her most useful activity is domestic travel; time spent in the office is merely the necessary connection between the two.

External Relations. (1) A lobbyist is paid to look like he's telling the truth when he's lying; a department's congressional liaison is paid to look like he's telling the truth when he really has nothing to say. (2) A reporter's brother-in-law who works for the government is known as an "informed source" when he's sober and a "leak" when he's drunk.
— Jim Kenworthy, Kansas City, Mo.

Kernan's Correlation. Every time you lend money to a friend you damage his memory.
— F. G. Kernan

Kernan's Fine Principles of Travel. (1) Whatever your friends told you, they are wrong. (2) You can't read at the beach. (3) Beware of smiling cabbies. (4) Avoid jolly groups, unless you are in one.
— Michael Kernan, *Washington Post*, April 14, 1985

Kerr's Rules. (1) The day the letter jackets or letter sweaters are given to an athletic team, it will be barely cold enough to wear them. (2) In most instances, there must be onions in fast foods and peanuts in candy. (3) Surplus toothpaste on the toothbrush results in a liquid that drops from the mouth but is solid enough to stick to the sink. (4) If you don't desire an elected office in a club or organization, you will probably be elected to it. **Corollary.** One sure way to be elected to an undesired office in a club is to be out of town the day of the election. **Corollary.** To prevent being elected to an unwanted office, chair the nominating committee.
— Bob Kerr, Amarillo, Tex.

Kesulab's Laws. (1) **Dictionaries.** Never look up a word you cannot spell. Never spell a word you cannot look up. (2) **Western Movie First Aid.** No matter where the good guy is

wounded, bandage the arm and shoulder. (3) **Band-Aids.** Band-Aids stick to children only when they are in traction.
— Gary O. Balusek, Xenia, Ohio

Kibble's Law. Miles per gallon are no problem if you occasionally forget to record a fill-up.
— G. V. Kibblewhite, Goldhurst, Kent, England

Kime's Law for the Reward of Meekness. Turning the other cheek merely ensures two bruised cheeks.
— Jack Kime, Las Cruces, N.M.

King's Law of Swimming Pools. When you build a swimming pool, hire a state highway engineer. They always build highways that hold water.
— John J. King, Pitts, Ga.

Kingfield's Constant. Nothing can be taken back. Everything is in the "record" . . . *always!!*
— Professor Kingfield in the television series "The Paper Chase"; from Steve Feinfrock

Kington's Law of Perforation. If a straight line is made in a piece of paper, such as a sheet of stamps or a check, that line becomes the strongest part of the paper. [Mr. Kington elaborates; "Actually, the most obvious example is a roll of lavatory paper. There is a subsidiary law which states that a sharp tug at a perforated lavatory roll pulls the whole roll on the floor (the only real life example I know of perpetual motion). The roll can never be rolled back."]
— Miles Kington, *Punch*

Kinsley's Law. Insincere flattery is even more flattering than sincere flattery. **Corollary.** All flattery is flattering.
— Michael E. Kinsley, *The New Republic,* January 20, 1985; from Joseph C. Goulden

Kinsley's Law of Magazines. New owners always replace the editor, especially if they begin by expressing complete confidence.
— Michael E. Kinsley, *The New Republic,* January 2, 1985; from Joseph C. Goulden

Kirshbaum's First Axiom of Publishing. There is always a shortage of the books that sell and an overabundance of the books that don't.
— Laurence J. Kirshbaum, President, Warner Books, quoted in the *New York Times,* January 18, 1988; from Joseph C. Goulden

Kissel's Cat Cause. Cats have an instinctive ability to detect those people who have severe allergies to them. Once a cat has found such an individual, it will first rub on the person's leg (to ensure the embedding of plenty of cat hair on the poor fellow's slacks), then proceed to jump on the person's lap and cling to it until it is removed with a crowbar or another prying device.
— Margo-Rita Andrea Kissell, Toledo, Ohio

Kissinger's Discovery. The nice thing about being a celebrity is that when you bore people, they think it's their fault.
— Henry Kissinger, quoted by Bob Swift in the *Miami Herald,* January 3, 1987

Kitman's Canons of TV Law. (1) The man on trial is never guilty. (2) The guilty person is in the court. (3) A lawyer whose name is in the title of the show never loses a case.
— Marvin Kitman, who studied for the TV bar by watching "Perry Mason," *Newsday,* May 25, 1986; also the following, which appeared in his column of September 16, 1984:

Kitman's First Law of Television. Each season is worse than the one preceding it.*

Klein's Law of Social Causation. The explanation for something being done that shouldn't be — or something not being done that should be — can usually be found by investigating who is or isn't making a buck on it.
— Larry Klein, *Stereo Review,* November 1976

Klein's Law of Utilitarian Discipline. You always have to keep a few screw-ups in the organization; otherwise, what would we use as a yardstick to judge our flawless performance?
— William S. Klein, Springfield, Ill.

Klein Theory of Neglected Composers and Compositions. There's a reason.
— from Lee Goodman, Prairie View, Ks., who writes; "Conceived after Michael Klein and I attended a recital of obscure works . . ."

The Klutz Factor. Philosophic argument always is imperfectly translated into public policy.
— Anonymous, quoted in George Will's column, December 3, 1978

Knight's Rules of Business. (1) Do business only with people whose word you consider to be as good as their written contract. (2) Then get it in writing anyway.
— Gary Knight, Baton Rouge, La.

---

*Not to be confused with his *Second Law,* which he discovered earlier during 1969–1970 season. It holds that pure drivel drives out absolute drivel.

Knopf's Rule of Best Selling Books. A historical novel has a woman on the jacket but no jacket on the woman.
— Alfred Knopf, quoted by Stefan Kanfer in *The New Republic,* August 11, 1986

Knowles's Law. The bumper sticker always stays on longer when the candidate wins.
— Robert P. Knowles, New Richmond, Wisc.

Knowlton's Law. One's belief in astrology is in inverse proportion to one's knowledge of astronomy.
— Mary Alice Knowlton, San Francisco, Calif.

Koch's Alcoholic Axiom. The effort and energy an intoxicated person spends trying to prove he is sober is directly proportionate to how intoxicated he is.
— Randall L. Koch, Kenosha, Wisc.

Kohn's Discovery. Intellectual tone of a paper is improved when it has at least one word in it that is unfamiliar to the readers.
— Alexander Kohn, Ness Ziona, Israel

Koolman's Truths. Clerical. Everything can be filed under "miscellaneous." **Dog's Life.** Life's a bitch, but even a bitch wags her tail when you scratch behind her ears. **Cats.** Anything you do to stop a cat from yowling outside your window at 3:00 A.M. will cause a neighbor to call the police.
— Ron Koolman, Golf Manor, Ohio

Kopcha's Commercial Reality. Often the smartest thing to do is the most obvious thing to do; it is also often the hardest thing to sell.
— Stephen C. Kopcha, Bloomfield Hills, Mich.; in the University of Missouri alumni magazine; from Bob Skole

Korologos's Kollection of 95 Percent Odds. (1) The odds are 95 percent that when you press the hold button on an elevator for one more passenger he will press a button for a floor below yours. The odds immediately go to 100 percent when you are in a hurry, at which time he will always hit a button on a floor below yours by mistake before punching the correct floor — which also is below yours. (2) The odds are 95 percent that every time you go into an underpass the radio announcer will immediately start saying something you want to hear. The odds immediately go to 100 percent when it is a newscast affecting you, a friend, or your business. (3) The odds are 95 percent that when your plane pulls into a gate at the airport the gate will be the farthest possible one from the terminal. The odds immediately go to 100 percent if there are no other planes at any gate. The reverse also is true: the odds are 95 percent that your boarding gate is the last gate in the terminal. The odds immediately go to 100 percent if you are carrying your own luggage. **Korologos' Laws.** (1) The length of your answer in a public hearing has a direct and inverse ratio to the truth. (2) The closer you get to Congressional recesses, the better good government you get. (3) Congresses do two things best — nothing and overreact. (4) When fifty-one senators tell you they'll be with you if needed, you've got a problem. (5) "Thank God! They killed the prayer amendment."
— Tom C. Korologos, Great Falls, Va.

Kostal's Observation. Select theaters aren't.
— Mark Kostal, Downers Grove, Ill.

Kramer's Rules. (1) Monday is a depressing way to spend one seventh of your life. (2) If you're at the top of the ladder, cover your ass; if you're at the bottom, cover your face. (3) Whatever is dreaded arrives promptly.
— Professor Mary Kramer, Lowell, Mass.

Krantz's Rule. If you ever pose for a magazine in an unlikely position — that's the shot they're going to use.
— author Judith Krantz, quoted in *The New Yorker*, October 13, 1980; from Mike Feinsilber

Kraus's Corrolation. The I.Q. of the power boat operator is inversely proportional to the cubic inch displacement of the engine.
— Paul A. Kraus, M.D., Waterbury, Conn.

Krauthammer's Law of Conservation of Indignation. Even in Washington the capacity for waxing indignant is not infinite.
— Charles Krauthammer, *Washington Post*, December 26, 1986

Kraver's Law. Their defective shopping cart will find Ruth Kraver.
— Ruth Kraver, on a Washington, D.C., radio call-in show

Krobusek's Law. As soon as you precisely figure out the wickets of any approval cycle, some bureaucrat will change one of the wickets. **Corollary 1**: You always have the obsolete form (or you never have the correct form.) **Corollary 2**: As soon as a procedure or checklist is developed, someone will change the physical hardware so that the procedure must be changed.
— Richard D. Krobusek, Plano, Tex.

Kroeger's Laws. Car Repair. After repair, your car will have more things wrong with it than it did before the mechanic worked on it. If you are lucky, it will still get you home. It will usually stop functioning as soon as the check clears. **File Storage Management.** The old files/records needed are requested in inverse proportion to the number of days since you discarded them. **Public Relations Account Management.**

The client on the smallest budget is the one that requires the most attention and account service time.
— Judi Kroeger, Allentown, Pa.

Krotky's Truism. You can't get an omelette and a chicken out of the same egg.
— Emil Krotky (1892–1963); from Larry Bryant

Krukow's Explanation. Even a blind dog finds a bone once in a while.
— San Francisco Giants pitcher Mike Krukow, on driving in a winning RBI

Kruse's Observation on Cultural Enlightenment. The more you try to cultivate people, the more you turn up clods.
— Stephanie Kruse, Chicago, Ill., who got it from her father

Kusche's Catch. Any event can be made to look mysterious, if relevant details are omitted.
— paraphrased from L. D. Kusche's *The Bermuda Triange Mystery — Explained*; from Steve Stine

L

Lada's Important Definitions for the Bureaucratic Environment. Committee. A work group created with the main purpose of finding and articulating reasons why a new idea will not work, or, failing that, why adoption of the new idea will cause more anguish within the institution that the idea's benefits are worth. **Policy.** A written statement, ordinarily using as many words as possible, to articulate an institutional position on a subject in a manner vague enough to

permit multiple contradictory interpretations. **Task Force.** A group organized to present the illusion of progress without the inconvenience of actually moving the institution forward.
— Stephen C. Lada, Wayne, Mich.

Ladof's Laws of Legal Services. (1) A client with a bagful of papers is trouble. Ditto for briefcases or any other containers. (2) Never take a case more seriously than your client does. (3) Most parents, when they demand custody, never seem to remember that it means they get the *kids.*
— attorney Anne Ladof, Emigsville, Pa.

Ladwig's Laws for Travel. (1) A light-year is defined as the time it takes to emerge from the middle of the plane upon landing when you have five minutes to make a connecting flight. (2) The speed of light is defined as how fast your connecting flight backs away from the gate as you come running down the concourse.
— Alan Ladwig, Office of Exploration, NASA, Washington, D.C.

Laithwaite's Rules. (1) Experiment is always right, the theory never! Experiment rules. (2) Never mind if you don't understand the theory, just have a go at using it.
— Professor Eric Laithwaite, Imperial College, London, quoted in *Felix,* October 9, 1981; from Tony Lang, London, England

LaLanne's Conclusion. I can't die. It would wreck my image.
— Jack LaLanne, *Los Angeles Times,* December 24, 1980; from Robert D. Specht

Lamb's Conclusion. The world meets nobody halfway.
— Essayist Charles Lamb (1775–1834)

Lament for Public Defenders. It's harder when they're really innocent.
— anonymous

Lament of the Parched. You get the most thirsty when traveling through areas where they tell you "don't drink the water!"
— in a *New York Times* travel column, November 1983

Lander's Law of Mind Over Matter. If nobody minds, it doesn't matter.
— Ann Landers column, February 10, 1986; from Tom Gill

Lang's Law of Bureaucratic Entropy. The total amount of bureaucracy in an organization can never decrease. It can only increase — and usually does.
— Tony Lang, Imperial College, London, England

Larson's Law of Social Interaction. For every action, there is an opposite but *more than* equal reaction.
— Curtis W. Larson, Chattanooga, Tenn.

Last Law of the Performing Arts. When thy opus becomes thy onus, thou art out on thy anus.
— quoted in concert by the late Steve Goodman; from Steve Stine

Lathrop's Universal Law of Applied Effort. If one is bad and doesn't work, then two times one must be the solution.
— from John A. Mattsen

Laub's Third Rule of Economics in Romance. Two cannot live as cheaply as one. Two cannot even live as cheaply as three.
— James A. Laub, Los Angeles, Calif.

Lauder's Law. When a person with experience meets a person with money, the person with experience will get the

money. And the person with the money will get the experience.
> — Leonard Lauder, President, Estee Lauder, Inc., from Mel Loftus, Alexandria, Va.

Laurel's Law. Honest people and stupid people have a common characteristic; they take it in the shorts a lot.
> — Laurel Siemans Moore; from D. F. Siemans, Jr.

Laver's Example of Murphy's Law. There are more j's and z's on my typewriter keyboard tjan the Englizj languzgue requires.
> — Murray Laver, Sidmouth, Devon, England

Lawson's Law of Analysis. Everything can be assessed rationally — from a distance.
> — John Lawson, Burlington, Ontario, Canada

Lawson's Laws of Travel. (1) If you get to the station early, the train will be late. (2) Postcards sent on a short vacation will arrive after you get home. (3) Any witty observations made on postcards will be obliterated by the postal cancellation. (4) Punctures in bicycle tires are more likely to occur in the rain than on a dry day. (5) If you exchange your money for a foreign currency, the likelihood of that currency then being devalued varies in proportion to the amount you have exchanged. (6) If someone giving you directions says, "You can't miss it," you will. (7) The discovery that you have forgotten the corkscrew will occur at the farthest point from which a corkscrew may be obtained. (8) If you are driving through several foreign countries and the fan belt breaks, it will break in a country in the language of which no one in your party knows the word for "fan belt."
> — Sarah Lawson, London, England

Lawton's Conclusion. The creation of random numbers is too important to be left to chance.
> — M. H. Lawton, Oakland, Calif.

Lawyer's Paradox. If it were not for lawyers, we wouldn't need them.
— A. K. Giffin, Dorval, Quebec, Canada

The League Principle. Enjoying the game is almost entirely a matter of having chosen the appropriate league to play in.
— Stu Goldstein, M.D., Danville, Calif.

Leavitt's Law of Pizza and Other Delicacies. There are two kinds of people in the world — the quick and the hungry.
— Jane Leavitt, East Peoria, Ill., who adds that her law is "to be uttered when someone in the group complains he didn't get his share"

Lederer's Law of Ferris Wheel Roulette. The more acrophobic the passenger, the greater the chance the Ferris wheel will come to a stop with that person parked at the top of the circle, the farthest point from terra firma.
— Rich Lederer, Concord, N.H.

Lee's Law of Business Competition. Always remember to keep your swash buckled.
— Gerald Lee Steese, Long Branch, Calif.

LeGuin's Strategy. When action grows unprofitable, gather information; when information grows unprofitable, sleep.
— Ursula K. LeGuin, in her science-fuction novel *The Left Hand of Darkness*; from Kenneth W. Davis

Lehrer's Explanation. When Henry Kissinger can get the Nobel Peace Prize, what is there left for satire?
— songwriter Tom Lehrer, explaining his retirement, *Los Angeles Times*, July 8, 1980; from Robert D. Specht

Leigh's Camping Discovery. Familiarity breeds in tents.
— Richard Leigh, Cheshire, England

Leonard's Warning. Never eat any product on which the listed ingredients cover more than one-third of the package.
— Joseph Leonard, quoted by Herb Caen in his column, March 3, 1986; from Janerik Larsson, Sweden

Leo's Law. Even a new windshield wiper will leave one smudged arc. **Corollary.** The smudged arc will always be at the eye level of the driver.
— Leo Kosowski, South Saint Paul, Minn.

Leslie's Law of Great Expectations. The richer the relative, the easier it is to remember his or her birthday.
— unknown; from Arlen Wilson

Leterman's Laws. (1) No rule for success will work if you don't. (2) A man should work eight hours and sleep eight hours, but not the same eight hours.
— Elmer G. Leterman, quoted in *Forbes,* May 20, 1985, and June 21, 1982.

Levey's Law of Thermogumular Dynamics. If you toss your gum around, you will sooner or later step in someone else's.
— Bob Levey, in his *Washington Post* column, November 25, 1987

Levin's Law. Any attempt to adjust the air conditioner will make it worse.
— Bernard Levin, *The Times* (London), July 9, 1980

Levinson's Lesson. Many people have come to expect too much of work. Work is work, no matter how you slice it.
— Dr. Harry Levinson, of *The Levinson Letter,* quoted in *Behavioral Sciences Newsletter,* July 25, 1983

Levy's Newtonian Corollary. Deadlines have gravity: the closer you get to them, the more pull they exert on you.
— D. Levy; from Richard Lederer

Lewis's Law of Travel. The first piece of luggage out of the chute doesn't belong to anyone, ever.
— Dave Lewis, Columbus, Ga.

Lichtenberg's Conclusions (a few of many). (1) Philosophy cannot fly in the face of facts without coming out with a bloody nose. (2) Man has climbed so far on the tree of knowledge that he finds himself out on a limb. (3) Talk is cheap, conversations dear. (4) Many atheists would believe in God if they were the ones being worshiped. (5) It is rootlessness that distinguishes man from vegetables. (6) Man is the problem-solving animal, thus also the problem-making one. (7) Life is an experiment in which you are the experiment. (8) Before you climb the ladder of success, find out who is holding it. (9) Friends often desert you in time of need. Enemies can be found anytime you need them. (10) People can prove anything they want to prove as long as they control the meaning of the word *proof*. (11) The best way to be completely flexible is to have no backbone. (12) To the adolescent, adult is spelled a-dolt. (13) You usually get fleeced before you get your sheepskin. (14) Self-expression is fine, but only if you have something worth expressing; every fart would prefer to be heard at a party rather than wasting itself in the solitude of the bathroom.
— Ben Lichtenberg, Varona, N.J.

Liddy's Revision. Obviously crime pays, or there'd be no crime.
— G. Gordon Liddy, quoted in *Newsweek,* November 10, 1986

Liebermann's Law. Everybody lies, but it doesn't matter since no one listens.
— anonymous; from Richard Leigh, Cheshire, England

Liebling's Revision. Freedom of the press is limited to those who own one.
> — the late A. J. Liebling, quoted in *Business Week*, June 15, 1981

Liggett's Law of Archaeology. (1) Dirt takes up to five times as much space outside the hole as it does inside. (2) No matter where you put the dirt you're going to have to move it. (3) The hole will eventually be deeper than your arm is long, and you will end up at the bottom of it, throwing dirt over your head.
> — archaeologist Barbara Liggett, quoted in the *Philadelphia Inquirer*, August 3, 1981; from Edward J. O'Neill

Lightfoot's Rules. (1) Great minds run around in the same circles. (2) Women aren't as stupid as men think they are. Men aren't as stupid as women think they are.
> — Fred Lightfoot, Greenport, N.Y.

Lilla's Distinction. The difference today between an old pair of suede shoes and a professor is that the former is given to Goodwill when it has served its purpose; the latter is given tenure.
> — Mark Lilla, in *The New Republic*; from Bernard Albert

Linden's Law. Any letter that opens with "Gentlemen:" is certain to be read first by an oversensitive feminist.
> — Carol Schuette Linden, Wilmette, Ill.

Lindsey's Law of Youth. The youth are always worse than the preceding generation were, in the opinion of the latter.
> — in Justice Ben B. Lindsey's *Revolt of Modern Youth* (1925); from Leon M. Louw

Lindvig's Law. If it's there, you'll step in it. If it's not, (1) it's already on your shoe, (2) it's on your car's floor mat, (3) it's on your new carpet.
— Larry Lindvig, Chicago, Ill.

Lipsett to Kelly to Lipsett Law, The. You don't know someone until you live with him, but you don't known him well until you divorce him.
— Donna Lipsett, El Paso, Tex.

Llarena's Law of the Bungle. If you are in a hurry, don't take shortcuts. Take the old beaten path — you will save more time that way.
— A. Francisco L. Llarena, Jr.

Lloyd-Jones's Advice to the Lazies. If you are always at the top of your class, you're in the wrong class. **Lloyd-Jones's Law of High Fidelity.** A good system is one sensitive enough to let you hear its own faults.
— David A. Lloyd-Jones, Tokyo, Japan

Lockhart's Law. He who laughs last . . . thinks slowest.
— Bob Lockhart, Middlebury, Conn.

Lodge's Law. The good old days are neither as good nor as bad as we remember them.
— from Tom Gill, who heard it from someone named Lodge

Logan's Beatitude. Blessed is he who has nothing to say, and cannot be persuaded to say it.
— C. Sumpter Logan, Sr., Lexington, Ky.

Lois's Law. What is logic to one is chaos to another.
— Lois Smith, Palo Alto, Calif.

Lone Star Cafe Motto. Too much ain't enough.
— New York City restaurant motto; from Judy Tillinger

Long's Law of Johns. Successful people never have to go to the bathroom. **Corollary.** All committee chairman have infinitely large bladders.
— Eugene A. Long, Boston, Mass.

Long's Rules of Hospital Care (a selection). (1) All conveniences such as radio, TV, telephone, and call button will in all cases be located on the identical side of your incision. **Corollary.** If your incision is in front, all conveniences will not function at all or function poorly. (2) There are very good nurses and very bad nurses. There is no such thing as a mediocre or average nurse. This rule does not apply to doctors for reasons of their omnipotence. (3) Although there are one hundred ways of getting in and out of bed, each one will result in the same amount of pain. (4) The length of stay will vary proportionately with the degree of pain. (5) The intensity of nursing care will vary inversely with the length of stay. (6) The nicest and most admired of all flower bouquets will come from the least expected person, usually your worst enemy or ex-wife.
— Eugene A. Long, Natick, Mass.

Lopez Axiom on Art and Crosswords, The. Just as some art exists only for its own sake, some words exist only for the sake of crossword puzzles. **The Lopez Dictum on Dining.** Waiters and waitresses generally wait until your mouth is full before asking how you like the food. Otherwise, how can they be sure you are really eating it? **The Lopez Law of Life.** Never be without a book. The day you forget to bring a book is the day you will get stuck in an elevator (traffic jam, etc.) for two hours and forty-five minutes. **Third Lopez Law of Life.** Never help your kids with their homework. Getting help with the homework defeats the purpose of education, which is to teach humility.
— Marsha Lopez, Westmont, Ill., who also submitted these from Manfred Lopez, age 13:

Lopez's Grade Point Principle. In American schools, your popularity is inversely proportional to your grade point average. **Lopez's Law of Lunches.** No matter what the school menu claims, it's really horsemeat.

Loren's Basic Principle for Bureaucratic Survival. The appearance of a bureaucracy is infinitely more important than its function.
— from John A. Mattsen

Louis's Lament. Has God forgotten all I have done for him?
— Louis XIV, after the French defeat at Malplaquet

Louw's Collected Laws. (1) If you think you may have forgotten something, you have. If you think you haven't forgotten something, you have. (2) The main trouble with self-evident truths is that they aren't self-evident. (3) The busiest day of the year is the worst day for the post office and the best day for the supermarket.
— Leon M. Louw, Melrose, South Africa

Lovell's Law. The closer to the bottom of the job scale, the higher the level of incorruptibility.
— Marc Lovell, in his novel *The Spy Game*; from William F. Deeck, College Park, Md.

Lovett's Observation on Gift-Giving. If you give a bald man a comb, he will never part with it.
— Aaron Lovett; from Raymond E. Lovett, Garrett Park, Md.

Lucht's Observation. The single most common mistake young achievers make in their bid for career advancement is to attempt to prove their competence.
— anonymous; from John A. Mattsen. See **Zimmerman's Corollary to Lucht's Observation.**

Luke's Law. When competence collides with custom, custom often wins at the expense of competence.
— Robert A. Luke, Jr., Bethesda, Md.

Lunt's Advice to Young Actors. Say the words so they can be heard, and don't bump into the stage furniture.
— Alfred Lunt; from Joseph C. Goulden

Lynn's Law. There are no part-time jobs. **Corollary.** Anyone with a part-time job works full-time for half salary.
— Denise D. Lynn, Woodstock, Conn.

Lytle's Third Law. Eat fat, be fat. Eat thin, be thin.
— the late Dr. Ivan Lytle, University of Arizona; from "an appreciative student," Meribeth Meixner Reed, Claremont, Okla.

 Mc

McAdoo's Rule of Political Self-Interest. Whenever a beneficial measure is opposed by powerful financial interests, the real reason for the opposition is never given. **McAdoo's Rules of Political Mendacity.** The first principle of political lying is to make the lie highly personal, for lies about a party or a class are too cold and abstract to arouse more than a faint public interest.

The second principle of the art is to create and disseminate a vague story, rather than one which hangs on precise data. The more vague and foggy it is the better, as it is likely to live longer than a detailed lie, which can be disputed by facts. Its vagueness is a sort of protective coloration; in the first place, it cannot be pinned onto its originator, for if it comes back to him and is slapped in his face, he will either deny it outright or declare that he was misunderstood. Vagueness leaves a great deal to the imagination, and people are likely to imagine the worst. The great lie-masters have learned by experience that much dependence can be placed on the widely diffused capacity for invention. All you have to do is to launch the lie in general terms, and the public will supply the details, so that the story grows by much retelling.

> — William G. McAdoo, Secretary of the Treasury under Woodrow Wilson, in *The Crowded Years,* from Joseph C. Goulden

McAfee's Law of Physical Material Balance. Matter can be neither created nor destroyed. However, it can be lost.

> — E. Ray McAfee.

McAfee's Theorem. A word to the wise is insipid.

> — Professor R. Preston McAfee, Purdue University

McAlister's Principle. The rate of cooling of coffee in a cup is inversely porportioned to the amount of time you have to drink it.

> — R. G. McAlister, Ukiah, Calif.

McBain's Constant. All ticket sellers always seem to be counting something no matter when you approach their windows. They are either counting money, or new tickets, or cancelled tickets, or stamps, or schedules, or sometimes they are counting their big toes, but they are always counting something, and they are always too busy with what they are counting to look up at you.

> — Ed McBain, *The Heckler;* from Bob Skole.

McCabe's Romantic Opera Rules. (1) The tenor always gets the girl. (2) They never get to live happily ever after. **Mc-**

Cabe's Law of Ultimate Uncertainty. Even if it already worked once, that could have been a fluke. **McCabe's Law of Relativity.** The older you get, the faster time seems to pass. **McCabe's Notation.** Ninety percent of the people in any group think that they are in the top 10 percent. **McCabe's Observation.** Sometimes you're the dog, sometimes the hydrant. **McCabe's Rules of Financial Planning.** (1) You must have a set of rules. (2) You must obey all the rules. (3) Never invest money with anyone who telephones from another state. (4) Do not pay retail prices for your investments. **McCabe's Rules of the Road.** When driving in the District of Columbia, you are in the greatest danger when (1) stopping for a red light or (2) going through a green light.
— Joseph M. McCabe, Washington, D.C.

McCaffery's Law. They — whoever they may be — can do whatever they want. **McCaffery's Reality.** When you finally join "them," you find out that McCaffery didn't know what he was talking about.
— James Manus McCaffery, New Orleans, La.

McCarthy's Warnings. (1) It is dangerous for a national candidate to say things that people might remember. (2) Remember that the worst accidents occur in the middle of the road. (3) (To new members of Congress) Vote against anything introduced with a "re" in it, especially reforms, reorganizations, and recodifications. This usually means going back to something that failed once and is likely to do so again.
— Eugene McCarthy, quoted in the *Washington Post*, September 4, 1984, and his article "Ten Commandments for New Hill Members," *Washington Post,* January 4, 1981

McConnell's Observation. The only thing that works in an old house is the owner.
— Spero McConnell; from his brother Ray, Miami, Fla.

McConnell's Organizational Observation. The purpose of organizations is to stop things from happening.
— Richard McConnell, San Francisco, Calif.

McCormick's Conclusion. You're either too young or old enough to know better, but you're never the right age.
— Peggy McCormick, San Mateo, Calif.

McCormick's Laments. (1) My problem is that my passport photos look like me. (2) When I finally get to the head of the line, I usually have forgotten what I was supposed to get or do when I got there.
— Ernest J. McCormick, West Lafayette, Ind.

McCullough's Laws of Inertial Reality. (1) When the situation starts to go down the tubes, it will complete the trip. A rolling stone gathers great momentum. (2) If you're getting nowhere in a hurry, you still won't get there any sooner. (3) If the Inertia of Reality heads downward, it will slow geometrically as it nears to bottom. Or, as apprehension increases with the certainty of a "worst possible outcome," Reality takes its own sweet time getting there and even longer leaving.
— D. Lee McCullough, Stonewall, Tex.

McDougal's Law. Planning never beat dumb luck.
— from Howard Hamer, Long Branch, N.J.

McEwen's Rule of Relative Importance. When traveling with a herd of elephants, don't be the first to lie down and rest.
— Robert A. McEwen, Maumee, Ohio

McGarry's Gynecological Givens. (1) When running an artificial-insemination-by-donor clinic, it is soon discovered that four-sevenths of women ovulate on the weekend. (2) The first and last people to take up any operation or technique are good doctors; the other ninety-eight are mediocre. (3) If, whilst on holiday in a strange town, a doctor enters a news agent to peruse a few girly magazines, he will be recognized and spoken to by an ex-patient (female) from his hometown, whose name he has forgotten.

— John McGarry, consulting gynecologist, Barnstaple, Devon, England

McGee's Law of Football. When you pass the ball, six possible things can happen, and five of them are bad.

— the character Travis McGee, in John D. MacDonald's *The Scarlet Ruse*; from Charles D. Poe

McGee's Sad Fact. All you need to become ill in our modern world is to follow ordinary patterns of diet and life-style.

— Dr. Charles T. McGee, in his *How to Survive Modern Technology*, quoted in *Time,* December 24, 1979

McGoorty's Warning. One of the worst things that can happen in life is to win a bet on a horse at an early age.

— Danny McGoorty, quoted in *The 637 Best Things Anyone Ever Said,* by Robert Byrne

McGregor's Revised Maxim. The shortest distance between two points is under construction.

— Scott D. McGregor, Moscow, Idaho

McGuire's Distinction. When a guy takes off his coat, he's not going to fight. When a guy takes off his wristwatch, watch out!

— sportscaster Al McGuire, quoted by Norman Chad in the *Washington Post,* April 21, 1986. Also this McGuireism, which first appeared in *Playboy:*

McGuire's Rule of the Table. The person who reaches for the check and doesn't get it never wanted it in the first place.

— from John Kessel

McKay's Dental Translations. (1) "It's deep." = I think you're going to need a root canal. (2) "This won't hurt," = It will. (3) "Don't worry." = Worry. (4) "Extensive." = Expensive.
— Michael S. McKay, D.M.D., Uncasville, Cal.

McKean's Law of Automotive 20/20 Hindsight. The sports car you really craved twenty years ago, but your father counseled was too frivolous and a bad investment because of low resale value, now has become a classic and sells for three to ten times the original purchase price . . . AND YOU STILL CAN'T AFFORD ONE.
— W. E. McKean II, Sioux Falls, S.D.

McKenna's Observations. (1) Legibility of handwriting declined proportionately with the proliferation of the ballpoint pen. (2) One who manufactures assumptions, then doles them out as facts, generally owns his own business. (3) Pessimism means never having to be disappointed.
— Thomas A. McKenna, Ardmore, Pa.

McKeon's Law of the College Catalog. The university catalog is much like the campus — it lies about the university.
— Thomas J. McKeon, Assistant Dean, Case Institute of Technology, Cleveland, Ohio

McKinney's Law. The probability of your knee hitting the leg of the table increases geometrically in direct relation to the amount of coffee in your cup.
— Bruce C. McKinney, State College, Pa.

McLaughlin's Query. What is it called when you spend 25 minutes looking for a restaurant, 20 minutes finding a place to park, 15 minutes standing in line to place your order, 10 minutes waiting for your food, and five minutes trying to locate an empty table? Fast food.
— Scott McLaughlin, quoted in Bob Levey's column, *Washington Post*

McMullin's Law of Excessive Acquisitiveness. Greed is its own reward.
— Roland McMullin, North Kansas City, Mo.

McNulty's Law. Never dive in a bikini.
— from Jeffrey Chamberlain, Nassau, N.Y.

McPherson's Reassurance. Three trees make a row.
— Professor of English David McPherson, University of New Mexico; from Sandra Adams, who says it is used to reassure students who want to make a point with a few examples

McSpiritt's Discovery for Garage Sale Shopping. To ensure finding the perfect item you've been looking for, at a good price, be certain the vehicle you're in is totally inappropriate. (Finding a magnificent solid-oak dining-room table with eight chairs, and you're in your old VW, or finally locating one hundred lbs of good-quality horse manure (unbagged), for your garden, and you're driving your Rolls Royce.
— F. D. McSpiritt, Flint, Mich.

Macrae's Law. In modern conditions of high elasticity of both production and substitution, we will generally create a temporary but large surplus of whatever the majority of decision-influencing people five or ten years earlier believed was going to be in most desperately short supply. This is because the well-advertised views of the decision-influencers tend to be believed by both profit-seeking private producers and consensus-following governments, and these two then combine to cause excessive production of precisely

the things that the decision-influencers had been saying would be the most obviously needed.
— Walter Macrae, *The Economist,* October 26, 1975; from Joseph C. Goulden

Macdonald's Moral. You have to be sincere to Sell Out; it's like making money — if your heart's not in it, the customer . . . sees through the imposture.
— Dwight Macdonald, quoted in the *New York Times* book section, November 21, 1982. It was invoked in the context of a story about Delmore Schwartz trying to write a "piece of junk" to win a $1,000 in a contest.

The MacEwan Principle. All benefits conferred on humanity by new inventions and discoveries will be applied in such a way as eventually to achieve (by other means) the same standard of misery as before.
— Douglas M. C. MacEwan, Kent, England

Macfarlane's Law. When a number of conflicting theories co-exist, any point at which they all agree is the one most likely to be wrong.
— G. Macfarlane, *Howard Florey, the Making of a Great Scientist*; from David L. Cowen, Jamesburg, N.J.

MacPherson's Law. No matter how good a bargain you have purchased, the first person you show it to could have got it cheaper if you had only told them. **Corollary.** If you ask the same people before you purchase, their supply has just run out, "can't get them for love or money."
— Ian MacPherson, London, England

Maddocks's Law of Thermopolitical Dynamics. If a less powerful person or group makes things hot for a more powerful person or group, that person or group is likely to make things an awful lot hotter for junior.
— Melvin Maddocks, in a *Christian Science Monitor* article

on whistle-blowers, February 20, 1981; from Steven R.
Woodbury

Magary's Principle. When there is a public outcry to cut the
deadwood and fat from any government bureaucracy, it is
the deadwood and fat that does the cutting. **Magary's Summation of Climatological Evolution.** Weather Man, Weather
Girl, Weather Person, Meteorologist.
— John T. Magary, Royal Oak, Mich.

Mahon's Silicon Valley Rule. Don't let your employees do to
you what you did to your former boss.
— Tom Mahon, *Charged Bodies: People, Power and Paradox
in Silicon Valley*; from Jack Limpert

Maine Haircut, How to Get One. If the name of the place
where you go to get your haircut does not contain the name
of the guy who is going to cut your hair, go somewhere else.
— in *The Wicked Good Book,* by Steve Bither

Main's Points. Phillips screwdrivers always have lead tips.
Bars of handsoap are molded around a thin, sharp plastic
sliver. If you overtip a waitress for good service, the busboy
will pick it up. Concrete never hardens until somebody has
initialed it.
— the late John A. Main, Yorba Linda, Calif.

Makower's Immutable Laws of Computing. (1) No matter
how much you know about computers, you can find an expert who can render everything incomprehensible. (2) You
will never run out of disks or printer ribbons during business
hours. (3) The price of a software package is in inverse proportion to the readability of its manual. (4) The size of a
computer error is in direct proportion to the importance of
the data lost. (5) For every computer error there are at least
two human errors, one of which is blaming it on the com-

puter. (6) No matter how long you delay your purchase of a computer product, a faster, cheaper, and more powerful version will be introduced within forty-eight hours. (7) The power never goes out at the beginning of a computing session. (8) If you back up a disk, the original is guaranteed not to fail. (9) Printers are not intended to work the first time you set them up. If they do, it is because you didn't follow instructions. (10) You never lose data you don't need.
— Joel Makower, Washington, D.C., in his book *Personal Computers, A to Z*

Malik's Observations. (1) Living on earth may be expensive, but it includes a free trip around the sun. (2) The same piece of tape that would not hold up your child's drawing will not come off the refrigerator. (3) When it comes time to sink or swim, procrastinators float.
— Julia Malik, Richboro, Pa.

Maller's Organizational Observation. The person who answers the phone in an organization knows the least of anyone. **Corollary.** The person you want to speak with is always in a meeting or away from the desk.
— Mark Maller, Chicago, Ill.

Mame's Lament. Life is a banquet, and most damned fools are starving to death.
— the character Auntie Mame in the play *Auntie Mame*

Manchester's Skeleton Theory. A man with nothing in the closet may have nothing in the attic either.
— author William Manchester, discussing John F. Kennedy on the CBS Evening News, November 8, 1983

Manning's Law of Inflation. What goes up doesn't always come down.
— Gerald Manning, Cork, Ireland

Manning's Maxim. Getting from one point to another known point is called navigation. Getting from one unknown point to another unknown point is called "being lost."
— Harvey Manning, *Backpacking One Step at a Time*; from Harvey O. Hays

Mann's Proposition. Any politician who perceives the problem insists upon full credit for its solution.
— Robert T. Mann, Chairman, Florida Public Service Commission; from D. Franklin Skinner, Miami, Fla.

Marcotte's Disaster Law. The first persons to arrive at the scene of any disaster are generally those least able to offer any type of aid or assistance.
— J. T. Marcotte, USCG, Opa Locka, Fla.

Marcus's Law. Never divorce the boss's daughter (or son).
— Stanley Marcus, Dallas, Tex., *Quest for the Best*

Margolis's Marcos Maxim. A dictator who doesn't even know how to steal elections is a total incompetent.
— Jon Margolis, *Chicago Tribune,* May 21, 1984; from Steve Stine

Margo-Rita's Hyphenated Name Law. People tend to ignore the second part of a hyphenated name. **Corollary.** When they don't eliminate the second name, they just eliminate the hyphen and mush the whole name together.
— Margo-Rita Kissell, Toledo, Ohio

Markgraf's Observation. Upon switching on a TV set, one will first see a commercial. *Or upon turning on* / WGN, one will hear three commercials.
— Richard Markgraf, Granville, Ohio

Mark's Dental-Chair Discovery. Dentists are incapable of asking questions that require a simple yes or no answer.
— Norman Mark, Chicago, Ill.

Marks's Law. Stand on any street corner in any city in the world. Close your eyes. Stick out your arms. You will touch a schmuck.
— William Marks, Chicago, Ill.

Marlin-Jones Conclusion. Most of us don't sell out because nobody wants to buy.
— critic Davy Marlin-Jones; from Marshall L. Smith

The Marshall Cook Theory. Jurors will give up the casual clothing they've been wearing for coats, ties, and formal dresses on the day their verdict is ready.
— named for a U.S. marshal in the court of Judge Aubrey E. Robinson, Jr., and reported in the *Washington Times* by Jay Mallin, July 11, 1986; from Joseph C. Goulden

Marshall's Distinction. A government could print a good edition of Shakespeare's works, but it could not get them written.
— economist Alfred Marshall (1842–1924); from Robert D. Specht

Marsolais's Law of Diminishing Credibility. Your trusty dependable lawn mower starts every time on the second pull, the only exception being when you're trying to sell it to your neighbor, at which time twenty-seven pulls are required to start it. **Marsolais's Law of Unfittingness.** No matter which utility company sends you a bill, the envelope they provide for its return to themselves is always one-quarter inch shorter than the bill.
— Maurice Marsolais, Fairfax, Va.

Martinez's Key. The key to effective verbal communication is to never state what the key to anything is. **Martinez's Observation.** In exactly 91.37 percent of all cases in which a percentage figure is cited, the percentage figure is incorrect.
— Daniel G. Martinez, University Park, N.M.

Martin's Discovery. Saying everything that is on your mind is one of the greatest sources of bad manners.
— Judith Martin, a.k.a. Miss Manners, quoted in *U.S. News & World Report,* December 6, 1982.

Martin's Rule. By the time you run into the house, get the binoculars, and run back outside, the strange bird will have left its perch.
— Lynn Martin, Mount Laurel, N.J.

Mary's Rule. All men/women have ten faults. Pick ten faults you can live with.
— Mary Williams; from her son Jon, South Melbourne, Australia, who adds that the rule can also apply to such things as cards, houses, and jobs

Mason's Law of Probability. Due to Brownian Movement, given enough time, everything will either disperse or turn into coal. **Mason's Law of Heat Transfer.** Light bulbs are always too hot to touch when they need replacement. **Corollary.** Flashlights, matches, and candles disappear when light bulbs burn out.
— H. Lawrence Mason III, D.M.D., Louisville, Ky.

Mattsen's Corollary to the Bureaucratic Oath [i.e., Don't rock the boat!]. Go ahead and rock the boat. The only people who will care are the ones who can't swim.
— John A. Mattsen, Finlayson, Minn.

Maverick's Observations. (1) You can fool some of the people all of the time and all of the people some of the time — and them's pretty good odds. (2) A cowards dies a thousand times; a hero only once. A thousand to one is pretty good odds. (3) "Work is all right for killing time, son, but it's no way to make a living."
— the old TV show "Maverick"; from Don Coles of St. Louis, Steve Stine, and Bernard L. Albert

Mayes's Law of Instant Retaliation. When forced to accept the dirty end of the stick, always shake hands with the guy who gives it to you. (Regrettably, this is effective only for right-handed people.)
— Colin D. Mayes, Hitchin, Herts, England

May's Maxim on Meetings. The only meeting that will ever start on time is the one for which you are late. **May's Observations on Meetings.** (1) Well-planned and -organized meetings do not run well. (2) Poorly planned and organized meetings run even worse, or not all.
— Bruce M. May, O.D., Reading, Pa.

Mead's Diplomatic Rule. Vows of eternal friendship and co-operation are the oldest tradition in diplomacy; the second oldest is breaking them.
— Walter Russell Mead, *Houston Chronicle*, June 10, 1988; from Charles D. Poe

Mead's Distinction. You are totally unique, just like everyone else.
— Margaret Mead; from Catherine Pfeifer

Means's Law of Restaurant Illumination. The harder it is to read the menu, the higher the prices on it.
— John Means, quoted in Bob Levey's column, *Washington Post*, November 12, 1985

Meier's Law. People are like electricity — they take the path of least resistance.
— Leroy W. Meier, Mt. Healthy, Ohio

Melbourne's Razor. If it were easy, everyone would be doing it.
— Marian Melbourne, Newport Beach, Calif.

Mel's Law. If it wasn't for the last minute, nothing would get done. *AMEN*
— Unknown, Radio call-in show, New York, N.Y.

Mendenhall's Axiom for Bailing Out. Never practice that which must be perfect the first time.
— Mo Mendenhall, former Marine fighter pilot, Camarillo, Calif.

Mendonça's Discovery. If a man wears one light brown sock and one dark blue sock to work, it is more than likely that he will have a similar pair at home.
— Jovit Mendonça, London, Ontario, Canada

Merilyn's Economic Analysis. I've never not had any money so much in my life.
— Merilyn "Rocky" Royce, *Ozark Graphic*; from Bill Ford, Doniphan, Mo.

Menkus's Principles of the Organizational Ecosystem. (1) Small failures are punished; big ones are rewarded — sometimes lavishly. (2) The value of an idea is more likely to be perceived in terms of the status/rank of its proponent rather than its inherent qualities. (3) Risk-taking furthers personal advancement; risk avoidance furthers personal survival.
— Belden Menkus, Middleville, N.J., from a longer list, *Journal of Systems Management*, August 1981

Meuse's Law. Anything with teeth sooner or later bites.
— Jim Meuse, Huntington Beach, Calif.

Meyer's Law of Human Relations. In all emotional conflicts the thing you find hardest to do is the one thing you should do.
— the character Meyer Meyer, in John D. McDonald's *Pale Gray for Guilt*; from Stephen M. Lonsdale, Abington, Mass.

Meyer Meyer's Rule. You never get a generous and delicious cocktail in a proper glass in a restaurant where the food is bad.
> — also Travis McGee's friend in *Cinnamon Skin,* by John D. McDonald; from Joseph C. Goulden

Michel's Iron Law of Oligarchy. The larger an organization grows in size, the more it oppresses its members.
> — Robert Michel; from Walter Shearer, Tokyo, Japan

Michener's Rules for Writers. If you have written a success-ful novel, everyone invites you to write short stories. If you have written some good short stories, everyone wants you to write a novel. But nobody wants anything until you have already proved yourself by being published somewhere else.
> — James Michener, quoted in Barbara Rowes's *The Book of Quotes*

Miller's Axioms for Football Betting with Tucker's Corollar-ies. (1) Place your largest bets on the game you win; never, never place a large bet on a game you lose. **Corollary.** You can't place your bets after the game. (2) The greatest team will have one terrible game each season; likewise, the most pathetic dogs will have one great game. **Corollary.** You never know when those games will be.
> — Chris Tucker, *D Magazine,* Dallas, Tex.

Miller's Axioms of Outdoor Grilling. (1) The fire is always at its peak fifteen minutes after dinner. (2) If you overhear the cook saying, "No problem, I'll just dust it off," it's time to visit the salad bowl.
> — Bryan Miller, *New York Times,* June 27, 1984; from Tom Gill

Miller's Principle. Abstinence makes the heart grow fonder.
> — Mark R. Miller; from Andrea Miller

Miller's Slogan. Lose a few, lose a few.
— Don Miller, Livermore, Calif.

Milligan's Formula. Middle age is halfway between your age and one hundred.
— R. D. Milligan, Rolling Meadows, Ill.

Mills's Law. The bigger the problem, the fewer the facts.
— Harlan D. Mills, *Mathematics and the Managerial Imagination*; from Mel Loftus

Milner's Distinction. A difference to be a difference must make a difference.
— T. H. Milner, San Francisco, Calif.

Milroy's Law. All machines have an innate sense of irresponsibility. **Mary Milroy's Corollary.** Machines are misogynists.
— Ian Milroy, Avon, England

Ming's Warning. Science will overcome all things. Even the human emotions.
— the character Ming the Merciless in "Flash Gordon" (1936)

Mintz's Law. The best things in life are messy.
— Ann Emmons Mintz, Philadelphia, Pa.

Mintzlaff's Law of Social Tolerance. Do not judge other people, just snicker at them.
— Charles Mintzlaff, Milwaukee, Wisc.

Missinne's Observations. (1) The most vocal opponents of water fluoridation are always people with false teeth. (2) It is one thing not to ask much of life, but it is another not to get anything.
— Jeff Missinne, Superior, Wisc.

Miss Manners's Travel Distinction. There are two classes of travel in America: Steerage and Steerage with Free Drinks. You pay a great deal extra for the free drinks, of course.
— Judith Martin, in her syndicated column, September 1, 1985

Mix's Law. There is nothing more permanent than a temporary building. There is nothing more permanent than a temporary tax.
— Averill Q. Mix, Los Gatos, Calif.

Mom's Law. Children only agree with you when they're on their way to something worse.
— the comic strip *Cathy*, July, 1986; from Tom Gill.

Mom's Law II. When they finally do have to take you to the hospital, your underwear won't be new or clean.
— Dennis Rogers

Montero's Principle. An attorney who informs the judge that he has "just one more question" will, invariably, keep the witness on the stand an additional half hour to forty-five minutes. However, if he informed the judge that he has "just several more questions," then the witness will be on the stand for several days.
— Wilson M. Montero, Jr., New Orleans, La.

Moore's Airline Constant. Departing connecting flights always leave on time.
— Bob Moore, Atherton, Calif.

The Moores' Definition of Insect Repellant. One of a number of gag items available in bait and tackle shops.
— Dick and Rick Moore, in their "Fishing Forecast," Anderson Valley *Advertiser*, April 17, 1985

Moore's Economic Discovery. Now I know why you rarely see a thin economist. It's because of all those words they have to eat.
— Mary Tyler Moore; from Bernard L. Albert

Moore's Observation on Irresistible Forces. Trailer parks attract tornadoes.
— David E. Moore, Wakefield, R.I.

Moore's Stages in the Development of a Movie Star. (1) Who's Dudley Moore? (2) Get me Dudley Moore. (3) Get me a Dudley Moore type. (4) Get me a young Dudley Moore. (5) Who's Dudley Moore?
— Dudley Moore; from Chad Hesting; a similar set of stages was attributed to the late Herschel Bernardi

Moran's Theorem for the Self-Employed. You spend the first half of your career wondering if people will buy your services and the second half wondering when they'll get around to paying for them.
— Frank J. Moran, Los Angeles, Calif.

Morgan's Correlation. The longer the vacuum cleaner cord, the sooner it gets caught on something.
— Karen Sorensen Morgan, New York, N.Y.

Morgan's Discovery. The average man is a little below average.
— humorist Henry Morgan

Morgan's Law of Air Travel. The occurrence of air turbulence will always coincide with the serving of the meal.
— Elizabeth S. Morgan, Gaithersburg, Md.

Morley's Credo. My theology, briefly, is that the universe was dictated, but not signed.
— Christopher Morley; from John Ohliger

Moulton's Law. The ease with which the toilet paper holder turns is directly proportional to the thickness of the toilet paper.
— D. N. Moulton, Argyle, N.Y.

Moyers's Discovery. The worst thing you can do to the liberals is to deprive them of their grievances.
— commentator Bill Moyers, at the Democratic National Convention, August 13, 1980; from Robert D. Specht

Moynihan's Architectural Solution.
Whereas in the fall of 1980 the frame of the New Senate Office Building was covered with plastic sheathing in order that construction might continue during the winter months; and
Whereas the plastic cover has now been removed revealing, as feared, a building whose banality is exceeded only by its expense; and
Whereas even in a democracy there are things it is as well the people do not know about their government: Now, therefore, be it
Resolved, that it is the sense of the Senate that the plastic cover be put back.
— New York Senator Daniel P. Moynihan, text of Senate Resolution #140, May 19, 1981

Moynihan's Revelation. Statistics will prove anything, even the truth.
— Sir Berkeley Moynihan; from Bernard L. Albert

Muir's (Latest) Observations. (1) There is no such thing as "a little dull." (2) Always buy thermometers in the summer because they come with more mercury.
— Frank Muir, on the BBC's "My Word"

Mulfinger's Laws. (1) Anything will conduct if the voltage is high enough. (2) Anything can be welded if the current is high enough.
— George Mulfinger, Greenville, S.C.

Munning's Favorite Saying. Life's short. Art's long.
— Dick Francis's character Alfred Munning, *In the Frame*; from Charles D. Poe

Munro's Rediscovery of Defoe's Law. Only Robinson Crusoe had everything done by Friday.
— C. A. Munro, London, England

Murphy's Discovery. Do you know presidents talk to the country the way men talk to women? They say, "Trust me, go all the way with me, and everything will be all right." And what happens? Nine months later you're in trouble!
— Maureen Murphy, on TV's "The Tonight Show"; from Robert D. Specht

Murphy's Law Number 51. If a plank doesn't warp, it will split.
— ad for the Trus Joist Corp. in *Engineering News Record*

Murphy's Posological Principle. For a particular ailment, the more remedies available, the less the chance of any of them working.
— Peter A. Murphy, Toronto, Ontario, Canada

Murray's Analogy. Law sufficiently complex is indistinguishable from no law at all.
> — Charles Murray, *National Review,* June 10, 1988; from Charles D. Poe

Murray's Law. The worst whistlers whistle the most.
> — Robert E. Murray, San Francisco, Calif.

Murray's Law (Another). The quality of restaurant food is in inverse ratio to the number of hanging plants.
> — David Murray, in a letter to the *New York Times,* July 26, 1983

Murray's Law (Yet One More). There are only twenty people in the whole world.
> — Jim Murray, GM of the Philadelphia Eagles. This law has been explored in several newspaper columns, including Tom Fox's in the *Philadelphia Inquirer,* January 9, 1983. Fox writes of Murray: "Just talk to twenty people, anywhere, anytime, and he says with total certitude, during the course of conversation with those twenty people you will find that you have some remarkable coincidence in common with at least one of them." From Mack Earle

Murray's Probability. If you have a 50 percent chance of being right, 90 percent of the time you are wrong. **Proofs.** (1) When trying to decide if the word is spelled "ie" or "ei," I'm wrong 90 percent of the time. (2) There are two lines at the post office window, the bank teller's windows, or the toll gates, and you pick the slow one 90% of the time.
> — Robert H. Murray, Wescosville, Pa.

Murray's Rule. Any country with "democratic" in the title isn't.
> — columnist Jim Murray, *Los Angeles Times,* August 3, 1980; from Robert D. Specht

Muzik's Tenet. To be a research scientist, you must have a high tolerance for ambiguity.
— Tom Muzik, Juball, Saudi Arabia

Myers's Observation. A parent who sends a child to school with the understanding that the child is to call if he is not feeling better should expect a call.
— elementary school principal G. E. Myers, Sumpter, S.C.

N

N–1 Law. If you need four screws for a job, the first three will be easy to find.
— Unknown, WRC Radio

Naden's Law. Any idea held by a person that was not put in by reason cannot be taken out by reason.
— Kenneth D. Naden, Bethesda, Md.

Nanna's Observations. (1) Saturday's newspapers are always smaller. (2) There is always a line for the ladies' room.
— R. A. Nanna, Toms River, N.J.

Napa Flood Rule. Trying to stop a flood with sandbags is like trying to shove a noodle up a tiger.
— observation by a Napa, Calif., man flooded out by torrential rains; spotted in the Sacramento *Bee* by Tom Gill

Napier's Completeness Law. The absolute conviction that a task has been completed is a good indication that part of it remains to be done.
> — Thomas M. Napier, West Lothian, Scotland, who discovered the law "as a consequence of throwing out the washing up water before finding more dishes to wash"

Nathan's Knowledge. There is never a day so bad that tomorrow couldn't be worse.
> — Harriet Nathan, Chicago, Ill.

Navy Maxim. A sailor never thinks that his ship is as good as the one that he was on before, or as nice as the one he wants to be transferred to.
> — from Vincent A. Orbish, LCDR USN (Retired), San Diego, Calif.

Nesman's Reassurance. Bomb threats are almost always false.
> — Les Nesman (Richard Sanders) on the TV show "WKRP in Cincinnati"; from Steve Stine

Nestor's Law. Anything worth doing makes a mess.
> — Sibyl W. Nestor; from Bonnie Nestor Johnson, Oak Ridge, Tenn.

Neudel's Laws. (1) Any organization created to unite a proliferation of splinter groups inevitably becomes another splinter group. (2) Any person hired by a bureaucracy to respond to public complaints has no power to remedy them. **Corollary.** The only people worth talking to in a bureaucracy are the ones who never deal with the public. (3) The spouse who snores always falls asleep first.
> — Marian Henriquez Neudel, Chicago, Ill.

Neuhaus's Rule. If you like a girl, her boyfriend is *always* a jerk.
— Robert Neuhaus, Chicago, Ill.

Nevers, An Assortment. (1) Never buy a portable TV set on the sidewalk from a man who's out of breath. (From Joseph C. Goulden) (2) Never trust a man with a tattoo on his face. (3) Never go to a dentist who has teeth painted on his lips. (From the *B.C.* comic strip) (4) Never start a project until you've picked out someone to blame. (5) Never buy real estate from a man who works out of a tent. (From *The Wizard of Id* comic strip)

Nevin's Nemesis. If reality won't fit the plan, then force it. If this fails, see **Lathrop's Universal Law of Applied Effort.**
— John A. Mattsen

Newchy's Law of Observation. The probability of being observed is in direct proportion to the stupidity of your actions.
— Newchy Mignone, Las Vegas, Nev.

Newlan's Truism. An *acceptable* level of unemployment means that the government economist to whom it is acceptable still has a job.
— anonymous; from John W. Gustafson

New Laws of Marriage. (1) Loose change on the bureau is community property. (2) Twice is always (i.e., if you forget to take out the garbage twice, you *always* forget to take out the garbage).
— anonymous

Newman's Discovery. Your best dreams may not come true; fortunately, neither will your worst dreams.
— R. A. Newman, Cherry Hill, N.J.

Newman's Law. It is useless to put on your brakes when you're upside down.
— actor Paul Newman, quoted in *Playboy*; from Shel Kagan

Nichols's Rule of Success. Success is when your mother reads about you in the newspaper.
— Mike Nichols, quoted by Henry Hanson in the *Chicago Magazine*, September 1982; from Joseph C. Goulden

Niebuhr's Law of the Jungle. Everyone out there is someone else's lunch.
— Mike Niebuhr, Dallas, Tex.

Nierenberg's Rule. There are times when you can't finesse any more.
— William Nierenberg, quoted in *Discover*, January 1984.

Nineteenth Hole Observation. The older I get, the better I used to be.
— overheard by reader and reported in Bob Levey's column, *Washington Post*, April 16, 1986

Nobel's Law of the Conversion of Trouble. Trouble is incompressible.
— Joel J. Nobel, M.D., Plymouth Meeting, Pa.

Nolan's Comment on Midlife Crisis. Sex takes up an infinitesimal amount of one's time, and to have to live with somebody who is listening to this crazy music while you want to listen to the Benny Goodman Quartet is a hell of a price to pay for a little sexual pleasure.
— Dr. William Nolan, quoted by Bob Swift in the *Miami Herald*, January 3, 1987

Nusbaum's Rule. The more pretentious the corporate name, the smaller the organization (for instance, the Murphy Cen-

ter for the Codification of Human and Organizational Law, contrasted to IBM, BM, AT&T . . .).
— Harvey Nusbaum, Rochelle Park, N.Y.

Nutter's Dictum. Good judgment comes from experience, and experience comes from bad judgment.
— economist G. Warren Nutter, quoted by Walter B. Wriston in the *New York Times,* November 4, 1983

O

Oakland School Bulletin Board Item.
———————— **Notice** ————————
THIS DEPT. REQUIRES NO PHYSICAL FITNESS PRO-
GRAM: EVERYONE GETS ENOUGH EXERCISE JUMPING
TO CONCLUSIONS, FLYING OFF THE HANDLE, RUNNING
DOWN THE BOSS, KNIFING FRIENDS IN THE BACK,
DODGING RESPONSIBILITY & PUSHING THEIR LUCK.
— found posted in an Oakland, Calif., school by Charles F. Dery, San Francisco

O'Harro's Law. Modesty is the opiate of the mediocre.
— Michael O'Harro, Washington, D.C.

O.J.'s Revision. It doesn't matter if you win or lose . . . until you lose.
— O. J. Simpson, on ABC's "Wide World of Sports"; from J. P. O'Shee

Old Economist's Razor. If you owe your bank a hundred pounds, you have a problem; but if you owe a million, it has.
— This has been attributed to John Maynard Keynes (for in-stance, in *The Economist,* February 13, 1982, and *Time,*

September 6, 1982; however, a letter from Theodor Schuchat of Washington, D.C., points out, "No one has found it in his writings, and Lady Keynes assured me, in writing, several years ago that to the best of her knowledge he never said it."

Oldfield's Explanation. Hey, I just want a condo, a Mercedes — be like the other amateurs.
> — shot putter Brian Oldfield, on why he tried to regain Olympic eligibility, quoted in the Anderson Valley *Advertiser*

The Old Teacher's Law. Minds at rest rust.
> — Unknown, from radio station WRC

Olly's Observation. When you remove a bread and butter plate, your thumb always goes where the butter was.
> — W. A. "Olly" Herold, Islington, Ontario, Canada

Organizational Inaction, The Four Theorems of. (1) The present is too soon (or too late) to discuss any important issue. (The time theorem.) (2) The topic is too narrow (or too broad) to be considered. (The subject matter theorem.) (3) The group is too small (or too large) for effective action. (The group size theorem.) (4) The topic is too controversial (or too dull) to deal with. (The excitement theorem.)
> — in "The Principles of Organizational Inaction," by J. Barnstep Clagg and Norma Mealstom, in *The Bureaucrat,* Summer 1979

Oristano's Laws of Personal Service Contract Negotiations. (1) If you want to play the game, you have to play the game. (2) When negotiating salary, let your conscience be your guide, plus 20 percent.
> — Mark Oristano, Arlington, Tex.

O'Shee's Observation. It always works better in the commercial.
> — J. P. O'Shee, Ville Platte, La.

O'Stee▮ ▮n will keep the child
home ▮ play (i.e., ball game).
(2) T▮

▮enn.

O▮ ▮ done so ineptly that the
f▮ ▮it worse.
▮, Foote, Cone and Belding

▮r that a politician is like a con-
▮reasonable feeling of security
▮d. **Ottinger's Law of the Execu-**
▮ a situation you "wouldn't touch
▮ duty is to seek out a store selling

▮Mercerville, N.J.

Ozark's ▮ ▮imitations are limitless.
— baseball ▮▮▮er Danny Ozark, on infielder Mike Andrews

Ozmon's Law. (1) If someone says they will do something
without fail, they won't. (2) The more people talk on the
phone, the less money they make. (3) People that go to conferences are the ones that shouldn't. (4) Pizza always burns
the roof of your mouth.
— Howard Ozmon, Richmond, Va.

P

**Pajari's Postulate Study (of particular interest to those de-
veloping proofs of hypotheses posed in math textbooks).** If
it couldn't be proved, it wouldn't be in the book
— George Pajari, Vancouver, British Columbia, Canada

Paliwoda's Premise. The best way to make money is not to lose it.
— Steve Paliwoda, Anchorage, Alaska

Palmer's Comment on Retirement. It really bothers me to think I may never throw a home-run pitch again.
— Jim Palmer, reflecting on his forced retirement from the Baltimore Orioles, quoted in *Sports Illustrated*

Pandora's Rule. Never open a box you didn't close.
— Mike Berman, Killeen, Tex.

Paper's General Law. Printing a text in any writing system other than Roman, Greek, or Cyrillic most likely results in text appearing either upside down or backwards.
— Herbert H. Paper, Hebrew Union College, Jewish Institute of Religion, Cincinnati, Ohio

Parkins's Deduction. If a system is too complex for one person to understand it, it is too complex for any finite number of people to understand it.
— Richard P. Parkins, Hampshire, England

Parkinson's Eighth or Tenth (who's counting?) Law. The chief product of a highly automated society is a widespread and deepening sense of boredom.
— C. Northcote Parkinson, in an interview that appeared in the *New York Times*, September 25, 1987

Parsons's Honesty Rule. If someone shouts a reply to your questions, "Well, to be honest . . .", you are entitled to assume that up to that moment he has been telling the most appalling lies. **Parsons's Rules for Collectors.** An essential factor in collecting anything at all is to start twenty years ago.
— Denys Parsons, London, England

Passman's Paradox of Flexible Mortality. There are plenty of things you can do to help you live longer; there is nothing that you can do to help you live forever.
　　— David L. Passman, Chicago, Illinois

Patinkin's Admonition. Never buy a used car if the radio buttons are all on hard-rock stations.
　　— Mark Patinkin, *Providence Journal*; from Ben Willis, Jr.

Pat's Subscription Law. If I want to know when my magazine subscription expires, the date on the sticker on the cover of the magazine is in a computer code that I can't decipher.
　　— Ralph C. "Pat" Wolfe, Walnut, Ill.

Patton's Laws of Immortality. No one is considered immortal until he is dead.
　　— Rick Patton, LaHabra, Calif.

Paul's Commentary. There is so much apathy in the world today . . . but who cares?
　　— Steven J. Paul, Rapid City, S.D.

Paulson's Solution for a Stagnant Career. Sex discrimination need not stifle your opportunities for career advancement if you are flexible enough to consider a sex change.
　　— Pat Paulson; from John A. Mattsen

Payack's Update. One hologram is worth 1,000,000,000 words.
　　— Peter Payack, *New York Times,* October 1, 1980.

Peachum's Principle. The road to good intentions is paved with hell.
　　— Ted Peachum, in Peter DeVries's *Consenting Adults*; from Robert D. Specht

Peacock's Laws of Teaching. (1) You never teach an easy class. Neither does anyone else. (2) Any lesson consists of 60 percent instruction, 40 percent discipline, and 5 percent embarrassing mistakes.
— Norman Peacock, Bedford, England

Pecor's Health Food Principle. Never eat rutabagas on any day of the week that has a "y" in it.
— Charles J. Pecor, Macon, Ga.

Pennsylvania Dutch Saying (paraphrased). Blondness don't last; brains do.
— in *The Gold Solution,* by Herbert Resnicow; from Charles D. Poe

Penny-Pincher's Rule. On the day your bill comes to $10.04, you won't be carrying any pennies. On the day you want to get rid of your pennies, it'll come to $10.00 exactly.
— Tom Gill, Davis, Calif.

People's Action Rules. (1) Some people who can, shouldn't. (2) Some people who should, won't. (3) Some people who shouldn't, will. (4) Some people who can't, will try, regardless. (5) Some people who shouldn't, but try, will then blame others.
— Bob Kerr, who says they apply to a host of activities, including driving, gambling, and drinking

Pepperoni Principle of Conflict Resolution. When facing a fight that cannot be won or that might prove too costly, order a pizza.
— from a August 14, 1987, *Christian Science Monitor* editorial in which it was pointed out that White House lobbyist Tom Loeffler had dropped by House Speaker Jim Wright's house with a pizza on the way to an agreement between the two

Pepys's Prediction. If we give women equal rights, the next thing you know, they'll want to send their children to the same schools as our children.
— Roy West, Philadelphia, Pa.

Perot's Political Polemic. What most politicians stand for is re-election. If you can organize the grass roots, you could probably get a law passed saying the world's square.
— H. Ross Perot; from Nick Kass

Persius's Point. How sweet it is to have people point and say, "There he is."
— Persius

Petersen's Law of Business Reports. The length of a report has an inverse relationship to the author's status in the organization.
— Dean M. Petersen, Memphis, Tenn.

Peterson's Rules. (1) Trucks that overturn on freeways are filled with something sticky. (2) No cute baby in a carriage is ever a girl when called one. (3) Things that tick are not always clocks. (4) Suicide works only when you're bluffing.
— Donna Peterson, San Gabriel, Calif.

Peter's Paradoxical Paradox. Man is complex — he makes deserts bloom and lakes die.
— Dr. Laurence J. Peter, *Los Angeles Times,* March 8, 1983

Peters's Secret. The secret of life is that there is no secret of life.
— Kurt M. Peters, San Francisco, Calif.

Peters's Third Law of Politics. The number of parking tickets issued declines in direct proportion to the number of days remaining before the next municipal election.
— Charles Peters, *Washington Monthly*

Petty's Pronouncement on Personal Pacing. In order to finish first, you must first finish.
— race car driver Richard Petty; from David Little

Pfeifer's Philosophy. All of life is rejection. Make sure you are thrown out by the best. **Pfeifer's Test for a Great Truth.** The opposite of one great truth is another great truth.
— Catherine Pfeifer, Milwaukee, Wisc.

Pfister's Law of Teaching. Overteach, because students underlearn and overforget.
— Fred R. Pfister, Point Lookout, Mo.

Phillips's Academic Laws. (1) **Practicality.** Anything that works is not scholarly. (2) **Clarity.** The best way to confuse people is to make something perfectly clear. (3) **Writing.** You can prove you have been a writer by producing what you have written. You can never prove you are going to be a writer. (4) **Competency.** To the extent a student is competent, he offends the teacher who is not. (5) **Promptness.** If you can't do it correctly, do it by the deadline. (6) **Plagiarism.** If you footnote every seventh line, you will never be accused of plagiarism.
— Gerald M. Phillips, University Park, Pa., from a larger collection

Pickle's Law. If Congress must do a painful thing, the thing must be done in a odd-numbered year.
— Representative Jake Pickle, quoted by James J. Kilpatrick

Pidduck's Principle. A pessimist only receives *pleasant* surprises.
— Ruth Piddick, Lachine, Quebec, Canada

Piper's Givens. (1) Fat people use more soap than thin people. (2) There is always plenty of good free cheese in a rat trap. (3) Today's gifts are tomorrow's yard sales. (4) Fifty percent of all doctors graduated in the bottom half of their class.
— James W. Piper, Concord, N.H.

Pirus Law of Cumulative Clutter. Accumulation of old magazines is directly proportional to the cost of the publications and their relationship to special interests, and inversely proportional to the number of persons in the household.
— Douglas I. Pirus, *The Journal of Irreproducible Results,* 1988; from Norman D. Stevens

Pitsinger's Law of Negative Motivation. The ability of anyone to do anything is reduced proportionally to the strength of the thought that one can't, until a point is reached where the individual believes they cannot and they truly can't.
— Roger Pitsinger, Lake Oswego, Ore.

Plato's Observation. People who campaign for the other party are called ward heelers. People who campaign for your party are said to be interested in ensuring the survival of the democratic system.
— Ed Karl, whose dog is named Plato

Plimpton's Correlation. There exists an inverse correlation between the size of a ball and the quality of writing about the sport in which the ball is used. There are superb books about golf, very good books about baseball, not very many

good books about football, very few good books about basketball, and there are no good books on beachballs.
— George Plimpton, quoted in *Sportswit,* by Lee Green; from Steve Stine

Plotnick's Lament. My pot of gold lies at the end of a circle.
— Bernard Plotnick, Pompano Beach, Fla.

Poer's Laws. Los Angeles Driving. You can't go around the block. **Motion Picture Production.** It's not the time it takes to take the take that takes the time; it's the time between the takes that takes the time.
— John M. Poer, Canoga Park, Calif.

Poe's Observations. (1) Sylvester Stallone is the thinking man's Chuck Norris. (2) Any accountant who has joined a band of antigovernment guerrillas is a revolutionary fiduciary.
— Charles D. Poe, Houston, Tex.

Pole's Law. Every American president makes his predecessor look good.
— J. R. Pole, *The New Republic,* May 16, 1983

Pollock's Discovery. Whichever way you stand, when you empty the Hoover bag, the dust always blows in your face.
— H. M. Pollock, Sevenoaks, Kent, England

Pollyanna's Educational Constants. The hyperactive child is never absent. The student who hit the teacher is the one with the lawyer. Just because the specialists find a label for a child doesn't mean they know what's wrong with him.
— Susan Ohanian, Troy, N.Y.

Pompey's Law of Harassment. If you are getting run out of town, get in front of the crowd and make it look like a parade.
— Sherman Lee Pompey, Florence, Ore.

Poole's Rule of Flattery. Always address recipients of typed correspondence as "Dr." You will be either correct or flattering.
— Charles Poole, Washington, D.C.

Poorman's Rule. (1) When you pull a plastic garbage bag from its handy dispenser package, you always get hold of the closed end and try to pull it open. (2) The defroster on the passager side of your car always works better than the one on the driver side. (3) It is always the up escalator that is being repaired.
— Paul A. Poorman, Akron, Ohio

Pope's Garage Sale Law. You will get your own junk back in three years. It will cost twice as much. You didn't need it until you sold it. You won't need it after you buy it back.
— William G. Pope, Somers, N.Y.

Posner's Distinction. Only tax-supported institutions are closed on a minor holiday.
— George E. Posner, Berkeley, Calif.

Pournelle's Pronouncement. Sometimes it may be better to have it Wednesday than perfect.
— Jerry Pournelle, *Byte,* December 1983; from Shel Kagan

Pratley's Prophecy. The fixing of one malfunction results in damage or malfunction to another part of the thing being fixed.
— James R. Pratley, Rancho Bernado, Calif., quoted in Jack Smith's column, *Los Angeles Times,* 1985

Pratt's Rules. (1) A travel clock must be wound at least every twelve hours or it will stop, unless it is in the suitcase at home — then it will run for three days without winding. (2) When the regulated want to make a change it is a laborious process; however, when the regulatory agency wants to make a change, a simple clarification of the regulations is all that is required.
— Harvey A. Pratt, Catonsville, Md.

Prince Philip's Rule. Never pass a bathroom.
— The Duke of Edinburgh; from Robert J. T. Joy, M.D., Bethesda, Md.

Prince's Actuarial Axiom. Destiny is statistics by another name.
— J. M. Prince, University of Tennessee, Knoxville

Principal's Principle. Star quarterbacks always take classes from teachers who give passing grades.
— principal Murdo I. MacLeod, Santa Ana, Calif.

Priorities, Two Laws About. (1) Nobody dies wishing they'd spent more time with their business. (2) Better to be king for a night than schmuck for a lifetime.
— from Steve Stine, who heard the second from the character Rupert Pupkin (Robert De Niro) in the movie *King of Comedy*

Proverbs Revised. (1) Early to bed gets the worm. (2) Two in the bush is the root of all evil. (3) People who live in glass houses are not too smart. (4) All's fair when you settle out of court. (5) A rolling stone gathers smashed objects in its path.
— the first two from James O. Stevenson, Bethesda, Md.; the second two written by schoolchildren and quoted by Johnny Carson on "The Tonight Show"; number 5 from Margie Mereen, Burnsville, Minn., who got it from her husband

Pryor's Observation. How long you live has nothing to do with how long you are going to be dead.
— Richard Pryor, on "The Tonight Show"

Pugh's Theory of the Individual Quotient of Vice. When abandoning a vice or vices, one will, sooner or later, substitute a new vice or vices which offset the vice or vices abandoned.
— restated from an article on this topic by Jodie T. Allen, *Washington Post* January 1, 1988. It is named for Robert Pugh of George Mason University. The principle also applies to cultural behavior. The author of the article asks, "What can so simply and satisfactorily explain the rise of pornography in this country as the concomitant disappearance of spitoons?"

Putt's Laws of Survival. (1) To get along, go along. (2) To protect your position, fire the fastest-rising employees first.
— Archibald Putt, in the periodical *Research/Development*; from Paul J. Lambeck

 Q

Qaddafi's Dietary Qualifier. We plant roses, we breed chickens, and we eat candy — but before we eat candy we must eat the kidneys of our enemies.
— Libyan dictator Muammar Qaddafi, quoted in *US News & World Report*

Quick's Law of Women's Panties and Men's Briefs. When one puts one's foot through the wrong hole, the undergarment must be completely removed before the situation can be corrected.
— David J. Quick, Brentwood, Calif.

Quigley's Law. Whoever has any authority over you, no matter how small, will attempt to use it.
— anonymous; received in an unmarked envelope

Quinn's Law. Whenever a golfer messes up a hole with a series of unfortunate shots and unaccountable tragedies before reaching the green, said golfer will invariably three putt.
— Eleanor and Floyd Taylor, Los Angeles, Cal.

Quinn's Rules to Eat By. (1) Never eat in a restaurant that calls itself a nightclub. (2) Never eat in any restaurant recommended by anybody who teaches in a college. (3) Never eat in an empty restaurant. Everybody who's not there must know something. (4) Never eat in any restaurant with a souvenir shop attached. (5) Never order bratwurst in a Chinese restaurant.
— from a much longer list that appears in *But Never Eat Out on a Saturday Night,* by Jim Quinn

Quinn's Understanding. Economists carry their projections out to two decimal points only to prove they have a marvelous sense of humor.
— Jane Bryant Quinn, quoted by Robert D. Specht in his *1986: An Expectation of Days*

Quisenberry's Theory of Relativity. I have seen the future, and it's a lot like the present, but much longer.
— Kansas City Royals pitcher Dan Quisenberry, quoted in the *St. Petersburg Times* by Roger Angell, April 8, 1985

Dr. Quoy's Laws of Fishing. (1) The biggest fish always hits the smallest rod. (2) If two lines can get tangled, they will. (3) Whatever bait you're using, the fish are hitting something else. (4) As the hook is bent, so goes the fish.
— Herbert C. Quoy, Ph.D.

R

Rabinowitz's Rule. Let a smile be your umbrella, and you'll get a lot of rain in your face.
— the character Gary Rabinowitz on the TV show "Archie Bunker's Place"; from Tom Gill

Racker's Remark. Scientific discoveries pass through three stages; firstly, they are disbelieved; secondly, they are believed but rejected as trivial; finally, they are accepted as correct and significant but dismissed as old hat.
— Efraim Racker; from David Welford, Birmingham, England

Radcliffe's Rule. There's no such thing as a single call to a federal agency.
— Charles W. Radcliffe, Minority Counsel, House Committee on Education and Labor, quoted in the *National Report for Training and Development,* Sept. 24, 1982; from Mollie N. Orth

Rae's Dilemma. When you move something to a better place for safe keeping, you can never remember the location of the better place.
— Mrs. Rae P. Jensen, San Francisco, Calif.

Ragucci's Collected Wisdom. (1) **The Purple Magnet Theory.** In any given crowd, the weirdo will automatically and immediately seek you out. (2) **First Truth of Love.** Love is exhausting. (3) **Hospital Law of Room Assignments.** Whenever possible, patients with similar sounding names will be put on the same floor in the same room.
— John J. Ragucci, Everett, Mass.

The Rainbow Ice Cream Co.'s Point. A person who doesn't like ice cream doesn't like a good laugh, goes to the beach and complains about the sand, sleeps in pajamas, and kisses with his mouth closed.
> — paraphrased from the aforementioned San Francisco institution by Bill Shea

Rajneesh's Razor. Experts consult; never wise men.
> — Shree Rajneesh; from Shel Kagan

Randall's Observation. The first person to spot and chastise a phony is either as big a phony as or a bigger phony than the one he passed judgment on.
> — Randall L. Koch, Kenosha, Wisc.

Randall's Reminder. The closest to perfection a person ever comes is when he fills out a job application form.
> — Stanley Randall, quoted by Patrick Ryan in *Smithsonian*

Randall's Rule of Economic Indicators. Increased productivity occurs when the number of unemployed not working is greater than the number of employed who are not working.
> — Warren Randall, Stony Brook, N.Y.

Rapoport's Rule on Eating at Cocktail Parties. You will eat just enough hors d'oeuvres to ruin your appetite for dinner but not enough to satisfy it.
> — Dan Rapoport, Washington, D.C.

Rappo's Law of Pediatrics (a selection). (1) Children are not small adults, although adults frequently act like large children. (2) Not all short physicians are pediatricians; some short physicians are anesthesiologists. (3) Children rarely outgrow things they like. (4) Mother's Day is not in May; it's the first day of school.
> — Peter D. Rappo, M.D., Brockton, Mass.

Rathbun's Generalization. Generalizations and value judgments are all bad. **Rathbun's Rule.** There is no harder nor more thankless taskmaster than the self-employed.
— J. M. Rathbun, M.D., Cumberland, Wisc.

Raub's Law. The more expensive the toy, the greater the tendency for the child to play with the box.
— I. Raub Love, Dayton, Ohio

Ravage's Rule of Foot. Excursions on foot will be approximately 58 percent uphill in both directions. This percentage will increase as the temperature rises.
— John M. Ravage, Philadelphia, Pa.

Raymie's Rule of Repair. No job is done until you bleed on it.
— Suzie Radus, Pittsburgh, Pa.

Reach's Rule. The secret of happiness is to let the other fellow do the worrying.
— A. J. Reach, of baseball and sporting goods fame, quoted in *Sporting News,* July 28, 1906

Reagan's Razor. Anything we do is in the national interest.
— Ronald Reagan, quoted in Lou Cannon's column, *Washington Post,* January 19, 1986. The president had uttered the line the previous July when asked whether sending helicopters to Bolivia for drug enforcement was in the national interest.

Recording Engineer, Ultimate Threat of. Don't tell me how to do my job, or I might do exactly what you say.
— from Steve Stine, who learned it at a recording engineer seminar in 1976 at Columbia College/Sonart Studios

Regan's Answer to the Question of How Social Security Will Be Funded in Fifty Years. I don't care, I'll be dead by then.
— Treasury Secretary Donald Regan, quoted in the *Washington Star*, April 18, 1981

Reidling's Rule for High School Football Broadcasts. The defensive end who falls on a fumble in his opponent's end zone is wearing a number that isn't on your program.
— from Paul Biler, who says that this is named for Jerry Reidling, Sports Director, WFRO, Fremont, Ohio. During a game, no one in the pressbox could identify a running back who ran for 175 yards and two touchdowns.

Reid's Reminder. If you are looking for one thing in a stack of stuff, if it is a horizontal stack, it will be at the back; if it is a vertical stack, it will be at the bottom.
— Rosemary Reid, San Francisco, Calif.

Reinstedt's Reminder. Just because you have an irrational fear of flying doesn't mean you're not going to crash.
— Bob Reinstedt; from Robert D. Specht

Reisman's Rule of Hustling Table-Tennis. First you need a good racquet, then you need a lot of balls.
— Marty Reisman; from J. M. McCabe

Reisner's Rule of Conceptual Inertia. If you think big enough, you'll never have to do it.
— John H. Reisner III

Reiss's Rule of Restaurant Ruination. No restaurant, diner, or other eating establishment has ever been improved by a change of ownership.
— Edward B. Reiss, Scottsdale, Ariz.

Renning's Maxim. Man is the highest animal. Man does the classifying.
— anonymous; from T. J. Nelson

Reston's Lesson to Journalists. You should always look around for the guys who are unhappy.
— James Reston, who got a number of scoops from the Nationalist Chinese during the Dumbarton Oaks conference of 1944 when the U.N. was created; from Joseph C. Goulden, who spotted it in Gay Talese's *Kingdom and the Power*

Reyna McGlone's Discovery. Lint, dog and cat hair, dirt, dust, etc., are most strongly attracted to objects of opposite color. **Corollary.** There is no such thing as a carpet that doesn't show dirt.
— Augustin Reyna McGlone; from Don Hall

Reynolds's First Law of Politics. Politicians will act rationally only when all other alternatives are exhausted.
— John Reynolds, Jr., Sandy, Utah

Reynolds's Law. It's just as easy to make a BIG mistake as a small one.
— Joan A. Reynolds, Hyattsville, Md.

Reynolds's Table Rules. (1) If you order your coffee without sugar, the waiter will bring it without cream. (2) You never make the right number of pancakes.
— C. Reynolds, M.D., Vancouver, British Columbia, Canada

Riberdy's Observations. (1) Dirty dishes attract surprise visitors. (2) Most swimmers will run for shelter at the first signs of rain. (3) If a picture hangs straight on the first attempt — expect it to fall. (4) Junk mail multiplies if left in the box.
— J. Riberdy, Windsor, Ontario, Canada

Rich Richard's Almanacation. When driving, don't look at anything lying on the road. If you look, chances are very good you'll see something you'll wish you hadn't. **Rich Richard's Truism.** God has given man the seemingly infinite capacity to remember telephone numbers and *ONE* zip code.
— V. Richard Smith, Willow Springs, Ohio

Rickover's Reminder. At any moment during a twenty-four-hour day only one-third of the people in the world are asleep. The other two-thirds are awake and creating problems.
— Adm. Hyman Rickover; from Jack Kime

Rinzler's Theory of Relativity. Traffic is never a problem when you're trying to kill time; it builds up in direct proportion to the urgency of your schedule.
— Carol E. Rinzler, in *Woman's Day*

Rippetoe's Certification Rule. Customer satisfaction at auto repair shops is inversely proportional to the number of mechanics on the staff who have passed written exams testing their mechanical skills. **Corollary.** No amount of practical evidence will convince college-educated liberals that written tests are worthless in judging mechanical skill. **Rippetoe's Motherly Musing.** Parenthood is the only job with a reverse apprenticeship. You start the job with no experience or practical knowledge and total responsibility for a helpless child; as you gain experience and knowledge your responsibility is gradually reduced to practically nothing.
— Rita Rippetoe, Citrus Heights, Calif.

Rist's Junk Drawer Discoveries. (1) All houses have a junk drawer. (2) Anything wanted from the junk drawer will be found at the bottom. (3) Once any item is removed from the junk drawer — no matter how large or small — the junk drawer will not close.
— Philip Rist, Cleveland, Ohio

Ritchie's Rules. (1) Everything has some value — if you use the right currency. (2) Paint splashes last longer than the paint job. (3) Search and ye shall find — but make sure it was lost.
— Peter Ritchie, Jr., Bowling Green, Va.

Rives's Discovery. Everything falls apart on the same day. [Rives calls this EFAOTS Day, and he pronounces it E fouts.]
— John Rives, Lafayette, Colo.

Rizzo Rule, The. If you are telling the truth, never take a lie-detector test. If you're not telling the truth, never take a lie-detector test.
— Daniel Rapoport, Washington, D.C., *Los Angeles Times*, November 6, 1981; from Robert D. Specht

Roberts's Restaurant Realization. If you don't like water, you don't like much.
— Dave Roberts; from Michael Sawhill, Buffalo, Wyo.

Robinson's Law of Restaurant Keeping. (1) When you are busy, it does not matter for what time they book — they will all arrive together. (2) No restaurant is ever as good as your best notice. **Corollary.** Neither is it as bad as your worst. (3) A client who is convinced that he is about to have a terrible meal is seldom disappointed. The reverse doesn't hold, but at least you have a better chance. (4) The one time the President wants to eat with you is midway during your annual holidays. (5) The clients in the biggest hurry are those who are still there after all the others have left. (6) If you run out of one item during service you will soon run out of others, each item in each course being the only thing on the menu the one customer really wanted. (7) All restaurants thrive on chaos — the successful ones are those which hide this fact from their clients, at least most of the time.
— Peter Robinson, who runs La Ferme Irlandaise, Paris, France

Robinson's Rationale for Grade Inflation. A student never complains about getting an A.
> — Associate Professor Judith Robinson, State University of New York, Buffalo

Robson's Rule. Learning always occurs after the job is finished.
> — Thayne Robson, University of Utah; from William D. Hickman

Rock and Roll Rules of the Road (a selection). (1) No one will request a song you know how to play. (2) Never challenge a heckler to come up and play it better than you just did. He or she will. (3) If necessary, a guitar is an excellent medium-range weapon.
> — T. C. Acres, Calgary, Alberta, Canada

Roddenberry's Realization. They say that 90 percent of TV is junk. But 90 percent of *everything* is junk.
> — TV producer Gene Roddenberry, quoted in *TV Guide,* April 27, 1974; from Don Nilsen

Roeper's Rules of the Universe (a selection). (1) Gas station attendants are hired based on their lack of knowledge regarding directions. (2) All men look like geeks for seventy-two hours after a haircut. (3) You will not get the hiccups when you are alone. You will get the hiccups in the middle of your bar exam, or at a funeral, or on a first visit to your future in-laws' house. (4) If you think your pants have split, they have. (5) If you think your nylon has a run in it, it does. (6) The question you will be asked most often in you life is "Do you want fries with that?"
> — Richard Roeper, *Milwaukee Journal,* February 18, 1987; from Catherine Pfeifer

Rogers's Boss Law. There will always be beer cans rolling on the floor of your car when the boss asks for a lift home from the office.
— Dennis Rogers

Rogers's Collected Thoughts. (1) Don't gamble; take all your savings and buy some good stock and hold it till it goes up, then sell it. If it don't go up, don't buy it. (2) There is only two sure ways to lose a friend. One is to go camping with him, the other is to loan him money. (3) Politics ain't worrying this country one-tenth as much as parking spaces. (4) Things will get better despite our efforts to improve them.
— Will Rogers; from various sources

Rolark's Reminder for Radicals and Revolutionaries. You never destroy the "establishment"; you simply replace it. If you do take over, *you* become the establishment.
— Bruno Rolark

Rooney's Laws. (1) You're much more likely to lock a member of your family out of your own house than a burglar. (2) You could be wrong. (3) When people say to me, "You're the boss," they don't mean it.
— Andy Rooney, respectively from "60 Minutes," *And More From Andy Rooney,* and his Tribune Media Service column of August 31, 1986

Roosevelt's Resolution. Do what you can, with what you have, where you are.
— Theodore Roosevelt

Rosato's Revelation. The world is full of sane people taking medicine to enable them to cope with all the insane ones who should be using medication but refuse to do so.
— Donald J. Rosato, M.D., Devon, Pa.

Rosenau's Law of Revolting Developments. There will be at least one.
— Milton D. Rosenau, Jr., Santa Monica, Calif.

Rosendahl's Corollaries. (1) All bad things happen at night, especially if the weather is up. (2) There is always one too few backup systems. (3) The manual left on shore is the one needed now. When you get the manual, the fine print will explain why you can't fix the problem. (4) There are no pleasant surprises. If you doubt it's right, then it's not; if you doubt it will work, then it won't; and when you think the repair is temporary, it is.
— Bruce Rosendahl, quoted in an article by Bob Wilson in the Duke University magazine on his scientific work in East Africa; from Steve Woodbury

Rosengren's Theorem. That which has already achieved the highest degree of perfection can be made even more perfect as long as it pays off.
— Bjorn Rosengren, head of the Swedish Municipal Workers; from Bob Skole

Rosen's Immutable Factory Outlet Law. Regardless of your actual summer destination, you will inevitably end up at a factory outlet.
— R. D. Rosen, *New England Monthly,* May 1985

Rosoff's Rugrat Rule. A baby learns to say Grandma within an hour after she has left on the 2,000-mile trip home.
— Denise Rosoff, APO, N.Y.

Rosoff's Rule of Thermodynamics. A scalding hot cup of coffee will be too cool one instant after it has been adjudged to be at a drinkable temperature.
— Henry Rosoff, APO, N.Y.

Rothman's Lemma. The accuracy of a forecast varies inversely with the extent of its publication.
— James Rothman, London, England

Roubin's Law. Why is it that no matter where you live or how many times you move, your neighbor's taste in music is always in inverse proportion to the volume it's played at?
— M. B. Roubin, Estes Park, Colo., *Stereo Review*, March 1988

Rough Rider's Dictum. Get action. Do things. Be sane. Don't fritter away your time. Create. Act. Take a place wherever you are and be somebody.
— quoted by Thomas Boswell, *Washington Post*, August 2, 1983, and applied to Baltimore Oriole catcher Rick Dempsey

Rowe's Law. Nobody's in a hurry when you are.
— Lynton S. Rowe, Epping, New South Wales, Australia

Royko's Law. Young people will always eat anything that is convenient, then wait until you buy some more convenient foods, and they will eat them too.
— Mike Royko, *Like I was Saying*; from Steve Stine. The following is in *Sez Who? Sez Me*; from Joseph C. Goulden:

Royko's Rule. In a strange bar, never use the phone more than once or they will think you are planning a stickup.

Royko's Rule of Public Broadcasting. No matter when I look, all I ever see on PBS is one of four shows: (1) Insects making love. (2) A lion walking along with a dead antelope in its jaws. (3) Some spiffily dressed, elderly Englishman sitting in a tall-backed chair in a room that is paneled in dark wood. (4) A station announcer talking about what great shows they have and urging us to send more money.
— Mike Royko, abridged from his column, June 4, 1986

Ruby's Remedy. The best bridge between despair and hope is a good night's sleep.
— Harry Ruby, quoted in the *Reader's Digest*, July 1952

Rucker's Law. If one asks the wrong question, the odds are very high that one will receive the wrong answer.
— Professor T. Donald Rucker, Ohio State University

Rudd's Discovery. You know that any senator or congressman could go home and make $300,000–400,000, but they don't. Why? Because they can stay in Washington and make it there.
— Hughes Rudd, *Los Angeles Times*, August 15, 1980; from Robert D. Specht

Rudd's Universal Explanation. Things like this happen.
— Unknown; from Ronald W. Tucker, Veracruz, Mexico

Runyon's Rules for Newspaper Columnists. (1) Never let them give you a desk, because they'll always know where they can find you. (2) Get mad as you want, but never get off the payroll. (3) Keep your byline in there every day. Otherwise, your readers might miss it — or worse yet, they might not.
— in the *Gossip Wars*, by Milt Machlin; from Joseph C. Goulden

Russell's Right. If it succeeds, it is right; if it fails, it is wrong.
— Martin Russell, Yonkers, N.Y.

Ruth's Law. When you have washed all the dishes, there is always one more piece of cutlery in the bottom of the dishpan.
— Mykia Taylor, Glenside, Calif.

Ryan's Gap. The interval between the election of your best friend and his hiring of your worst enemy to be his administrative assistant. On the average, Ryan's Gap is thirty-seven hours and twelve minutes.
— John L. Ryan, quoted in *Conservative Digest*, April 1981; from Joseph C. Goulden

Ryder's Reminders. (1) The person(s) who has all the answers understands none of the problems. (2) Never mistake activity for progress.
— Bruce A. Ryder, Richmond, Va.

 S

Sacramento Manifesto. When you're out to make your mark in the world, watch out for guys with erasers.
— spotted by Tom Gill on a T-shirt in the California capital

Sadat's Rule. Never review the troops until you *know* whose troops they are.
— D. H. Lee, University of Louisville, Ky.

Sailor's Dictum. If you don't make waves, you're not under way.
— Leonard P. Gollobin, Fairfax, Va.

Saki's Advice to Travelers. Never be flippantly rude to elderly strangers in foreign hotels. They always turn out to be the King of Sweden.
— author Saki, quoted in *A Dictionary of Catch Phrases*, by Eric Partridge and Paul Beale

Salak's Observations. (1) Nothing makes you more tolerant of a neighbor's midnight party than being there. (2) Don't try to step into a revolving door behind someone and expect to come out ahead.
— Joseph C. Salak, Deland, Fla.

Saliers's Law. Whenever two of anything are tossed to the same person, they will arrive at the same time. You will catch neither. **Tennis Corollary.** People enjoy tossing balls so they arrive at the same time.
— Richard R. Saliers, Grandville, Mich.

Sally's Collected Conclusions. (1) **Witch Doctor's Fail-Safe.** If the spell works, the witch doctor takes the credit. If it fails, the patient gets the blame. (This fail-safe also works well for diet doctors, psychotherapists, and self-improvement gurus of every stripe.) (2) **Mail.** Junk mail never goes astray. (3) **Child Expert's Chide.** Whatever children really like is bad for them. (4) **Animal Acquisition Axiom.** Free kittens eat expensive lunch. **Cat-Lover's Corollary.** They are worth it.
— N. Sally Hass, Sleepy Hollow, Ill.

Sam Goldwyn's Rule. Never name a movie character "Joe."
— per *The Takers,* by William Flanagan, 1984; from Joe Goulden

Sam's Law. Only fools can be certain; it takes wisdom to be confused.
— the character Sam in the TV show "Quincy"; from Steve Feinfrock

Sanders's Counterpunch. Mayor Jimmy Walker once said that no girl was ever ruined by reading a book. If I believed that, I'd throw away my typewriter.
— novelist Lawrence Sanders, quoted in the *New York Times* Book Review, June 8, 1982

Sandia Rules. (1) I don't know what I want to hear until I hear what I don't want to hear. (2) The more important a thing is, the less time you are given to do it. (3) There are more ways to do something wrong than there are to do it right.
— James D. Plimpton, Albuquerque, N.M., who reports that they have been "floating around" Sandia National Labs for a while

Santulis's Personal Computer Corollary. Personal computers will always remain inexplicable to the layman. **Proof.** The person frustrated with these conditions sets out to rectify this information gap by learning about computers and then explain them to others without the use of jargon that makes the layman's eyes glaze over. The problem is that when a certain amount of knowledge on computers is attained, the former novice immediately loses the detail of his or her former ignorance and becomes just as unintelligible to a layman as any other "winky-blink." Thus computers will always remain complicated and mysterious to the general public, and people who use them will always seem slightly odd to those that don't.
— Kevin Santulis, Oregon, Wisc.

Sauget's Law of Education. Sit at the feet of the masters long enough, and they'll start to smell.
— John Sauget, Urbana, Ill.

Saul's Screwing Saw. When fastening down something held by several screws, don't tighten any of the screws until all of them are in place.
— M. Saul Newman; from Steve Stine

Savage's Law of Expediency. You want it bad, you'll get it bad.
— Richard C. Savage

Sawhill's Rule. Potential is finite.
— Michael Sawhill, Buffalo, Wyo.

Sayers's Observation. It is always pleasant to see a fellow creature toiling still harder than one's self.
— Dorothy L. Sayers, *Busman's Honeymoon*; from David F. Siemens, Jr.

Scanlan's Law. Wedding presents always come in pairs: two toasters, two blenders, two umbrella stands.
— Phyllis Scanlan, Ellyn, Ill.

Schaefer's Rule of Distance. The floor moves further away when you bend over.
— Don Schaefer, Park Ridge, Ill.

Scharringhausen's Conclusion. Self praise stinks.
— William L. Scharringhausen, Park Ridge, Ill.

Schmidt's Theory of Highway Velocities. You will always feel safer from the law if you are speeding in the right lane of the highway. If you go the same speed in the left lane, it's a whole different feeling.
— Marty Schmidt, Glen Ellyn, Ill.

Schmitz's Law of Television Viewing. If you watch a show twice during the year, the second time will be a rerun of the first.
— Edward J. Schmitz, Vienna, Va.

Schnepper's Secret. You can fool some of the people all of the time, and all of the people some of the time, but if you work it right, that's all you need to make a comfortable living.
— Jeff Schnepper, American College, Bryn Mawr, Pa.

Schorr's Theological Comment on Investigative Reporting. Apparently they will not forgive us our presspasses.
— Daniel Schorr, on National Public Radio, March 12, 1985; from James E. Farmer

Schrumpf's Law. The most benefit is derived from money spent on items used between you and the ground. For example, shoes, mattresses, and tires.
— Lee Schrumpf, Bridgeton, Mo.

Schulman's First Law. Books will exceed bookshelving.
— J. Neil Schulman, *The Rainbow Cadenza*; from Neal Wilgus

Schumacher's Conclusion. It is amazing how much theory we can do without when work actually begins.
— E. F. Schumacher; from Steven Woodbury

Schumer's Law of Traffic. You can never catch a red light when you really need to.
— Bob Schumer, Jenkintown, Pa.

Who just turned 40?

Doc Scoggins's Reminder. You're only young once, but you can be immature all your life.
— Charles Scoggins, M.D., quoted in the *Internist* June 1981, in reference to his avocation as a member of a rodeo roping team; from Bernard Albert

Scott's Theory. Younger men aren't better until they get older.
— Jenna Scott; from Robert L. Stakes, El Paso, Tex.

Scoville's Law. The most complicated rules, regulations, and procedures are created by people who don't have to make them work. **Corollary.** Complex rules, regulations, and pro-

cedures are created by people who need to appear busy to
keep their job.
— Wilber E. Scoville, Oshkosh, Wisc.

**Seckel's Explanation for Such Things as People Who Invoke
the Healing Power of Quartz Crystals to Fix Their Cars.**
There are a lot of people with their umbilical cords out looking to stick it into something, to remove responsibility.
— physicist Al Seckel, quoted in the *New York Times*, April
8, 1988; from Joseph C. Goulden

Seeberg's Law. Whenever you approach a car in a parking
lot with its lights left on, the doors will be locked.
— Marge Seeberg, Northbrook, Ill.

Seersucker Principle. For every seer, there is a sucker.
— from Steven Stine, who heard it in an old "Alfred Hitchcock Presents" rerun. A character played by Jack Klugman
says it to a character played by E. G. Marshall.

Seleznick's Theory of Holistic Medicine. Ice cream cures all
ills. Temporarily.
— Mitchel J. Seleznick, M.D.; from Sol G. Brotman

Sellen's Observation. It doesn't *take* all kinds; we just *have*
all kinds.
— Robert W. Sellen, Georgia State University, Atlanta

Serjak's Law. If you wait long enough, you'll be there all day.
— Jacob Serjak; from Gordon Serjak, North Miami, Fla.

Servan-Schreiber's Law. Democracy is completely dependent on oil.
— Jean-Louis Servan-Schreiber, *The World Challenge*
(1980); from Charles D. Poe

Seymour's Beatitude of the Bureaucracy — on the treatment of employee complaints. The first time you're a disgruntled employee. The second time you're a pain in the ass. The third time you're a nut.
— John Seymour, Bayonne, N.J.

The Shah's Invocation. Let the good times roll.
— named for the Shah of Iran, by Va. legislator Ray Garland

Shales's TV Testimonial. Well, of course, you can't avoid watching television, I mean, what would life be but an endless series of real experiences.
— critic Tom Shales, *On the Air!*

Shaw's Solution. If you can't get rid of the family skeleton, you may as well make it dance.
— George Bernard Shaw; from Catherine Pfeifer

Shaw's Syllogism. If a statement, either written or spoken, begins with, "As a matter of fact . . ." whatever follows is likely to be a downright lie.
— George Bernard Shaw; from Francis J. Hennessy

Shea's Discovery. Unlimited warranties are usually neither.
— Bill Shea, Daly City, Calif.

Sheehan's Law. As the quality of government goes down, the number of meetings increases.
— anonymous; WRC radio

Shephard's Law of Flubdubbery. Problems are simple. It's just that people are simpler.
— W. W. Shepherd; from G. B. Shepherd, Santa Ynez, Calif.

Shephard's Query. Dirt is a universal constant universe; why push it around?
— anonymous WRC radio

Sherekis's Rules of the Road (abbreviated). (1) Gas is always five cents cheaper at the station two miles down the road from wherever you fill your tank. (2) Everything is farther than you think. (3) The windshield washers, wipers, and defrosters on the passenger side of all automobiles, domestic or foreign, will work with the force and efficiency of a car wash, while those same accessories on the driver's side will leave a three-inch wide band of mud, moth intestines, and steam at the exact eye level of the driver, whatever size he or she may be. (4) Five individuals make all the calls into all the all-night talk shows in the country. One is a 52-year-old male who belongs to the National Rifle Association, the American Legion, the Baptist Church, and the Possee Comititas, and who believes that Ronald Reagan is good on the economy but soft on communism. Two are hopeless alcoholics past middle age, one of each sex, who are known by their first names to all the talk-show hosts and who feel that everything would be okay if people would be nicer to each other. (5) If a motel advertises that a "single" is anywhere from $12.50 to $22.95 per night, the same room will be available for a party of two or more for $52.80, including tax. (6) The pungent, earthy smell of manure in the countryside will generate more tasteless jokes and gross accusations among people under eighteen than any other single phenomenon.
— Rich Sherekis, from a larger collection he published in the *Illinois Times,* September 1984.

Shively's Rule. Your favorite song always comes on the car radio when you reach your destination.
— Cynthia Shively, Lawrence, Kans.

Is this why WGN doesn't play music?

Shoe-Shopper's Rule. If it feels good, it's ugly. If it looks good, it hurts.
— N. Sally Hass, Sleepy Hollow, Ill.

Shoe's Instructions for Rest Room Hand Dryer Machines. (1) Push button. (2) Rub hands gently under nozzle. (3) Wipe hands on pants.
— Jeff MacNelly's *Shoe* comic strip, June 19, 1980

Shorris's Assumption. Assumptions keep us awake nights.
— Earl Shorris, quoted in *Forbes,* February 9, 1987

Shula's Computer Age Razor. If it can't fit in a few filing cabinets, is it really that important?
— columnist Jeff Shula, Waldo (County, Maine) *Independent,* on a local high-school principal's request for a $29,000 computer to store school records

Siegel's Law of Knife Sharpening. The first thing a freshly sharpened knife cuts is the sharpener's thumb or one of his fingers.
— Peter V. Siegel, Jr., APO, San Francisco, Calif.

Silverman's Sagacities. (1) What man can think of, man can do! — I think. (2) Man gets irritated and winds up with ulcers, oysters get irritated and wind up with pearls.
— Isador Silverman, University Heights, Ohio

Simon's Translation. In my country we have a name for sushi . . . bait.
— comedian Jose Simon, quoted in Bob Swift's column, *Miami Herald,* January 3, 1987

Sisley's Second Law. We exist in a state of overcorrection.
Sisley's Third Law. Life is a soap opera, only a little slower.

194 · PAUL DICKSON

Sisley's Fourth Law. The misdeeds of a member of any minority are attributed to all the persons in that minority, while the misdeeds of a member of the majority are attributed to that individual alone.
> — John R. Sisley, Jr., Utica, N.Y. who notes, "Sisley has no first law. It is very much more impressive to begin with a second law."

Sister Cheyney's Universal Mother's Response. Alright! Share!
> — F. D. McSpiritt, Flint, Mich., who adds that it applies to all situations save those involving razor blades or matches

Skole's Perfection Principle. Anything named perfect should be suspect.
> — Bob Skole, Solna, Sweden, in a letter complaining about a piece of computer software with "Perfect" in its title. Also:

Skole's Statistical Law. The statistic you want is hard to find; the statistic you need is impossible to find.

Skye's Rules. (1) Never make friends with a person whose nickname is "Gator," "Moose," or "Flower." (2) You can't throw away a trash can. (3) A watched pot never boils over.
> — J. Skye, San Antonio, Tex.

Slay's Rule. Don't do anything dumb. **Slay's Corollary.** I'll decide what's dumb.
> — General Alton D. Slay; from Lt. Col. William P. Campbell

Slevin's Rule. The more a person is confused by what you say sincerely, the more likely they are to agree with you in principle.
> — Martin Slevin, Whitmore Park, Coventry, England

Slous's Contention. If you do a job too well, you'll get stuck with it.
> — Roy Slous; from T. S. Durham

Slug's Constant. No matter how fast a computer is, inefficient programs will evolve so that the machine will appear to run at the same speed as always.
> — John Dvorak, *PC Magazine*, May 12, 1987; from Shel Kagan

Smith's Rule of Bar Decorum. Never take a punch at a man named Sullivan.
> — the late H. Allen Smith, *Life in a Putty Knife Factory*; from Joseph C. Goulden

Smith's Suggestions to the New Graduates (a selection). (1) Dirty laundry never goes away. (2) There's no such thing as a "friendly" divorce. (3) A few years after graduation, everyone becomes a high-school letterman.
> — Wes Smith, "Welcome to the Real World," *Modern Maturity*, June-July 1985

Smith's Commuter Observations. (1) If your lane moves faster than all the others, it's time to change lanes. (2) There is always room to merge behind a diesel bus.
> — Dan Smith, Walnut Creek, Calif.

Smith's Cosellian Dilemma. I have tried hard to like that man, and I have failed miserably.
> — the late Red Smith, on Howard Cosell, quoted by Shirley Povich, *Washington Post*

Smith's Final Reflections. (1) No man is an s.o.b. to himself. (2) A straight line is not the shortest distance between persons. (3) Only he who tickles himself may laugh as he

pleases. (4) The spiritual overshadows and purifies the religions. (5) Rules of life are plural, willy-nilly.
— from a longer list by T. V. Smith, in his autobiography *A Non-Existent Man*, 1962. Smith was a philosopher who became a congressman. From Wayne I. Boucher

Smith's Glue Givens and Adhesive Axioms. (1) Regardless of its intended purpose, an adhesive will always stick to your fingers best. (2) When the sophisticated two-part adhesive systems are measured accurately and mixed and timed precisely, they can be expected to work every bit as good as model airplane cement. (3) If you break the handle on a coffee cup, consider the new space age adhesives and then buy a new cup.
— V. Richard Smith, LaGrange, Ill., who also discovered:

Smith's Hypotheses. (1) Wear white pants, no one will ask you to do dirty work. (2) When you are young you think that everyone is watching you. After twenty, you try to get people to notice you, and it is only when you get old that you realize that no one was *ever* looking. (3) The best seat on a commercial airplane is the one behind the one with its back stuck in its upright position. (4) The sales receipt that you are most likely to lose is the one that you need to return with a rebate *and* I would like to be able to buy the special glue that they use on the bottle labels that must be removed to accompany a rebate *and* might we be able to make a nice dent in the "National Debt" with all the money that is not redeemed on rebates.

Smith's Law of Dietary Certainty. People who eat natural foods will die of natural causes.
— Robert H. Smith, Oceanside, Calif.

Smith's Observation. At a sit-down dinner at the family reunion, the probability of the cuckoo clock striking during the

pre-meal prayer varies directly with the number of children seated at the table.
— Dr. Terry B. Smith, Kirksville, Mo.

Smith's Political Dictum. When caught with your hand in the cookie jar, it's easy to explain to your enemies, but try to explain it to your friends.
— James R. Smith, Petoskey, Mich.

Smolik's Law. A politician will always be there when he needs you.
— Richard C. Smolik, St. Louis, Mo.

Smythe's Laws. (1) If you want to hide a needle, don't put it in a haystack; put it in a box of needles. (2) You get screwed to the extent that you prostitute yourself. (3) You can catch more flies with honey than with vinegar, but if you really want to catch flies, use putrid hamburger.
— anonymous; from Marshall L. Smith

Snyder's Data Processing Rule of Thumb. The usefulness of a computer printout is inversely proportional to its weight.
— Timothy H. Snyder, letter to *Business Week,* November 23, 1987

Snyder's Law. In any situation involving more than one person doing similar jobs, the important information will be given to the person not involved in the project, and he will forget to pass it along as it does not involve him.
— Daniel K. Snyder, Pearl City, Hawaii, who offered this example: "While researching material for the completion of a job, my cohort was informed that the job was cancelled, a fact that I was informed of two days later upon completion of the job."

Sod's Law of Change. The more you want something to change, the more it stays the same. The more we want things to stay the same, the more they change.
— John Emsley, *New Scientist*, April 2, 1987

Soika's Law. Wherever you park your car in the summertime, when you get back the sun will be shining on the driver's seat.
— George R. Soika, Oshkosh, Wisc.

Solomon's Explanation. The only function of economic forecasting to is make astrology look respectable.
— Stanford economist Ezra Solomon, *USA Today*, June 26, 1984

Sommers's Official Explanation of Why a Cold Makes One Miserable. There's no point in having a cold if it doesn't make you miserable.
— Jeffrey Sommers, Cincinnati, Ohio

Soudriette's Observation. You can never tell which way a pickle will squirt until you bite it.
— William C. Soudriette, New York, N.Y.

Spano's Law of Nutrition. The tastiness of any food is directly proportional to the amount of cholesterol contained within. **Corollary.** If it tastes good, spit it out.
— Franco J. Spano, M.D., and Gregory G. Spano, M.D., Chicago, Ill.

Specht's Discovery. A condominium is just an apartment with a down payment.
— Robert D. Specht, Santa Monica, Calif.

Spence's Admonition. Never stow away on a Kamakazi plane.
— T. R. M. Spence, Sydney, Australia

Spring's Olfactory Axiom. It doesn't smell until you step in it.
— Bernard Spring, D.D.S., Windsor, Ontario, Canada

Springer's Observation. There are no failures at a class reunion.
— Jerry Springer; from Anthony McMullin

Staedler's Reaction. Television is like throwing a diamond in an outhouse. There is something good in there, you just have to dig through so much crap to find it.
— John A. Staedler, Merced, Calif.

Stanton's Law of Minimum Requirements. Bad breath is better than no breath at all.
— Marsha Stanton, Dhahran, Saudi Arabia

Stapley's Laws. (1) Interviewers. Never ask a politician for a short answer, as the politician will then give a longer answer than if one had not been so specific about its length. **(2) Young People.** Marry an ugly girl/boy; then in thirty years' time, you won't notice the difference as much. **(3) Denial.** The louder or bigger or more frequent the denial, the more likely it is that the original accusation was correct.
— Nigel Stapley, Dyfed, Wales

The Stark Theorem on Lobbyists. The more boring and incomprehensible a piece of legislation is and the fewer taxpayers it affects, the more lobbyists it will attract.
Or,

$$L(3) = \frac{P}{I}[AF^2 \times D] - 93(AFDC + SSI + \text{food stamps})$$

(L(3), the Length of a Line of Lobbyists, equals the Population of the Nation (P) divided by the Number of Individuals Impacted (I). This figure is then multiplied by the square of Arcaneness Factor (AF) times the Dullness Factor (D) minus 93 times the number of references to poor people.)
— Representative Pete Stark, Calif., whose findings were reported in the *Washington Weekly,* October 22, 1984. The inspiration for his theorem was the scant number of lobbyists who show up for Medicare hearings (affecting 26,758,000 people) contrasted with the hordes who lobby for lower corporate taxes.

Stasny's Elevator Strategy. If you're in the front of a packed car and hear footsteps down the hall followed by the words, "Hold the elevator!" here's a way to mollify everybody: Lunge for the control panel, but deliberately miss the "Door Open" button. The person staring at you from the outside will think you tried, and the restless mob behind you will be glad you didn't.
— Jim Stasny, "Surviving the Shaft," *Washington Post,* November 12, 1987

Steger's Law of Sound Stewardship. Ten saved dimes total the dollar with which, by careful shopping, you may be able to buy a dime's worth.
— (Ms.) Shelby Steger, Berkeley, Calif.

Steinert's Rule. Whenever you need somebody, you can never find them, but when you don't need them you can't get rid of them.
— Terrell W. Steinert, FPO, San Francisco, Calif.

Stern's Constant.
When you have a bad back,
Anything that can fall — does!
— Rhoda Stern, Skokie, Ill.

Stine's Laws and Rules. Communication. Communication is 90 percent reception. **Relative Beauty.** If you make something yourself, all you see in it is the mistakes. **Bedtime Stories.** You cannot underestimate a child's capacity for repetition. You cannot underestimate a child's capacity for repetition. **Finding Restaurants and Gas Stations While Driving on Limited Access Highways.** If you can't see it from the road, it doesn't exist. **Mumblers.** If somebody mumbles something, and you ask them to repeat it, you will understand it all, except the part you didn't get the first time. **Techno-Logic.** In any technical subject, the more basic information is, the harder it is to find out. **Thinking.** When people get lost in thought, it is usually because they are in unfamiliar territory. **Trouble Shooting.** Just because you've fixed a problem doesn't mean you've fixed the problem.
— Steve Stine, Skokie, Ill., who is also responsible for the following:

The Stine Dialogue for Marital Bliss. My wife, Diane, says there are two things that are essential to a successful marriage: communication and simple politeness. I replied, "That's stupid, and I don't want to talk about it."

Stockmeyer's Stock Quotations. (1) Closet space is like money — you will use up as much as you have. (2) The more expensive the dress, the smaller the size you will be able to fit into.
— Claire Stockmeyer, Washington, D.C.

Stoebner's Law. Do not pour any more milk for the child than you want to wipe up.
— Ben E. Stoebner, Tehachapi, Calif.

Stoll's Laws. (1) People who try to make things better usually make them worse. (2) The more expensive the suit, the

greater the size of the waist in proportion to the size of the jacket.
— Austin Stoll, Chicago, Ill.

Stones's Track and Field Maxim. Never turn your back on the javelin competition.
— Olympic high-jumper Dwight Stones; from Sally G. Pecor, Washington, D.C.

Story's Laws. (1) Even failures aren't perfect. (2) Accordion players always wear a ring. (3) An apple a day keeps the doctor away, but why stop there? An onion a day keeps everyone away.
— Thomas W. Story, Antioch, Calif.

Straus's Axioms. Everything the government touches turns to solid waste. (2) After the government turns something to solid waste, it deregulates it and turns it into natural gas.
— V. Michael Straus, Washington, D.C.

Stump's Flu Shot Law. If everyone else has a flu shot, you don't need one.
— Richard B. Stump

Summer Help. And some are not.
— R. F. Heisey, Arlington, Va.

Suplee's "Self-Help Book" Conclusion. There's a succor born every minute.
— Curt Suplee, *Washington Post,* October 17, 1982

Surprenant's Law of Gardening. The easiest vegetables to raise in a garden are those you like least (and vice versa). Tastes of insects and animal pests are directly proportional to your own.
— Donald T. Surprenant, Barrington, Ill.

Susan's Law. Before you ask, don't.
— Unknown, WRC Radio

Sutton's Second Observation on Mental Health. When you have searched your pockets five times over and looked high and low for your car keys, and no possible explanation for their loss or whereabouts is forthcoming, don't lose heart. Things could be much worse. Think of those poor people who do not have cars — but, nevertheless, are looking for their car keys.
— Francis W. A. Sutton, St. Austell, Cornwall, England, who also offers a number of other laws, including these fine examples:

Sutton's Laws. (1) If at first you don't succeed, don't try again until you have successfully identified the bastards who are against you. (2) Extreme desirability never survives acquiral. (3) The emergence of a good business opportunity always occurs at a period of peak load.

Svaglic's Rule. The ability of a professional person is inversely proportional to the amount of credentials he displays on his office wall.
— James M. Svaglic, Webster Groves, Mo.

Svensson's Law. If spring arrives on Monday, that's the day you have to work.
— translated from the original by Valfried Skapenhuggare (*Dagens Nyheter,* February 5, 1988); from Bob Skole

Swain's Statement on the Transfer of Knowledge. The lecture method is the single best way that a lecturer or public speaker can transfer the information from his notes to the notebooks of his audience, without passing through either of their heads.
— Wayland R. Swain, Grosse Ile, Mich.

Swanson's Lament. I'm still big. It's the pictures that got small.
— Gloria Swanson, in *Sunset Boulevard*

Swanson's Law of Poverty. Everyone thinks everyone else has money.
— Eugene D. Swanson, Waco, Tex.

Sybert's Law. Ignorance is blissful only to the intelligent.
— Christopher Sybert, Lutherville, Md.

Symons's Law of Flirting. When a girl appears not to know you exist, it means she is definitely interested in you. Or that she is definitely uninterested in you. Or that she does not know you exist.
— Don Symons, Santa Barbara, Calif.

Szadokierski's Law of the Street. When the sign says walk it means run.
— Mark Szadokierski, Charlottesville, Va.

Szasz's Observation. Why is it that when you are between 7 and 12, the children of your parents' friends are always of the opposite sex; but when you're between 15 and 20, they never are.
— Ferenc M. Szasz, Albuquerque, N.M.

The Tammeus/Case Scientific Theory. All otherwise inexplicable phenomena of science can be explained by magic.
— Bill Tammeus, in his column, *Kansas City Star,* June 5,

1988. This is a law he learned in eighth grade from David Case. The next rule is a Tammeus original:

Tammeus's Rake Rule. The last 50 leaves take as long to rake as the first 5,050.

Taylor's Law of Taxis. Taxis are soluble — they dissolve in rain.
> — Rod Taylor, in the movie *Sunday in New York*; from Dick J. Hessing

The Teacher's Truism. The only time parents are willing to accept their child as "average" is at the moment of birth.
> — unknown; from Richard E. Fisher, Homestead, Fla.

Teaford's Observations on Sewing Machine Personality/Functioning. (1) One "damnit" restores machine's functioning. (2) Two "damnits!" are self-cancelling. (3) One "sonofabitch" will cause a full bobbin to immediately run out of thread. (4) Crying helps a lot.
> — Robert M. Teaford, Napa, Calif.

Teller's Truism. Fail-safe prescription bottle caps are always filled by the pharmacist, for whatever ailment, to those people who have arthritis in their hands.
> — Herbert J. Teller, Spruce Pine, N.C.

Temps's Discovery. You can't lead a cavalry charge, if you think you don't look good on a horse.
> — Mable L. Temps, Fremont, Calif.

Thermodynamics, First and Second Laws in Layman's Terms. (1) When you put a spoonful of fine wine into a vat of sewage -- you get sewage. (2) When you put a spoonful of sewage into a vat of fine wine — you get sewage.
> — from "Cleve" Bishop, who heard it elsewhere

Thien's Distinction. You can always tell a home that has a 5-year-old in it. You have to wash the soap before using it yourself.
— Alex Thien, in the *Milwaukee Sentinel*

Thomas's Reality Check. If the Super Bowl is the ultimate game, why is there another one next year?
— former Dallas Cowboy Duane Thomas, quoted in *Time*, January 24, 1983

Thomas's Rules of School Life. (1) Ink smudges, however long it is left to dry. (2) Pens always run out of ink during dictation. (3) Five-hundred-word essays always lose 100 words between writing and handing in to be marked. (4) Pencil sharpeners do no such thing. (5) Homework is always for this Thursday, not next Thursday. (6) The amount of homework given on Fridays is directly proportional to the number of parties, etc. that you had planned to go to. (7) Excuses have always been heard before. (8) Teachers expect miracles. (9) Miracles never happen.
— schoolboy Matthew Thomas, Mid-Glamorgan, South Wales

Thompson's Corollary. With an expense account, anything is possible.
— writer Hunter Thompson, who is oft-quoted on this tenet of his self-styled brand of "gonzo" journalism

Thomson's Law. Ten percent of your subcontractors will give you 90 percent of your aggravation.
— Kenneth D. Thomson, San Francisco, Calif.

Thorn's First Law of Return. The closer the alumni live to the old hometown, the less likely they are to show up at the twentieth anniversary reunion.
— Bill Thorn, quoted in Clarence Page's *Chicago Tribune* article on reunions, July 24, 1985

Thoreau's Query. It is an interesting question how far men would retain their relative rank if they were divested of their clothes.
— Henry David Thoreau; from Bernard L. Albert

Throckmorton's π Rebuttal. Pie are not square. Pie are round. Cornbread are square.
— Robert J. Throckmorton, Las Vegas, Nev.

Tiger's Rule. The bigger and more abstract the activities an organization has to perform, and the less real human contact is necessary to maintain a steady state, the more its form of written communication will depart from vernacular speech.
— anthropologist Lionel Tiger, *The Manufacture of Evil*; from George L. Whally

Tigner's "You Can't Take It With You" Truism. You never see a Brinks truck following a hearse.
— Dr. Steven S. Tigner, University of Toledo; from Margo-Rita Andrea Kissell

Tillinger's Rule. Moderation in all things, including moderation.
— Judy Tillinger, New York, N.Y.

Tilp's Equation. Progress plus people produce pollution or People plus pollution produce progress.
— the late Frederick Tilp, Alexandria, Va.

Timothy's Principle of Crawling Infants. Any infant who can crawl tends toward the most expensive accessible object. **Corollary 1.** Nothing is inaccessible to a crawling infant. **Corollary 2.** All babies crawl, especially when you are not looking.
— Peter H. Dolan, M.D., Anchorage, Alaska

Tim's Admonition. They can't chase you if you don't run.
— Pat Jett, Hillsboro, Mo., to her fourth-grade son, Tim, who was being chased at school by sixth graders

Titanic Laws. (1) If you worry about missing the boat — remember the *Titanic*. (2) If you've got to sail on the *Titanic* — you might as well go first class.
— from John Kessel, Boulder, Colo.

Tobin's Pearls of Wisdom. First Pearl. Nobody can do everything at the same moment — you have to do one thing after another. **Further Pearl.** In traffic, as elsewhere, just because it's permissible doesn't mean it's a good idea. **Splendid Pearl.** A mistake is not a failure. **Ultimate Pearl.** Nothing ever happens by itself. **Exuberant.** *This* is the day to be happy — there is no other. **Empirical.** Things always seem to come in bunches. **Travel.** When in Rome, do what you feel like. **Psychological.** A fault is when somebody does things in a way you don't like.
— Art Tobin, Longueuil, Quebec, Canada

Todd's Laws. (1) Facts are not judgments, and judgments are not facts. (2) Emotion is a rotten base for politics. (3) Envy is the root of all evil. (4) The most damaging lies are told by those who believe they're true.
— Dick Francis, *In the Frame*, 1976; from Charles D. Poe

Tom's Catechism. On Investing. You will get in too late and get out too soon. **On Becoming a Millionaire.** You will not win the lottery. **On Sudden Business Lunches.** Blue socks and brown socks match in a dark restaurant. **On Movie-Going.** Meryl Streep will have an accent. **The Corollary to "All Important Phone Calls Are Missed."** If you buy an answering machine, you will forget to turn it on. If you turn it on, you will forget to rewind the tape. If you do everything right, the only people who will call are those you don't want to talk to — you are now obligated to call them back. **On Hosting.** There is not enough ice. You will run out of brie before you run out of bread. You will have made too much onion dip. **Maxim.** News travels fast. Bad news travels faster. **On Cracker Jack Prizes.** It's Sticker Fun. It's Jokes No. 2. It's not a whistle. **On the Classification of Insects.** It's big. It's ugly. It will fly at your face.

— Tom Cipullo, Hialeah, Fla. Also:

Tom's Reminder. You will need a No. 2 pencil.

Toner's Theory of Parenthood. Parents never live up their children's expectations.

— Mike Toner, Parkville, Md.; from Christopher Sybert

Toni's Solution to a Guilt-Free Life. If you have to lie to someone, it's their fault.

— Toni Schmitt; from Mary Lou Waddell, Oak Ridge, Tenn.

Torch's Laws. (1) The more important the meeting, the more likely one is to make an embarrassing noise sliding into a restaurant booth. (2) Thin envelopes seldom contain good news. (3) Most people get well by themselves; in fact, most people get well by morning. (4) People who call you Doc do not pay bills. (5) The essence of discretion is silence.

— Evan M. Torch, M.D., Medical College of Georgia, Augusta

Townsend's Law of Life. Everybody wants to go heaven, but nobody wants to die.

— O. J. Bud Townsend, Canoga Park, Calif.

Trace's Law. Whenever a political body passes legislation on behalf of the consumer, the consumer will wait longer and pay more for the same product or service.

— Richard W. Trace, Kingston, Mich.

Travelers, Advice to. It is wise to travel in pairs so there is always someone to blame for leaving the insect repellent at home.
> — from *Far Eastern Economic Review,* Hong Kong, and quoted in *Reader's Digest*

TRB's Law of Scandals. When wrongdoing is exposed, the real scandal is what's legal.
> — Timothy Noah, *the New Republic,* July 11, 1988

Trillin's Conclusion. Immigration laws have been traditionally based on bland food. **Trillin's Rule for Finding Good Food in a Strange City.** Stick with the cooking of ethnic groups large enough to have at least two aldermen on the city council.
> — Calvin Trillin, quoted by Phyllis C. Richman in the *Washington Post,* May 18, 1983

Tristan's Law of Disappearances in the Bermuda Triangle and Other "Dangerous" Sea-Areas. The more people there are in any given sea-area, the more novices, fools, and incompetents there will be, and therefore the more inexplicable disappearances.
> — Tristan Jones, *Adrift,* 1979

Tromberg's Revisions. (1) Stitches take time at nine. (2) A sneeze in time saves polyps.
> — Shelly Tromberg, Washington, D.C.

Tron's Law of Liquid Assets. Money is the least viscous of all substances.
> — Andrew Tron, Toronto, Ontario, Canada

Trudeau's Discovery. This is the only country in the world where failing to promote yourself is widely regarded as being arrogant.
— cartoonist Garry Trudeau, commenting on his reluctance to grant interviews, *Newsweek,* October 6, 1986

True Theorem. Thodium pentathol.
— Charles Poole, Washington, D.C.

Truman's Triple Tenet. Three things can ruin a man — money, power, and women. I never had any money. I never wanted power, and the only woman in my life is up at the house right now.
— Harry S. Truman, quoted in *Scandals in the Highest Office,* by Hope Ridings Miller, 1973. Also, this forwarded by Nick Kass:

Truman's Truism. When the "amens" get too loud in the back of the church, that's the time to go home and lock the smoke house.

Trumm's Law. You can't make a fact out of an opinion by raising your voice.
— Bruce Trumm; from Robert D. Gillette, M.D., Cincinnati, Ohio

Tuppeny's Truism. (1) We are all in this alone. (2) Put the burden on the other guy — where it belongs. (3) Good news never comes before 9:00 A.M. Good news never comes registered mail. (4) Always means "more than once." (5) It's impossible to "drown your trouble" in cottage cheese. (6) The fancier the car, the uglier the driver.
— Peg Tuppeny, Chicago, Ill.

Turcotte's Law. If we weren't all a little crazy, we'd go nuts.
— Dorothy Turcotte, Grimsby, Ontario, Canada, who learned it from her son Paul

Turner's Law of Modesty. The nurse never inquires about a patient's bodily functions unless there is a roomful of visitors. The nurse inquires by shouting from the doorway.
— Ms. Sidney P. Turner, Baltimore, Md.

Tussman's Law. Nothing is as inevitable as a mistake whose time has come.
— anonymous, quoted by John Petrella in a letter to the journal *Integra*; from Neal Wilgus

Twain's Warning. Be careful about reading health books. You may die of a misprint.
— Mark Twain, quoted in Rich Lederer's column, *Concord Monitor*, November 18, 1985

Udall's Admonition. Don't shear the sheep that laid the golden egg that is going to cause the well to run dry. **Udall's Fourth Law.** Any change or reform you make is going to have consequences you don't like.
— Representative Morris Udall, quoted in the *Congressional Record*, October 31, 1985, and the *Washington Post*, June 14, 1981; from Joseph C. Goulden

Umhoefer's Rule. Articles on writing are themselves badly written.
— Joseph A. Umhoefer, editor and writer; from Frederick C. Dyer, who notes that Umhoefer "was probably the first to

phrase it so publicly; however, many others must have thought of it long ago."

Uncle Ed's Rule of Managerial Perception. You always think the boss is a son-of-a-bitch until you're the boss. **Uncle Ed's Rule of Thumb.** Never use your thumb for a rule. You'll either hit it with a hammer or get a splinter in it.
— Edward Karl, Urbana, Ill.

Uncle Irving's Three Phases of Life.
First, youth.
Then middle age.
Then "Gee, you look wonderful."
— quoted by Bob Levey in the *Washington Post,* September 3, 1979

Underwood's Banking Maxim. The greenest and/or slowest tellers are invariably assigned to the drive-up windows, especially Friday afternoons.
— Dale M. Underwood, Santa Rosa, Calif.

Underwood's Distinction. The extent to which a service organization has become a bureaucracy is measured by the degree to which useless work has driven out useful work. In pure bureaucracy all work is useless and tends only to perpetuate the bureaucracy. In pure service all work is useful, altruistic, and of greater ultimate value than the organization itself.
— the Rev. John F. Underwood, King of Prussia, Pa.

Unruh's Understanding of Political Alliances. If I had slain all my enemies yesterday, I wouldn't have any friends today.
— the late Jesse Unruh, Calif. State Treasurer; from Tom Gill. Unruh also uttered one of most quoted lines of his time: "Money is the mother's milk of politics."

Vacation Rule No. 1. Thou shalt never answer a telephone before 8:00 A.M.
— Armen Keteyian, *Sports Illustrated*, March 31, 1986

Vancini's Discovery. In a bureaucracy, good ideas go too far.
— John Vancini, Brooklyn Center, Minn.

van der Byl's Law of Progress. It is far better to get nowhere fast than to get nowhere slowly.
— A. R. van der Byl, Transvaal, South Africa

Van Dongen's Law of Heredity. Twits beget twits.
— Van Dongen, Saskatoon, Saskatchewan, Canada

Van Herik's Discovery. Any combination of commercially mixed vegetables will invariably be made up of an oversupply of inedible broccoli stalks.
— Doris E. Van Herik, West Chicago, Ill.

Van Tassel's Computer Graffiti. (1) They say it's automatic, but you really have to push the button. (2) It is easier to change a program than to change a bureaucracy. (3) Some of the best programs owe their greatness to the fact that all the work was lost halfway through the project. (4) If computers are so fast, why do we spend so much time waiting around the computer center?
— Dennie Van Tassel, Santa Cruz, Calif., *Introductory Cobol*

Verbov's Explanation. A police officer directing the traffic is the usual explanation for the long traffic delays.
— Julian Verbov, M.D., Liverpool, England

Verplanke's Discovery about Snobs. I have never known a superior person who was a snob.
— Hans Verplancke, Leiderdorp, The Netherlands

Vernooy's Law of Psychopharmacology. The antidepressant medication that makes you feel like having sex again will cause anorgasmia (or impotence).
— Diana Vernooy, Teaneck, N.J., *American Journal of Psychiatry,* September 1987

Vest's Laws of Air Travel. (1) No matter where you sit in an airplane, the person in the seat in front of you will recline the seat into your lap. (2) No matter where you sit in an airplane, the person in back of you will stick their feet against your elbow or stick knees against the back seat. (3) No matter where you sit in an airplane, there will be, no further than three seats away, a woman with a hyper three-year-old child who will alternatively scream or throw food.
— C. R. Vest, Washington, D.C.

Vijlee's Cosmic Principle. In most cases, real life performance will not match laboratory test results.
— A. Vijlee, McKees Rocks, Pa., from his article in *Machine Design,* April 23, 1987; from Lee A. Webber, Huntington Beach, Calif.

Vincent's First and Fourth Laws. (1) As the intelligence of the participants at conferences increases, so disagreement among them increases by geometric progression. (4) Authors expand; editors abridge; publishers cut.
— Ben Vincent, Radlett, Herts, England

Vito's Rule of Nonviolent Encounters. Never get in a battle of wits without ammunition.
— unknown, WRC radio

Vlachos Law. There is always one more squeeze in the tooth-paste or the lemon.
— unknown; from Mykia Taylor

Voell's Three Laws. (1) They never put the executive suite in the basement. (2) Living in the king's house does not make one the king. (3) An illusion is a conviction waiting for a place to fail.
— James W. Voell, M.D., Silver Spring, Md.

Vogel's Observation of Office Behavior. When an executive on vacation picks up pebbles and small shells from the beach and flippantly tosses them into the air, it is merely a contin-uation of his career-long habit of zipping rubber bands at the back of the head of his busy secretary.
— Arthur R. Vogel, Evanston, Ill.

Vogel's Nevers. Never attempt levity while filling out your insurance forms. Never think you can lose both gloves. Never get in a gun fight with seven men when you only have a six-shooter.
— W. J. Vogel, Toppenish, Wash.

Wade's Law of Performance Appreciation. The likelihood of a standing ovation is directly proportional to (1) (for profes-sional performances) the fame of the performer(s); (2) (for amateur performances) the number of relatives and close friends of the performer in the audience. **Corollary.** There is no relationship whatsoever between the likelihood of a standing ovation and the quality of the performance.
— Luther I. Wade, Hammond, La.

Wallner's Rule. If a thing is worth doing, hire it out.
— Marilyn Wallner, Carmichael, Calif.

The Wall Street Journal Rule. In order to learn from mistakes, you have to first recognize you are making mistakes.
— *Wall Street Journal* editorial, January 9, 1982

Walter's Rule. All airline flights depart from the gates most distant from the center of the terminal. Nobody ever had a reservation on a plane that left from a close-in terminal.
— Robert Walters, Washington, D.C.

Ward's Conversational Dictum. No meaningful verbal exchange ever takes place anywhere except the exact narrowest portion of a doorway.
— C. F. Ward, San Diego, Calif.

Warner Swayze Axiom. When small men begin to cast large shadows, it is a sure sign that the sun is setting.
— in a Warner Swayze ad; from Robert E. Blay

Warren's Dilemma. Life ain't worth living, but what else can you do with it?
— Grace A. Warren, Sacramento, Calif.

Warren's Law. Nobody does anything for one reason.*
— Bill Warren, Hollywood, Calif.

Warson's Truths. (1) If you can't join them, beat them. (2) Sometimes it is too late to win. But it's never too late to lose. (3) Every action is imperfect. (4) If a picture is worth a thou-

---

*"Except perhaps," writes Warren, "throw up, but you want laws that are in good taste."

218 • PAUL DICKSON

sand words, one act is worth a thousand pictures. (5) It is "expensive" only if it can't get the job done.
— Tom Warson, Santa Fe, N.M.

The Washington Rule. No one is ever to be held accountable for anything done in the course of business. **Corollary.** In official Washington, you can try to murder a foreign leader by day and make small talk with his ambassador that evening.
— columnist Richard Cohen, *Washington Post,* January 14, 1986

Wearing Hats, Law of. Never wear a hat that has more character than you do.
— hatmaker Michael Harris; from Bill Spivey, San Francisco, Calif.

Weber's Law. If you have no trouble finding a place to park, you won't be able to find your car.
— Philip Weber, Sacramento, Calif.

Webster's Law. The damage rarely exceeds the deductible.
— Doug Webster, Hartford, Conn.

Weed's Axion. Never ask two questions in a business letter. The reply will discuss the one in which you are least interested, and say nothing about the other.
— Brian J. Weed, Carmel, Calif.

Weight-Lifters' Law. If you can't place it down easy, don't pick it up.
— sign seen at a Chicago Health Club; from Steve Stine

Weiss's Nine "Nevers" of Organizational Nuance. (1) Never blame on malice what can be explained by stupidity. (2) Never assume a letter of complaint is sincere if it also im-

plies the virtue of the writer. (3) Never stop beating a dead horse until the boss administers the burial. (4) Never confuse agency policy with agency intentions; nor expect either to be necessarily reflected in agency actions. (5) Never assume priorities transcend an organizational change, even if it is a minor one. (6) Never regard as accurate a policy decision flow chart with more than one feedback loop. (7) Never claim a particular piece of data was necessary to support a policy, since it might turn out to be wrong. (8) Never use all your data in supporting a decision if you expect someone to question it later on. (9) Never believe a sentence that uses the phrase (a) comprehensive review, (b) cooperative process, (c) total systems analysis, (d) final decision, (e) final budget projections, or (f) long-term policy.
— Martin H. Weiss, Springfield, Ill.

Weissman's Discovery. When a man says he's "separated," it means he hasn't seen his wife since breakfast.
— Rozanne Weissman, Washington, D.C.

Welch's Potluck Principle. At any gathering, there will never be enough meat, vegetables, etc., but there is always enough Jell-O.
— Patrick Welch, Clearwater, Fla.

Welford's Dilemma. It is the students who least require assistance that are most forthcoming in asking for it.
— David Welford, Birmingham, England

Westmeyer's Collegiate Constant. No matter where you build the sidewalks, students will find a shortcut across the grass. If you build a sidewalk on the shortcut path, students will construct another shortcut between it and the original sidewalk.
— Paul Westmeyer, San Antonio, Tex.

West's Rules. Lex Logica. The logical man has a shorter life expectancy than the practical man, because he refuses to look both ways on a one-way street. **Efficiency.** A well-fed wastebasket will serve you better than the best computer. **Publishing.** Go ahead and print it — the readers will proof it anyway. **Academia.** There is nothing so funny that a professor of Folklore can't flatten it with an academic paper. **Legislation.** The more pork in the barrel, the faster it rolls. **Cash Flow.** If he can shut off your water, pay him first. **Boat Ownership.** The next best thing to having a friend with a boat is having a boat.

West's Latest Discoveries. (1) Artificial hearts are no big deal; they've been around since the first banker. (2) When generals and admirals finally grow up, they go into retirement. (3) Social sobriquet: The cream rises to the top; unfortunately, so does the scum. (4) Journalism is a suffix of irresponsible.
> — Roy W. West, Philadelphia, Pa., who is also responsible for the following:

West's Mushroom Cloud Theory of Barbecuing. Use enough fluid and you can start cinderblocks.

West's Time Constant. A split second is the time that elapses between the moment you step into a perfectly adjusted shower and someone turns on the washing machine and the dishwasher and flushes every toilet in the house.
> — Robert T. West, Minneapolis, Minn.

Wexford's Law. In a two-car family, the wife always has the smaller car.
> — in Ruth Rendell's *The Best Man to Die*; from D. J. Camp, Plymouth, England

Whatley's Axioms. (1) No auto clock ever worked right, if at all. (2) No Hudson was ever recalled. (3) Money usually ruins a good idea.
— Craig Whatley, San Rafael, Calif. Also:

Whatley's Truths. (1) There's more than one way to skin a knee. (2) Four out of five doctors recommend another doctor. (3) Anything is impossible. (4) Build a better mousetrap and the world will beat a path across your face. (5) Everything sounds romantic in French. Everything sounds like an order in German. Everything sounds like an argument in Italian. (6) What's right or wrong depends on which end of the food chain you're on.

And still more:

Whatley's Plerophories. (1) Practical jokes aren't. (2) Money doesn't talk — it just never shuts up. (3) Religion is the last refuge of the religious. (4) Still water runs deep, but the fishing stinks. (5) They don't even make plastic like they used to. (6) Forgive thine enemies, then kiss them off. (7) Fat is hereditary — you get it from your government.

Wheel Wisdom. (1) Before the squeaky wheel gets the grease, check first to see if it isn't just spinning. (2) If you insist on telling everyone you are a big wheel, in due time "little" wheels will let you carry the load. (3) The inventor of the wheel must have decided that life did *not* have to be a drag.
— Chuck Werle, Chicago, Ill.

Whipple's Law of Organizations. In any pecking order, the ratio of peckers to peckees is always greater than one.
— Donald G. Whipple, Torrance, Calif.

White's Corollary of Taxation. Taxes are not designed to be fair, they are designed to raise money.
— Gordon White, Alexandria, Va., letter to the *Washington Post,* September 15, 1980

White's Dilemma. Old age is a special problem for me because I've never been able to shed the mental image I have of myself — a lad of about 19.
— essayist E. B. White

White's Discovery. He from whom you first ask the way will be a stranger too.
— Leonard White, Camberley, Surrey, England

White's Laws. (1) If you are paid to make a decision, then bloody well make a decision, even if it is a wrong one. (2) If it is the wrong one, you can always change it tomorrow.
— Reg White; from Alan Kilburn, England

White's Medical Rule. The less we know about a disease, the more medicines are available to treat it.
— Robert I. White, M.D., Johns Hopkins University School of Medicine, Baltimore, Md.

White's Medical Rule II. In the practice of medicine (and I suspect other fields of endeavor, too), gratitude received bears no relation to effort expended.
— Benjamin V. White, M.D., West Hartford, Conn.

White's National Security Rule. Security declines as security machinery expands.
— E. B. White, quoted in *Federal Times,* October 29, 1979; from Joseph C. Goulden

White's Political Rule of Thumb. Political campaigns do not truly start until the guys in bars stop arguing about the World Series.
— Teddy White, quoted in *National Review,* July 8, 1988; from Charles D. Poe

Whitney's Distinction. A diamond ain't nothing but a lump of coal with a migraine.
— L. P. Whitney, Blue Hill, Me.

Whittet's Observations. (1) Enemies are more likely to activate you than friends. (2) It is easier to fool the eye than any of the other senses. (3) In any improbable situation, the only solution is another improbability. (4) It is not winning I enjoy so much as defeating you.
— George Sorley Whittet, Carshalton, Surrey, England

Wilgus's Principles of Cultural Inflation. (1) Everything once a subject is now a Field. (2) With the Knowledge Explosion, new Fields are constantly being created. (3) Everyone who once had an interest in a subject is now an Expert in a Field. (4) Everything you need to know about a Field can be covered in a five-minute TV interview with an Expert.
— Neal Wilgus, Albuquerque, N.M.

Wilkes College Guide for Students. When in doubt, cut. When confused, drop.
— anonymous, Wilkes-Barre, Pa.

Willets on Aging. There is an engaging legend abroad in the land that advancing years mellow one and somehow bring out the kindliest impulses of one's nature; that the countryside swarms with repentent Scrooges. My own observation has been that when a bastard grows old, he simply becomes an old bastard.
— Isabel M. Willetts, LeClaire, Iowa

Willey's Discoveries. (1) The length of stay of out-of-town guests is inversely proportional to their desirability. (2) There are three absolute maxims for the handyman — your garden hose, extension cord, and ladder are always too short.
　　— Boots Willey, Lehigh Acres, Fla.

William Lyon Phelp's Second Law. The value of an earned doctorate varies in inverse proportion to the extent of its use by the recipient.
　　— in *Context,* March 15, 1980; from Jeffrey Chamberlain

Williams's Diet Advisory. Throw out all women's magazines, they'll drive you schizo. Page 1 is a diet. Page 2 is a chocolate cake. It's a no-win situation.
　　— the late Kim Williams, in her *Book of Uncommon Sense;* from Joseph C. Goulden

The Willis Catch-55. When the speed limit is raised from 55 to 65 mph, it actually becomes 75 because motorists think they won't be ticketed unless they exceed the limit by more than 10 mph. **The Willis Catch-88.** No matter who he is, the next president of the United States will be perceived to be a failure, because his duties have been multiplied dramatically, while his hands will be tied by a crippling national debt and deficit, and by a Congress which is oversensitive to the "wish lists" of single-issue pressure groups, including ex-congressmen turned professional lobbyists.
　　— Jane B. Willis, letter to the *Sarasota Herald-Tribune,* April 15, 1988; from Ben Willis, Jr.

The Willis Contradiction. The most important things in life aren't things. **The Willis Reminder.** "All natural ingredients" sounds super wholesome, but arsenic, cyanide, coal dust, and manure are all natural too.
　　— Ben Willis, Jr., McLean, Va.

Will's Law. All economic news is bad, and all news is economic news.
— George F. Will, *Newsweek*, April 23, 1984

Wilson's Definition (for economics and political science professors). The difference between communism and capitalism is this: in capitalism, man exploits man; in communism, it's the other way around. **Corollary.** By the time you learn this, you've probably been teaching it backwards for years.
— Professor John R. M. Wilson, Mid-America Nazarene College, Olathe, Kans., who developed it with Gary Moore and Steve Cole

Wilson's Laws of Flight. (1) You want a drink and the smallest bill you have is a twenty. (2) Offering a flight attendant a $20 bill for a $2 drink is like spitting on an Alabama state trooper. (3) On arrival, passengers without time constraints are the first to fill the aisle.
— Louis D. Wilson, from a much longer list of flight laws published in the *Wall Street Journal*, June 30, 1986

Wilson's Rule of Annoyance. A caller who dials the wrong number will call a second time as soon as you have comfortably returned to your living room chair, and will act as if he or she is the one being inconvenienced.
— Mike Wilson, Jackson, Mich.

Winterhalder's Wisdom. Cop-outs aren't necessarily lies; in fact, the best cop-outs are absolutely true.
— unknown

Wolf's Laws of Cookery. (1) **Liquid Sugar.** A drop of honey, molasses, or other liquid sugar will spread itself in a layer one molecule deep over every available surface. **Corollary.** Double this area if small children are present. (2) **The absolutely necessary ingredient.** You don't have it. **Corollary 1.**

You can't get it at any shop within fifty-mile radius. **Corollary 2.** It's gone bad. (3) **Measurements.** The most fabulously fascinating recipe available will be expressed in terms of grams (if you have no scales) or firkins (if you do). (4) **Company.** Your soufflé falls when, and only when, there are guests. (5) **Double-boilers.** (a) If you turn your back on it, it will boil dry. Or burn. (b) If you watch it like a hawk, it will boil dry or burn when the phone rings. (6) **Bread-and-telephone Law.** The telephone will ring only at the messiest stage of kneading. (7) **Drop-ins.** If you have the reputation of being a good cook, your mother-in-law will drop in when, and only when, you are serving canned beans. (8) **Leftovers.** It turned green. **Corollary.** The probability of fur-bearing leftovers increases logarithmically on days when you have (a) morning sickness, (b) flu, (c) a hangover.

— Molly Wolf, cook and biochemistry student, Halifax, N.S., Canada, from a longer list

Woolridge's Razor. It's one thing to hear about it from your coach, but when you wife tells you it stinks, you tend to work on it.

— Orlando Woolridge of the Chicago Bulls on why he raised his free-throw percentage

Wright's Perspective. Give me the luxuries of life and I will willingly do without the necessities.

— Frank Lloyd Wright; from Bernard L. Albert

Wyle's Law of 2 1/2. When the U.S. government is involved, it takes twice as long, and twice as much money, to do anything, and then you get only one-half as much done.

— Frederick S. Wyle, San Francisco, Calif.

XXcellent Mxssagx from thx Coach. Who makxs a txam a succxss? Evxn though my typxwritxr isn't a nxw modxl, it works quitx wxll xxcxpt for onx kxy. I had wishxd sxvxral timxs that it workxd pxrfxctly. It is trux that thxrx arx 41 othxr kxys opxrating wxll xnough, howxvxr just onx not making thx xffort makxs all thx diffxrxncx.

Somxtimxs it sxxms to mx a txam can bx somxwhat likx my typxwritxr . . . not all of thx mxmbxrs arx xxpxnding xnough xffort. Pxrhaps, you txll yoursxlf "Wxll, I'm only onx pxrson. I won't makx or brxak our txam." But it doxs makx a diffxrxncx bxcausx a txam to bx xffxctivx nxxds activx participation from xvxry singlx pxrson, xvxn thosx on thx bxnch.

So thx nxxt timx you think you arx only onx playxr, and your xfforts arx not nxxdxd, rxmxmbxr my old typxwritxr and txll yoursxlf, "I am a kxy pxrson on thx txam and I am nxxdxd vxry much."
    — John Kessel, *Thoughts and Quotes for Volleyball Coaches,*
      1986

Yauger's Law of Backstabbing. When you talk about someone behind their back, their back will be right behind you.
    — David Yauger, Leesburg, Va.

Yearwood's Admonition. To err is human, but do not use up the eraser before the pencil.
    — R. L. Yearwood, Hereford, Tex.

Young's Rule. When using humor in a speech, the laughter at the end of the joke should be directly proportional to the time invested to obtain the laughter.
— Jeff C. Young, Phoenix, Ariz.

Zais's First Postulate. As long as you retain the capacity to blush, your immortal soul is in no particular danger.
— Elliot Zais, Corvallis, Ore.

Zawada's Conundrum. The easier it is to correct mistakes, the more often mistakes will be made.
— Donald F. Zawada, Lisle, Ill., who adds, "First discovered ten years ago while watching computer programmers at interactive terminals: rediscovered more recently while watching our secretary at a word processor."

Zeek's Discovery. The key to flexibility is indecision.
— Valentino J. Zeek, Maitland, Fla.

Zimmerman's Corollary to Lucht's Observation. Looking competent is just as ineffective as being competent.
— John A. Mattsen; see **Lucht's Observation**

Zipf's Principle of Least Effort. Learning favors methods that require the least writing, the least new learning, and the least memorizing.
— Unknown, U.S. Department of Agriculture Press Release

Zisla's Discoveries. (1) A good administrator tries to do as little as possible; a bad administrator tries to do as much as possible. (2) Don't concern yourself too much with the "bottom line." There will be a new one tomorrow or even before. (3) It doesn't matter how many catastrophes you survive, living will still kill you. (4) It is possible to paint zebra stripes on an elephant — it won't do much good as a disguise: the zebras will know it is still an elephant and even though they will be puzzled, maybe even confused, so will the other elephants.

— Harold Zisla, South Bend, Ind., who is also responsible for the following:

Zisla's Law. If you're asked to join a parade, don't march behind the elephants.

Zmuda's Principle. It's a lot easier to work on a nonexistent problem because there are fewer — if any — obstacles to overcome.

— Joseph Zmuda, San Francisco, Calif.

FELLOWSHIPS

One of the benefits that accrue to the folks who help the Murphy Center with its research is their appointment as a fellow of the Murphy Center. The value of such a title should be reckoned by the fact that it can be given only by the director and cannot be bought (cheaply)!

In addition, there is the position of senior fellow, which is reserved for those whose contributions have been extraordinary. What follows momentarily are lists of the senior fellows and fellows who have contributed to this effort.

Meanwhile, the Center plans to press on with its vast and vague research agenda and looks forward to hearing from people who have solved a piece of the puzzle. Your laws, rules, formulae, maxims, and six-figure research grants will be accepted by

Paul Dickson, Director for Life
The Murphy Center
Box 80
Garrett Park, MD 20896-0080

At some point in the near future, the Center plans to reissue and combine its first two works, *The Official Rules* and *The Official Explanations,* in a new, blockbuster edition. This monster will be annotated with comments, revisions, and corrections on the original material. Such comments and amendments will be most welcome.

————————————— SPECIAL —————————————

Senior Fellows

Theodore C. Achilles	Joseph C. Goulden
Joseph E. Badger	Shel Kagan
Russell Dunn Sr.	Martin Kottmeyer
Fred Dyer	Herbert H. Paper
M. Mack Earle	Charles D. Poe
Tom Gill	Bob and Monika Skole

Robert D. Specht
Steve Stine
Neal Wilgus

Bennett Willis Jr.
Steve Woodbury

──────── **SPECIAL** ────────

Fellows

William John Abley
Bob Ackley
T. C. Acres
A. W. Adams
Sandra Adams
Don Addis
Betsy Adkins
Jerry Adler
Bernard L. Albert, M.D.
George Albrecht
Nancy Alden
Brooks Alexander
Joan C. Alkula
John Allcock
Mary Allen
Patrick J. Allen
Stephen Allen
Onesimo T. Almeida
Don Alt
Wayne Aman
Jim Amis
Jo Anderson
Lance Anderson
Ron Anjard, M.D.
R. Armitage
James S. Armstrong
Russell Ash

Roger Backhouse
Kent Bailey

Bill Bain
J. Stacey Baird
Nicholas Bakalar
Ross K. Baker
Scott R. Baker
William Luther Balliew IV
Gary O. Balusek
Jim Banks
Phil Barker
Dawn Barry
Karen Marie Bartol
Al Batt
Joshua M. Bear
Virginia Beckwith
J. R. Belcher
Charles A. Belov
H. Bennett
Michael Berla
Mike Berman
Ian Beste
John A. Beton
Richard Beville
Melvin Bierman
Paul Biler
C. B. "Cleve" Bishop
Stephen Bishop
Barney C. Black
Alexander W. Blackwell
Robert E. Blay
Judith Ilene Bloom

Bernard B. Borkon D.M.D.
Bruce Boston
Sharon Boucher
Wayne I. Boucher
Richard D. Boyd
Charles P. Boyle
Karyn Brady
Wayne Branstadt
Steven Ronald Brattman
Christopher R. Brewster
Judye Briggs
Thomas E. Briggs
Ken Brinnick
D. R. Brock
William Brodersen
John C. Brogan
Wally Brooks
Jon Broome
Ben Brown
Bruce "BB" Brown
David S. Brown
Doris Brown
Larry Bryant
Dean Bunn
Catherine Burns
Betty Joe Byars

David B. Cagle
Thomas H. Callen II
D. J. Camp
Gardner Campbell
James G. Campbell
Lt. Col. William P. Campbell III
Phil Cannon
Ann Carmel
Don Caron
Simon Carrington
Tom Carvlin

James A. Cassidy
Richard E. Cavanagh
Jeffrey Chamberlin
Howard Channing
Stephen J. Chant
Stephen M. Chaplin
O. L. Chavarna-Aguilar
Ed Chensky
Shelby Chism
Tom Cipullo
John Clark
Dean Travis Clarke
Kelly H. Clifton
Nonnee Coan
Paul W. Cochran, M.D.
Reed Cockrell
Robert V. Cohen, M.D.
John W. Colburn
Don Coles
D. S. Collins
A. J. Comer
John Condon
Mike Connolly
Charles A. Conrard III
Bob Cooper
Ed Cooper
Marsha J. Corrales
G. F. Corvin
Alan Cosnow
Claudia Costello
W. Roy Couch
H. Coucheron-Aamot
Lady Curzon Couper
David L. Cowen
Geoff Cox
John S. Craig
C. D. Crenna
Joseph Crescimbeni

Don Crinklaw
Mark Cristano
Donald Critchfield
Terry L. Crock
Donald K. Crowell
Caroline Curtis

Michael Dale
William J. Daugherty
Jeffrey P. Davidson
Stan Gebler Davies
Kenneth W. Davis
Lee A. Davis
M. I. M. Davis
Norman M. Davis
Jim Dawson
Kevin A. H. Dean
Kevin Dean
William F. Deeck
Robert L. Delaney
Ron Denham
Calvin E. Deonier
Al deQuoy
Glenna deQuoy
Doug DeRock
Charles F. Dery
Yvonne G. T. DeVault
G. H. DeViney
John H. Dickey, Ph.D.
Isabelle C. Dickson
Mary Distin
Mike Dixon
Peter H. Dohan, M.D.
Michael Dolan
Van Dongen
Franz Dousky
William G. Downs
Delores Drakenberg

Myron DuBow
Bob Dunning
Raymond H. Dupuy
T. S. Durham
Alicia K. Dustira
Edward J. Dwyer
Denise Dykema

Euan F. Eddie
Bob Einbinder
Stan Eling
Gerald S. Ellenson
Owen Elliott
Andy Ellis
Mary Ellis
Beverly Ellstrand
Raymond F. Elsner
Daniel Emmanuel
David Ennes
Gareth J. Evans
George Evans
James T. Evans
John E. Eyberg

James E. Farmer
Lloyd A. Fassett, M.D.
Mike Feinsilber
Monroe Feldman
Eve M. Ferguson
Larrie Ferreire
Russell Fillers
Owen Findsen
Steve Finefrock
David Finger
Richard E. Fisher
John F. Fitzloff
Helen Fleischer
K. C. Flory

Brian M. Foley
Bill Ford
George Fortner
Marguerite H. Foster
Nicholas Foster
Don D. Fowler
John C. Fraraccio
Alex Fraser
Victor Fresco
Randall L. Fullner
William D. Futch, M.D.

William P. Gannon
Joel R. Garreau
Walt Giachini
Ron Gibson
Mike Gilbert
Thomas Gill
Robert D. Gillette
W. Harper Girvin
Guy Godin
Joyce Godsey
Stu Goldstein, M.D.
Leonard P. Gollobin
Andor Gomme
Frank J. Gongola
B. B. W. Goodden
Lee Goodman
Dr. Kurtis J. Gordon
Eugene Gramm
Michael Grant
Paul Gray
Cindy Graziano
Jay Green
Walter Gregory
Jack Gren
John C. Grice
Dave Grissom

Stephen J. Grollinger
Sidney Gross
David S. Grubnick
Al Gudeman
Ben W. Gunn
Tony J. Gunter
John W. Gustafson
Scott B. Guthery

Timothy Haas
David K. Hackett
Irving Hale
Donald M. Hall
Robert A. Hall
Robert Scott Hallen
Judith Halperin
Howard Hamer
Alfred Hanlon
Gary W. Hanson
James Hardie
R. J. Harkness
C. Jack Harrel
Arnold Harris
R. C. Harrison
Paul Harwitz
David Haslam, M.D.
N. Sally Hass
Richard Arthur Hassell
Herman Hassinger
Jan Hatwell
Georgia E. Hauser
H. Gordon Havens
Harvey O. Hays
John Hazlitt
John M. Hebert
Gene Hegel
Jeffrey H. Heileson
Bob Heimberg

George A. Heinemann
R. F. Heisey
Hugh Hembree
Joe C. Henderson
Francis J. Hennessy
R. A. Herold
W. A. Herold
Louis D. Hertz
Gisela Herzfeld
Dick J. Hessing
Chad Hesting
Paul C. Hewett
Colin Hewitt
John H. Hewitt, M.D.
Bill Hickman
James W. Hiestand
Joan O'Steen Hill
Robert P. Hilldrup
C. Elton Hinshaw
Archie Edward Hinson
Judy Hirabayashi
Wilbur W. Hitchcock
Aksel Hoff
E. P. Hoff
Gene F. Hoffnagle
Stephen Holben
William M. Holden
Edgar Holland
Phillip Holliday
Scott Holloway
Joseph Holmes
R. Hoover
C. M. Hopkins
Stanley Horowitz
Joseph A. Horton, M.D.
Betty Hoyle
Dr. Jo H. F. Huddleston
Joseph M. Humpert, M.D.

David H. Humphreys
Daniel Humphreys
Freddy Huygen
Jeremiah Hynes

Charles Issawi

Norma Jacob
Lewis G. Jacobs
Roberta B. Jacobson
Alice James
H. L. James
Andrew F. Jardine
Jan Jennier
Lynn Jensen
Mrs. Rae P. Jensen
Dick Jesson
Pat Jett
Fred R. Jewell
Christopher John
Bob Johnson
Bonnie Nestor Johnson
Frank Johnson
Willis Johnson
Helen E. Jolliffe
Richard K. Jolliffe
Janis Jones
Tristan Jones
Robert J. T. Joy, M.D.
Wally Juall
Gary Jump
Rev. Christian F. Just

Miriam Kachur
Alida Kane
Ed Karl
Nicholas E. Kass
Robert Katz

George Keelerick
Bob Kehr
Michael Kehr
John R. Kelley, Jr.
Thomas W. Kelly
Walter J. Kenneven
Jim Kenworthy
Bob Kerr
John and Laurel Kessel
G. V. Kibblewhite
Jack Kime
John J. King
Miles Kington
Margo-Rita Andrea Kissell
William S. Klein
George A. Kling
Gary Knight
Erwin Knoll
Robert P. Knowles
Mary Alice Knowlton
Alexander Kohn
Ron Koolman
Tom C. Korologos
Mark Kostal
John Paul Kowal
Mary Kramer
Paul A. Kraus, M.D.
Richard D. Krobusek
Judi Kroeger
Stephanie Kruger

John R. Labadie
Stephen C. Lada
Anne Ladof
Alan Ladwig
Paul J. Lambeck
Tony Lang
Curtis W. Larson

James A. Laub
Caroline Laudig-Herschel
Murray Laver
John Lawson
Sarah Lawson
M. H. Lawton
Jane Leavitt
Rich Lederer
D. H. Lee
Richard Leigh
Bernard Levin
D. Levy
Alan G. Lewis
Dave Lewis
Mike Lewis
Ben Lichtenberg
Fred Lightfoot
Jack Limpert
Carol Schuette Linden
Larry Lindvig
Donna Lipsett
David Little
David Lloyd-Jones
Bob Lockhart
Scott Lockwood
Mel Loftus
C. Sumpter Logan, Sr.
Ed Logg
Eugene A. Long
Stephen M. Lonsdale
Manfred Lopez
Marsha Lopez
Leon M. Louw
I. Raub Love
Raymond E. Lovett
Elizabeth Lundgren
Robert A. Luke, Jr.
Denise D. Lynn
Sharon Lynn

E. Preston McAfee
E. Ray McAfee
R. G. McAlister
Joseph M. McCabe
James Manus McCaffery
Richard McConnell
Spero McConnell
Ernest J. McCormick
Peggy McCormick
Lee McCullough
Robert A. McEwen
John McGarry
Scott D. McGregor
David McKay
Michael S. McKay
W. E. McKean II
Thomas A. McKenna
Thomas J. McKeon
Bruce C. McKinney
Anthony McMullin
Roland McMullin
F. D. McSpiritt

Douglas M. C. MacEwan
Cynthia MacGregor
Murdo I. MacLeod
Ian MacPherson
Carlisle Madson
John T. Magary
John A. Main
Joel Makower
Julia Malik
Mark Mallar
Charles Mann
Gerald Manning
Richard Manning
Stanley Marcus
Norman Mark
Richard Markgraf

Harriett Markman
Steve Markman
William Marks
Maurice Marsolais
Daniel G. Martinez
H. Lawrence Mason III
Steve Masse
John A. Mattsen
Carl Mattson
Bruce O. May
Colin D. Mayes
Barbara K. Mehlman
Leroy W. Meier
Marian Melbourne
Mo Mendenhall
Jovit Mendonça
Belden Menkus
Margie Mereen
Jim Meuse
Newchy Mignone
Andrea Miller
Don Miller
Mark R. Miller
R. D. Milligan
T. H. Milner
Ian Milroy
Ann Emmons Mintz
Charles Mintzlaff
Jeff Missinne
Averill Q. Mix
Wilson M. Montero, Jr.
Ann L. Moore
Bob Moore
David E. Moore
Frank J. Moran
Henry Morgan
Elizabeth S. Morgan
D. N. Moulton
George Mulfinger

C. A. Munro
Peter A. Murphy
Lloyd Murray
Robert E. Murray
Tom Muzik
G. E. Myers

Kenneth D. Naden
R. A. Nanna
Thomas M. Napier
Harriet Nathan
Leslie Nelson
Robert Nelson
T. J. Nelson
Marian Henriquez Neudel
Robert Neuhaus
Gary Neustadter
R. A. Newman
Mike Niebuhr
Don Nilsen
Joel J. Nobel, M.D.
Harvey Nusbaum

Susan Ohanian
Michael O'Harro
Edward J. O'Neill
Vincent A. Orbish
Mollie N. Orth
J. P. O'Shee
Charles Ottinger
Mac Overton
Howard Ozmon

George Pajari
Steve Paliwoda
Richard P. Parkins
Denys Parsons
David L. Passman

Rick Patton
Steven J. Paul
Charles J. Pecor
Sally G. Pecor
Kurt M. Peters
Dean M. Peterson
Donna Peterson
Catherine Pfeifer
Fred R. Pfister
Gerald M. Phillips
Ruth Piddick
Richard C. Pierce
Jean Pike
James W. Piper
James D. Plimpton
Bernard Plotnick
John M. Poer
H. M. Pollock
Sherman Lee Pompey
Charles Poole
Paul A. Poorman
William G. Pope
George E. Posner
Harvey A. Pratt
J. M. Prince

David J. Quick
Herbert C. Quoy

Efraim Racker
Susie Radus
John J. Ragucci
Warren Randall
Dan Rapoport
Peter D. Rappo, M.D.
J. M. Rathbun
John M. Ravage
Ross Reader

Rosemary Reid
John H. Reisner III
Edward B. Reiss
C. Reynolds
Joan A. Reynolds
John Reynolds, Jr.
J. Riberdy
Rita Rippetoe
Philip Rist
Peter Ritchie, Jr.
John Rives
Peter Robinson
Dennis Rogers
Bruno Rolark
Donald J. Rosato, M.D.
Milton D. Rosenau, Jr.
Denise Rosoff
Henry Rosoff
R. H. Roth
James Rothman
Lynton S. Rowe
T. Donald Rucker
T. J. Ruhoff
Martin Russell
Bruce A. Ryder

Joseph C. Salak
Richard R. Saliers
Robert W. Sallen
Tony Sandy
Kevin Santulis
Irvin J. Sattinger
John Sauget
Richard C. Savage
Michael Sawhill
Phyllis Scanlan
Don Schaefer
Marty Schmidt

Jeff Schnepper
Marilyn Alt Scholl
Kenneth L. Schorr
Bob Schumer
Peter Scott
Wilber E. Scoville
Edward J. Schmitz
Lee Schrumpf
Thedor Schuchat
Marge Seeberg
Mitchel J. Seleznick, M.D.
Robert W. Sellen
Gordon Serjak
John Seymour
Bill Shea
Walter Shearer
G. B. Shepherd
Rich Sherekis
Cynthia Shively
Francis Shoemaker
Peter V. Siegel, Jr.
D. F. Siemans, Jr.
John R. Sisley, Jr.
B. Franklin Skinner
J. Skye
Martin Slevin
Roy Slous
B. V. D. Smith
Dan Smith
James R. Smith
Lois Smith
Marshall L. Smith
Brother Ray Smith, CSC
V. Richard Smith
Robert H. Smith
Dr. Terry B. Smith
Richard C. Smolik
Bob Snider

Daniel K. Snyder
Dennis R. Solomon
Jeffrey Sommers
William C. Soudriette
Franco J. Spano, M.D.
Gregory G. Spano, M.D.
T. R. M. Spence
Bill Spivey
Bernard Spring
John A. Staedler
Robert L. Stakes
Diana K. Stanley
Marsha Stanton
Nigel Stapley
Ashley Steele
Gerald Lee Steese
Shelby Steger
Terrell W. Steinert
Rhoda Stern
Norman D. Stevens
James O. Stevenson
Carol T. Stewart
Diane Stine
Claire Stockmeyer
Ben E. Stoebner
Austin Stoll
Thomas W. Story
V. Michael Straus
Richard B. Stump
Donald T. Surprenant
Francis WA Sutton
James M. Svaglic
Wayland R. Swain
Eugene D. Swanson
Don Symons
Mark Szadokierski
Ferenc M. Szasz

Bill Tammeus
C. L. Taylor
Eleanor and Floyd Taylor
Robert M. Teaford
Herbert J. Teller
Mable L. Temps
Thomas Terry
D. Park Teter
Matthew Thomas
Kenneth D. Thomson
James Thorpe III
R. J. Throckmorton
Judy Tillinger
Frederick Tilp
Dr. Joel A. Tobias
Art Tobin
Evan M. Torch, M.D.
O. J. Bud Townsend
Richard W. Trace
Sheldon Tromberg
Andrew Tron
Chris Tucker
Ronald W. Tucker
Peg Tuppeny
Dorothy Turcotte
Brian J. Turk
Ms. Sidney P. Turner

Dale M. Underwood
Rev. John F. Underwood

John Vancini
A. R. van der Byl
Lloyd W. Vanderman
Doris E. Van Herik
Julian Vebov, M.D.
Diana Vernooy

Hans Verplanke
C. R. Vest
Elaine Viets
Ben Vincent
James W. Voell, M.D.
Arthur R. Vogel
W. J. Vogel
Stuart G. Vogt
Bob Vopacke

Mary Lou Waddell
Luther I. Wade
Bradford Walters
Robert Walters
C. F. Ward, M.D.
Bill Warren
Grace A. Warren
James Warren
Tom Warson
Judie Wayman
Philip Weber
Doug Webster
Brian J. Weed
Martin H. Weiss
Rozanne Weissman
Patrick Welch
David Welford
Stephen Brent Wells
Chuck Werle
Philip B. Wershba
Robert T. West
Roy W. West
Paul Westmeyer

George Whally
Craig Whatley
Donald G. Whipple
Gail White
Leonard White
Benjamin V. White, M.D.
Robert I. White, M.D.
L. P. Whitney
George Sorley Whittet
Boots Willey
Mary Williams
Meridith G. Williams
Arlen Wilson
E. A. Wilson
John R. M. Wilson
Mike Wilson
S. Michael Wilson
Molly Wolf
Ralph C. "Pat" Wolfe
Ashley C. Worsley
Frederick S. Wyle

David Yauger
Barry Hugh Yeakle
Robert Yoakum
Jeff C. Young

Elliot Zais
Donald F. Zawada
Valentino J. Zeek
Harold Zisla
Joseph Zmuda

DISCLAIMER

the guarantee. Product must be used only for its intended purpose and in accordance with manufacturer's specific warning. Read and follow label instructions. Any amount paid is not refundable without proof of purchase (UPC) and cashier's receipt showing date and place of purchase with the amount paid for this product encircled.

This message is intended for the private use of our readers and any reproduction, rebroadcast, or any other accounts of this message without the prior written consent of the National Football League is strictly prohibited. Check local zoning laws before ordering; slightly enlarged to show detail. We make no warranty, either expressed or implied, including, but not limited to, any implied warranties of merchantability or fitness for a particular purpose, regarding these materials, and make such materials available solely on an "as is" basis. Close cover before striking.

For external use only and occupancy by over ten persons is prohibited by the Fire Marshall and the laws of this state. If a rash, irritation, redness, or swelling develops, discontinue use. Pat. pending, Reg. U.S. Pat. Off. Copyrighted, trademark on file with the Federal Trade Commission, and failure to reduce speed so as to avoid collision with any vehicle on, near, or entering the highway is in violation of I.C.C. 9-4-1-57(a). Tumble dry only.

The sole and exclusive liability, regardless of the form of action, shall not exceed the purchase price of the materials described herein. Do not exceed recommended dosage and those who brought you this message are solely responsible for its content. Which, by the way, contains NO sodium, carbohydrates, or polyunsaturated fats; it is LOW sugar and is caffeine free. Before using consult your doctor.

Tested and rated by Underwriter's Laboratories; avoid extreme temperatures and store in cool, dry place. No artificial colors or flavoring has been added; hard hat and safety goggles are required. We reserve the right to refuse service to anyone regardless of race, creed, color, or national origin, and we are not responsible for lost articles or personal property, public or private. You break it, you bought it! Do not place near a magnetic source.

Recommended for adults over 21 only and in no event shall we be liable to anyone for specific, collateral, incidental, or consequential damages in connection with or arising out of purchase or use of these materials. Some restrictions apply. Do not use if safety seal is broken.

Any resemblance to actual persons, living or dead, is unintentional and purely coincidental. This warranty gives you specific legal rights which vary from state to state. Sorry, we cannot be responsible for errors in typing, typography, or photography. The possibility of electrical shock does exist if you remove the cover and leave any of the devices plugged in and/or turned on. Be sure to unplug the device from the power outlet and clean only with a soft, dry cloth. Keep away from moisture, rain, snow, gloom of night, and so forth. User assumes full responsibility.

The Surgeon General of the United States has warned that smoking this product could be hazardous to your health and that the best safeguard, second only to abstinence, is the use of a condom. Except as provided herein, no employee, agent, franchisee, dealer, or other person is authorized to give any warranties of any nature. Some states do not allow the limitation or exclusion of incidental or consequential damages, so the above may not apply to you.

We make no warranty as to the design, capability, capacity, or suitability for use except as provided in this paragraph. Do not fold, mutilate, or spindle. Money orders or cashier's check only. Terms and specifications may change without notice. All returns must be accompanied with a Credit Return Authorization number on shipping carton.

To avoid accidental erasure, remove appropriate tab or cover write-protect notch with tape. No part of this message covered by the copyright herein may be reproduced or copied in any form or by any means—graphic, electronic, or mechanical, including photocopying, recording, taping, or information storage and retrieval systems—without written permission of the author and publisher. No admittance by anyone under 17 unless accompanied by an adult. Shut off engine.

Do not puncture, incinerate, or store above 120 degrees Fahrenheit. Avoid contact with eyes and skin and avoid inhaling vapors. Do not clean with abrasives and do not use on suede, leather, vinyl, or plastic or allow to come in contact with paint finish or chrome.

Information in this message is subject to change; see your representative for the latest information. An equal housing lender. Do not leave unattended. Live, except on the West Coast.

Connect ground wire to avoid shock. Do not remove protective covering. Price and availability subject to change. Four-week clearance on personal checks. Compatibility not guaranteed. Add 3 percent for Visa and MasterCard, 5 percent for American Express. Texas residents add 8.25 percent sales tax. Color monitor not included. Do not remove protective cover. Do not remove this tag under penalty of law. Return shipments are subject to a restocking fee. Add 3 percent for shipping and handling. We reserve the right to substitute equivalent items. Bridge freezes before highway.

Payment in U.S. currency only. Warranty does not cover accidental damage, misuse, misapplication, or damage resulting from modification or service other than an authorized service center. Minimum order $10.00; some shipments subject to additional freight. Watch for fallen rock. An equal opportunity employer. No shoes, no shirt, no service.

The purpose of this warning is to advise service personnel that using anything but factory-specified components may affect the approval or safety of the unit. It is recommended that only direct replacement parts be used, and that extreme care be taken in servicing items in hazardous or potentially hazardous locations.

UL approval requires that only the specified battery for which the unit was designed is used. Use of any other battery may invalidate the UL listing. Substitute of components may impair intrinsic safety. Do not recharge mercury batteries and do not dispose of batteries in fire as an explosion may occur.

Furthermore, the purchase or use of this product or service shall not be deemed to grant either directly or by implication, estoppel, or otherwise, any license under the normal nonexclusive royalty free license to use that arises by operation of law in the sale of a product.

Caution: Federal law prohibits the transfer of this product to any person other than the patient for whom it was prescribed and the law further prohibits dispensing without a prescription. (Harmful if swallowed and minor allergic skin reaction may occur whether swallowed or administered to any portion of the body.) Take with food or milk.

Note: This warning label may self-destruct and/or the paper on which it is printed can burn if placed in an environment capable of combustion (i.e., where oxygen and an ignition source are available). If this document/label should ignite, place in a nonflammable container, remove to a safe area, preferably out-of-doors, and either extinguish using methods approved by fire safety codes in your area and the State Fire Marshall's Office or cover container with a fireproof material to eliminate oxygen supply to burning substance.

Offer limited to one coupon per specified product. Any other application constitutes fraud. Reproductions will not be honored.

If this document is burning, do not inhale fumes or permit smoke to get in your eyes nor should you touch the material at any time.

We offer no extensions or exceptions to the manufacturer's warranty policies. All defective products shipped by us will be handled in accordance with the manufacturer's stated warranty terms in the owner's manual of the defective product.

We reserve the right to correct any shipping error. Any customer receiving an incorrect product, which is not the product ordered, must contact us within five working days after receiving the incorrect product to obtain return authorization. The product must be returned within twenty-one days. After receipt, the product will be promptly inspected to ensure it is in "new condition." After inspection, we will promptly reship the product at our expense.

Products shipped but not accepted will be refunded less a restocking fee of 10 percent of the original purchase price but not less than ten (10) dollars. Second, shipping costs will also be deducted from the refund. We ship only *new* products; therefore, once a customer orders and accepts an order it cannot be returned for a refund or credit, as it is then considered *used* merchandise.

To avoid danger of suffocation, do not use in cribs, beds, carriages, or playpens. This warranty does not cover misuse, accident, lightning, flood, tornado, tsunami, volcano eruption, earthquake and other Acts of God, neglect, damage caused by improper installation, incorrect line voltage, improper or unauthorized repair, broken antenna or marred cabinet, missing or altered serial numbers, blasting by mine crews, jack-hammering, or sonic boom vibrations and customer adjustments that are not covered in the instruction book.

Warranty valid only on products purchased and used in the United States. Warranty is *not* valid if incident occurs owing to an airplane crash, ship sinking or taking on water, motor vehicle crashing, or because of dropping item. This warranty does not cover fallen rock, leaky roof, broken glass, or mud slide, forest fire, or projectile (which can include, but not be limited to, arrows, bullets, shot, BB's, shrapnel, lasers, napalm, torpedoes or emissions of X rays, Alpha, Beta & Gamma rays, darts, knives, stones, etc.).

Liability for loss, delay, or damage to baggage is limited, unless a higher value is declared in advance and additional charges are paid. A coat, umbrella, pocketbook, camera, binoculars, infant food, and reading material for the trip are carried free and not included in the free baggage allowance. Baggage is subject to tariffs, including limitations of liability therein contained.

Passenger shall comply with government travel requirements, present exit and entry and other required documents, and arrive at airport by the time fixed by carrier or, if time is not fixed, early enough to complete departure procedures.

No agent, servant, or representative of carrier has authority to alter, modify, or waive any provision of this contract.

No merchandise will be accepted without a current return authorization number clearly shown on the outside of the package. Return authorizations are obtained through our Customer Relations Department.

"Lovely to look at, delightful to hold; but if you break it, consider it sold."

The user takes full responsibility for everything and anything that could and/or does go wrong resulting in any kind or type of problem, difficulty, embarrassment, loss of money or goods or services or sleep or anything else whatsoever. We are not responsible for lost articles.

The preceding was a paid political announcement.

(The preceding Universal Disclaimer [UD] was assembled by Joseph E. Badger of Santa Claus, Indiana, who proposes that it appear on all new products. He was kind enough to allow the Murphy Center, which assumes no responsibility for its use, to pioneer its use as a book disclaimer.)

INDEX

Abstinence. Miller's.
Absurdity. Bombeck's.
Academia. Colburn's, Cross's,
Farbinger's, Fenster's, Gray's,
Issawi's, Kennevan's, Lilla's,
Phillip's.
Accents. Cohn's, West's.
Accomplishment. Andersen's.
Accountability. Ellenson's.
Accounting. Accounting,
Grollinger's, Poe's.
Acting. Feldman's.
Action. Larson's.
Additions. Alida's.
Adjustment. Ancient.
Advertising. ACW's, Advertising,
Bokum's, Ebert's, O'Shee's.
Advice. Advice, Amis's, Brecht's,
Clifton's, Dull's, Field's,
Granger's, Hynes's.
Age. (p. 2), Blake's, Fraser's,
Granger's, Humpert,
McCormick's, Milligan's,
Nineteenth, Szasz's, White's,
Willets.
Agendas. Couch's, Kagan's.
Agriculture. Gill's.
Air-Conditioning. Levin's.
Air Force. Air Force.
Airplane / Aviation. Airline,
Collins's, Crescimbeni's,
Fowler's, Goldthwait's,
Gunter's, Hanlon's, Hoff's,
Moore's, Morgan's, Reinstedt's,
Smith's, Vest's, Walter's,
Wilson's.
Alcohol. Alcoholic, Breslin's,
Bunn's, Hewett's, Koch's.
Ambiguity. Addis's, Muzik's.

Analysis. Lawson's.
Anger. Horowitz.
Animals. Goldthwait's, Sally's.
Anonymity. Anonymity.
Answers. Andersen's, Ryder's.
Anthropolgy. Jones's.
Antiques. Craig's.
Apartments. Specht's.
Apathy. Paul's.
Apology. Gallagher's.
Appearance. Doris's.
Appliances. Morgan's.
Appreciation. Diminishing.
Archaeology. Boyle's, Liggett's.
Architecture. Jones's, Moynihan's.
Argument. Harlan's.
Army. Advice, Ben's, Draftees,
First.
Art. Lopez, Munning's.
Assumption. McKenna's, Shorris's.
Asthma. Comer's.
Astrology. Knowlton's.
Astronomy. Fraknoi's, Gill's,
Knowlton's.
Atmosphere. Clovis's.
Author. Asa's, Bakalar's.
Automatic / Automation.
"Automatic," Parkinson's.
Automotive. (p. 6), Andrea's,
Avery's, Badger's, Belcher's,
Beton's, Boswell's, Burns's,
Clifton's, Corrales's, Couch's,
Cynthia's, Ellis's, Evans's,
Hall's, Hansen's, Hardie's,
Hertz's, Hiestand's, Hoffman's,
Jeff's, Just's, Kibble's,
Kroeger's, Leo's, McKeen's,
Newman's, Patinkin's, Petty's,
Poer's, Poorman's, Rich,

Automotive (*cont.*)
Rippetoe's, Roeper's, Sherekis's,
Soika's, Stine's, Tuppeny's,
Wexford's, Whatley's.
Average. Friedman's, Morgan's.
Avoidance. Fortner's.
Axiom. Foster's.

Baby. Alden's.
Backpacking. Clifton's.
Baldness. Burma, Lovett's.
Banking. Underwood's, West's.
Barbecue. Hilldrup's, West's.
Baseball. Berra's, Brabender's,
Durocher's, League, Ozark's,
Palmer's, Plimpton's.
Basketball. Bishop's, Plimpton's,
Woolridge's.
Bathroom. Burn's, Foster's,
Moulton's.
Beauty. Stine's.
Beer. Bunker's, Rogers's.
Behavior. Cumming's.
Belief. Hardy's.
Betrayal. Cosgrave's.
Birds. Cosnow's.
Birthdays. Leslie's.
Blacks. Ellison's.
Bladder. Kelley's.
Blame. Ellenson's.
Bluffing. Blount's.
Boats. Kraus's, West's.
Boiling. Ellis's.
Books. Almeida's, Bakalar's,
Burn's, Emerson's, Godsey's,
Goulden's, Hasting's, Irving's,
Katz's, Kirshbaum's, Knopf's,
Plimpton's, Sander's.
Boredom. Clark's, Doolittle's,
Hawkeye's.

Bosses. Confusion, DeViney's,
Gross's, Irving's, Roger's,
Rooney's.
Bottom Line. Green's.
Boxes. Pandora's.
Boy Scouts. Anon's.
Brains. Gudeman's.
Bridge. BB's.
British Army. Advice.
Budget. Issawi's.
Bureaucracy. Adler's, Backhouse's,
Bureau, Cavanagh's, Chandler's,
Federal, Grubnick's, Karl's,
Kenworthy's, Krobusek's,
Lada's, Lang's, Loren's,
Magary's, Mattsen's, Neudel's,
Seymour's, Underwood's, Van
Tassel's.
Business. Bierman's, Carvlin's,
Hepler's, J's, Knight's, Kopcha's,
Lee's, Peterson's, Sutton's.

Cadillacs. Avery's.
Camping. Leigh's, Rogers's.
Cards. BB's.
Career. Boyle's, Lucht's.
Carpentry. Chensky's, Murphy's.
Cash. Boston's, Col's.
Cat. Addis's, Clay's, Distin's,
Kissel's, Koolman's, Sally's.
Catholicism. Evans's.
Changes. Allen's, Blake's, Sod's,
Udall's.
Character. Harrel's.
Cheating. Bangs!'s.
Check. Armstrong's, Col's.
Cheese. Piper's.
Children. Achilles', Alden's, Alt's,
Anjard's, Buxbaum's, Covert,
Dickson's, Doherty's, Foster's,

Gannon's, Geist's, Helen's, Hewitt's, Hopkins's, Mom's, Myer's, O'Steen's, Peterson's, Pollyanna's, Rappo's, Raub's, Rosoff's, Sally's, Stine's, Thien's, Timothy's.

Chocolate. Batt's, Bloom's.

Christmas. Christmas, December.

Citations. Goulden's.

Cities. Holden's, Jacob's.

Civilization. Flashman's.

Cleanliness. Draftee's.

Cliché. Asa's.

Closets. Stockmeyer's.

Clothing. Doris's, Dwyer's, Formal, Helen's, Kohn's, Jolliffe's, McNulty's, Roeper's, Smith's, Stockmeyer's, Stoll's, Thoreau's.

Clowns. Hawkeye's.

Coffee. Findsen's, Gunter's, McAlister's, McKinney's, Reynold's, Rosoff's.

Collecting. Johnson's, Parson's.

Colleges / Universities. Brotman's, Farbinger's, Harmer's, Kennevan's, McKeon's, Smith's, Springer's, Thorn's, Welford's, Westmeyer's, Wilkes.

Columnists. (p. 1).

Concrete. Main's.

Committee.

Commodities. Adkins's.

Communication. Allcock's, Balliew's, Bangs!'s, Celine's, Covert, Huddleston's, Martinez's, Stine's.

Commuter. Smith's.

Competence / Incompetence. Luke's, Zimmerman's.

Compromise. Macdonald's.

Computer. Basham's, Data, Doctor, Guthery's, Jacob's, Makower's, Santulis's, Shula's, Slug's, Van Tassel's.

Confusion. Fenster's.

Congress. Galbraith's, Kelleher's, Korologos's, McCarthy's, Moynihan's, Pickle's, Rudd's, Stark.

Conservation. Brooks's.

Conservative / Liberal. Carver's, Fresco's, Greenfield's, Hall's.

Consistency. Gustafson's, Haven's.

Consolidation. Fitzloff's.

Constants. Allen's.

Consulting. Beck's.

Consumerism. Duke, Exxon, Trace's.

Contracts. Bierman's, Chuck's, Hinson's, Oristano's.

Conventions. Hanson's, Ozmon's.

Coping. Branstadt's.

Corporations. Corporate, General, Hembree's.

Correctness. Air Force.

Cost. ACW's, Alice's, Baker's, Braffman's, Holben's.

Courage. Boyle's, Maverick's.

Courtship. Neuhaus's, Weissman's.

Cowboys. Amis's.

Crap. Flory's, Hemingway's.

Creationism. Evans's.

Creativity. Alice's.

Credibility. Marsolais's.

Cricket. Dunstan's.

Crime. Abrey's, Liddy's.

Crisis. Boyd's, Gilbert's.

Criticism. Almeida's, Campbell's.

Crowds. Brogan's, Gallagher's.

Culture. Kruse's.

Customers. Byar's, Emmanuel's.

Dam. (p. 9).

Danger. Cozgriff's, Nesman's, Tristan's.

Data Processing. Data, Kroeger's, Snyder's.

Deadlines. Levy's, Pournelle's.

Death. Cooper's, Cronkite's, DeVault's, LaLanne's, Passman's, Patton's, Pryor's, Townsend's.

Debate. Hegel's.

Debt. Hoover's, Smith's.

Deception. Bangs!'s.

Decision / Decision-making. Macrae's, White's.

Definitions. "Automatic," Hegel's.

Democracy. Chaplin's, Murray's, Servan–Schreiber's.

Dentistry. McKay's, Mark's.

Design. Clifton's.

Diamond. Whitney's.

Diet. Dieter's, Ellstrand's, Elsner's, Spano's, William's.

Dilemmas. Branstadt's.

Diplomacy. Mead's.

Dirt. Fran's, Reyna, Shephard's.

Disasters. Cassandra's, Marcotte's.

Discontinuity. Collins's.

Discretion. Doctor.

Distance. McGregor's, Schaefer's.

Distinction. Milner's.

Divorce. Cynthia's, DuBow's, Marcus's.

Doctorates. Boyle's, Poole's, William.

Doctrine. Keeleric's.

Documentation. Documentation, Kingfield's, Rosendahl's.

Dog. ACW's, Canine, Clay's, Henderson's, Humphrey's, Koolman's, Krukow's, McCabe's.

Doing. Dunn's.

Do-It-Yourself. Bennett's.

Domestic Life. Albert's.

Doom / Doomsday. (p. 9), Hackett's.

Doors. Ehre's, Salak's.

Dreams. Newman's.

Drink. (p. 3), Alcoholic, Bars, Brotman's, Bunker's, Bunn's, Koch's, Meyer, Hewett's, Smith's, Tuppeny's.

Driveways. Carl's.

Dues. Dickson's, Granger's.

Dullness. DeRock's, Muir's.

Dust. Pollock's.

Ears. Boyle's.

Eating. Batt's, Ellstrand's, Harriet's.

Economics. Ackley's, Baker's, Hart's, Harwitz's, Heinlein's, Laub's, Moore's, Newlan's, Old, Quinn's, Solomon's, Steger's, Will's, Wilson's.

Editorial Laws. Bremmer's, Garreau's.

Education. Bartlesville, Bonham's, Brattman's, Brown's, Lloyd-Jones's, Lopez's, Oakland, Pollyanna's, Robinson's, Robson's, Sauget's, Thomas's, Welford's, Zipf's.

Efficiency. Beville's.

Elections. Kerr's, Knowles's, McCarthy's, Ryan's.

Electricity. Culkin's, Gongola's, Meier's, Mulfinger's.

Electronic. Albrecht's, Electronic.

Elephants. Zisla's.
Elevators. Epps's, Fassett's,
 Stasny's.
Emergency. Gretchen's.
Emotion. Fraser's.
Employee. Emmanuel's.
Energy. Brooks's, Exxon's,
 Hubbard's.
English. Bartlesville.
Enthusiasm. Diana's, Hardie's.
Entrepreneurs. Kahn's.
Environment. Broom's,
 Cassandra's.
Epigram. Asa's.
Equality. Gunn's.
Errors. Ellenson's.
Escalators. Poorman's.
Events. Allcock's, Bill's.
Evil. Bailey's.
Evolution. Babbitt's, De-
 Evolutionary.
Examples. Chuck's, Fullner's.
Excess. Lone.
Exhaustion. Baird's.
Expectation. Bloom's.
Expediency. Savage's.
Expense Accounts. Condon's,
 Thompson's.
Experience. Barbara's, Holden's.
Expert. Rajneesh's.
Explanation. Fortner, George's,
 Krukow's.
Exploitation. Barbara's.
Expression. Lichtenberg's.
Expressways. Beton's.

Factory. Barnes.
Failure. Bartol's, Canfield's,
 Fortune, Hebert's, Titanic,
 Tobin's.
Fame. Persius's.

Family. Achilles', Albert's, Alt's,
 Rogers's, Shaw's.
Fashion. Barbara's.
Fate. Crowell's.
Favors. Alinsky's.
Federal Funds / Grants. Flory's.
Feet. Jean's, Ravage's.
Ferris Wheel. Lederer's.
Fighting. McGuire's.
Filing. Berla's.
Finance. Bronfman's, Kennedy's.
Finesse. Nierenberg's.
Fingernails. Johnson's.
Fire. Federal, Humphrey's.
Fishing. Moores', Quoy's.
Flattery. Kinsley's, Poole's.
Flexibility. Hallen's Lichtenberg's,
 Zeek's.
Flies. Crock's, Evans's, Smythe's.
Flirting. Symon's.
Flooding. Napa.
Flubs. Beck's.
Folk Dancing. (p. 3).
Food. Airline, Bartol's, Brewster's,
 Callie's, Clovis's, Grant's,
 Chensky's, Cockrell's, Cuomo's,
 Dieter's, Dillon's, Ellenson's,
 Fenster's, Hancock's, Harriet's,
 Holleran's, Johnson's, Kerr's,
 Leonard's, Lopez, Miller's,
 Murray's, Olly's, Pecor's,
 Quinn's, Rapoport's, Reynold's,
 Riberdy's, Roeper's, Royko's,
 Simon's, Smith's, Spano's,
 Story's, Trillin's, Whatley's,
 Wolf's.
Fools. Bodine's, Helmer's, Mark's,
 Sam's.
Football. Eddie's, Elway's,
 McGee's, McLaughlin's, Miller's,
 Plimpton's, Principal's,

Football (*cont.*)
Reidling's, Thomas's.
Forecasting. Goodhardt's,
Rothman's.
Formal Attire. Formal.
Fortune cookies. (p. 4), Fortune.
Freeway. Ellis's, Hebert's.
Friendship. Gallagher's, Rogers's.
Frustration. Silverman's.
Fudgsicles. (p. 5).
Future. Crenna's.

Garage Sale. Pope's.
Garbage. Cagle's, Janitorial,
Poorman's.
Garden. Bennett's, Blackwell's,
Dickson's, Farmer's, Gibson's,
Gill's, Hauser's, Horowitz,
Jewell's, Surprenant's.
Gasoline. Kibble's, Stine's.
Generalization. Rathbun's.
Genius. Alice's.
Genuine. Hammer's.
Geography. Emery's.
Geometry. Baker's.
Gifts. Piper's.
Glasses. Drakenberg's.
Glue. Gilbert's, Smith's.
Goals. Addis's.
Golf. (p. 9), Dickson's, Nineteenth,
Plimpton's, Quinn's.
Government. Baker's, Brooks's,
Bureau, Chism's, Cuomo's,
Federal, Haldane's, Marshall's,
O'Toole's, Posner's Sheehan's,
Straus's, Wyle's.
Governors. Baker's.
Grammar. Bob's.
Grandchildren. Gannon's, Rosoff's.
Grants. Baker's.
Grass. Gibson's.

Greed. McMullin's.
Greenhouse Effect. (p. 9).
Groups. BB's.
Guests. Holliday's, Willey's.
Guilt. Beichman's, Gross's.
Gynecology. McGarry.

Habits. David's.
Hair. Cooper's, Distin's, Maine,
Roeper's.
Halley's Comet. (p. 8).
Hands. Fran's.
Happiness. Camus's, Reach's.
Hardware. Anderson's.
Harassment. Pompey's.
Harvard. Dolan's.
Hats. Wearing.
Health. Cochran's, Cohen's.
Hearing. Sandia.
Heckler's. Harlan's.
Height. Anjard's.
Heredity. Achilles', Van Dongen's.
Hero. Fast.
Hiccups. Roeper's.
Hierarchy. Driscoll's, Gramm's,
Hebert's, Kramer's, Lovell's,
McCabe's, Whipple's.
History. Bettman's, Grice's.
Hobbies. Brattman's.
Holes. Grissom's.
Home. Albert's, Alice's, Alida's,
Caroline's, Dykema's, Elliott,
Hilldrup's, McConnell's,
Rooney's, Willey's.
Honesty. Laurel's, Parson's.
Horses. Kempley's, McGoorty's,
Temp's.
Horticlture. Bennett's.
Hospitals. Long's, Mom's,
Ragucci's, Turner's.
Hot. Jensen's.

Hotel. Dickson's, Greene's.
Hubris. Bower's.
Human Condition. Cosgrave's,
Cowan's, Crinklaw's,
Hassinger's, McCaffery's,
Mead's, Melbourne's, Meyer's,
Niebuhr's, Rooney's, Rudd's,
Smith's, Tim's, Warren's,
Warson's.
Human Statistics. Chaipis's.
Humility. Gene's, Kime's, Zais's.
Hydrogen. Ellison's.

Ice Cream. Elliot's, Rainbow,
Seleznick's.
Ideas. Amos's, Breslin's,
Hesting's.
Ignorance. Bentov's, Sybert's.
Illness. Cohen's, McGee's.
Image. Alden's, Beck's.
Immortality. Grollinger's.
Immutables. Immutability.
Improvement. Clarke's, Hutber's,
Rogers's.
Incest. Bax's (p. 3).
Income. Alice's.
Incompetence. Hardie's.
Index. James.
Indignation. Krauthammer's.
Industrial. Barnes, Industrial.
Inertia. Air Force, Reisner's.
Inflation. Cranston's, Manning's.
Influence. Dull's.
Information. Bentov's, LeGuin's,
Snyder's.
Insects. Tom's.
Inspection. Kass's.
Institutions. Hoffer's.
Insurance. Cochran's, Insurance,
Webster's.
Intellectuals. Beichman's.

Intelligence. Alex's, Callen's,
Carlisle's, Condon's, Dean-Boyd,
Hall's, Pennsylvania.
Intentions. Peachum's.
Interest. Cagle's.
Investments. Bronfman's, Dines's,
Tom's.
I.Q. Alex's, Callen's, Carlisle's,
Kraus's.
Irony. Daniel's.
Itching. Gomme's.

Jive, Hewitt's.
Jobs. Denham's.
Jokes. Bloom's, Whatley's,
Young's.
Journalism. Bagdikian's,
Chapman's, Davis's, Kerr's,
Liebling's, Reston's, Runyon's,
Schorr's.
Judgment. Dawn's.
Junk. Rist's, Roddenberry's.
Justice. Chapman's.

Kissing. Holmes's.
Knives. Siegel's.
Knowledge. Allen's, Bentov's,
Cerf's, Fraraccio's, Gray's,
Holloway's, Lichtenberg's,
Swain's.
Kohoutek. (p. 8).

Lament. Plotnick's.
Language. Adler's, Bartlesville,
Chavarria–Aguilar's, Cohn's,
Paper's, Whatley's.
Laughter. Black's, Lockhart's,
Smith's.
Laundry. Cotter's, Halperin's.
Law / Lawyers. Bloom's, DuBow's,
Herberrger's, Kelly's, Ladof's,

Law / Lawyers (*cont.*)
Lament, Lawyer's, Marshall,
Montero's, Murray's.
Leadership. Clark's.
Learning. Gray's.
Legal Advice. (p. 5).
Letters. Bailey's, Brian's,
Claudia's, Cox's, Issawi's,
Linden's, Marsolais's.
Liberals / Conservatives. Fresco's,
Greenfield's, Hall's, Moyer's,
Rippetoe's.
Library. Alkula's, Hasting's,
Heisey's.
Lies. Corrales's, Liebermann's,
Rizzo, Shaw's, Todd's.
Life. Alex's, Allen's, Andersen's,
Blake's, Brook's, Bunn's,
Cooper's, Evan's, Fraser's,
Greene's, Hovancik's (p. 3),
Howard's, Kramer's, Lopez,
Mame's, Mintz's, Mintzlaff's,
Missinne's, Munning's, Peter's,
Smith's, Uncle, Warren's,
West's, Willis.
Lighting. Alden's, Greene's,
Mason's, Pfeifer's.
Limitations. Ozark's.
Lines. McCormick's.
Liquid. Cooper's.
Lobbying. Kenworthy's, Stark.
Location. Brenner's, Eddie's.
Locker. Jardine's, Jim.
Logic. Dunstan's, Lois's, West's.
Lone Ranger. Brady's.
Longevity. Hinshaw's.
Loss / Lost. Alicia's, Bastl's,
Berla's, Helen's, Hertz's,
Hinson's, Joliffe's, Juall's,
McAfee's, Manning's, Miller's,
O.J.'s, Reid's, Ritchie's.

Love. Ann's, Brown's, Fraser's,
Ragucci's.
Luck. Amundsen's, Dorothea's,
Horton's, Stern's.
Lunch. Condon's.
Luxury. Wright's.

Machine. Guthery's, Helen's,
Milroy's.
Magazine. ACW's, Depuy's,
Kinsley's, Krantz's, Pat's, Pirus.
Mail. Armstrong's, Byar's, Gill's,
Hale's, Riberdy's, Sally's,
Torch's.
Man. Peter's, Renning's.
Management. Abley's, Aman's,
Boyd's, Cavalary, Cavanagh's,
Condon's, Invisible, J's,
Mahon's, Heinemann's,
Hoffnagle's, Uncle, Zisla's.
Manufacturing. Grollinger's.
Marketing. Carlin's.
Marriage. Abley's, Agel's,
Carvlin's, Cher's, Churchill's,
Crinklaw's Horowitz, Jump's,
Lipsett, Mary's, Neudel's, New,
Scanlan's, Stapley's, Stine's.
Marxism. Helprin's.
Matchmaking. Jacobson's.
Math. Katz's, Lawton's.
Matter. Boehm's.
Media. Beck's.
Medicine. Advertising, Briggs's,
Futch's, Haslem's, Kesulab's,
Long's, Murphy's, O'Steen's,
Piper's, Rappo's, Rosato's,
Sally's, Seleznick's, Solomon's,
Stump's, Teller's, Torch's,
Tromberg's, Turner's, Vernooy's,
White's.
Mediocrity. Crudup's, McGarry's.

Meetings. Colburn's, Condon's, Foley's, General, Sheehan's, Torch's.

Memory. Haven's.

Men. Adams's, Lightfoot's, Scott's.

MENSA. Gudeman's.

Mental Health. Sutton's, Turcotte's.

Mess. Nestor's.

Mice. Addis's.

Military. Anon's, Buxbaum's, Cavalry, Goulden's, Hall's, Sadat's, West's.

Milk. Adkins's.

Mind. Albrecht's, Lander's, Lightfoot's, Manchester's, Old.

Minorities. Sisley's.

Miseries. MacEwan.

Mistakes. Boyle's, Dale's, Reynold's, Tussman's, Wall, Yearwood's, Zawada's.

Mistress. Haught's.

Moderation. Tillinger's.

Modesty. Galbraith's, O'Harro's.

Money. Alice's, Baird's, Bakalar's, Boyle's, Burns's, Dart's, Foster's, Gold's, Graziano's, Gross's, Hewitt's, Hunt's, Issawi's, Jacobson's, John's, Kernan's, Klein's, Lauder's, McCabe's, Merilyn's, Paliwoda's, Penny, Schrumpf's, Swanson's, Tom's, Tron's, Truman's, Whatley's.

Morality. Corporate.

Motel. Dickson's.

Mothers. Nichol's, Rippetoe's, Sister.

Motion. Gordon's, Henderson's.

Motivation. Pitsinger's.

Motorcycles. Haught's.

Movies. Captain, Ebert's, Fenster's, Hanlon's, Kempley's, Kesulab's, Kostal's, Moore's, Poer's, Poe's, Sam, Swanson's, Tom's.

Moving. Alicia's, Rae's.

Multiplicity. Ensminger's.

Murphy Center for the Codification of Human and Organizational Law. (pp. 1–11).

Murphy's Law. (pp. 6–10), Gayer's, Laver's, Murphy's.

Murphy's Law, Exceptions to. (pp. 6–10).

Music. Boucher's, Burns's, Hall's, Holliday's, Klein, Last, Murray's, Patinkin's, Rock, Roubin's, Shively's, Story's.

Mystique. Jeff's, Kusche's.

Myth. Johnson's.

Name. Beste's, Boxmeyll's, Boyle's, Fuchs's, Margo, Nusbaum's, Skye's.

National Security. Celine's, Reagan's, White's.

Nationalism. Chesterton's.

Nature. Clovis's, Dean's, Heilson's.

Navy. Allen's, Navy.

Nevers. Brodersen's, Daugherty's, Hazlitt's, McNulty's, Nevers, Vogel's, Weiss's.

New York. Brotman's, Dixon's.

News. (p. 5), Bagdikian's, Beck's, Brady's, Bremner's, Harris's, Nanna's.

Nicknames. Boxmeyll's.

Nitroglycerin. (p. 8).

Noses. Fran's.

Nostalgia. Lodge's.

Obesity. Amis's, Lytle's, Piper's,
Whatley's.
Objects. (p. 4), Alicia's.
Observation. Newchy's.
Obviousness. Bear's.
Ocean. Boucher's.
Odds. Korologos's.
Office Rules. Ferguson's,
Vogel's.
Official. Hammer's.
Oil. Hubbard's, Industrial, Servan–
Schreiber's.
Opera. McCabe's.
Opinion. Allen's, Avery's,
Trumm's.
Opportunity. Bishop's.
Optimism. Carson's, Higgins's.
Organization. Conway's,
Denham's, Density, Fitzloff's,
Hinshaw's, Klein's, McConnell's,
Menkuss's, Michel's, Neudel's,
Organizational, Tiger's, Weiss's.
Ovation. Wade's.
Oxymoron. Boston's.

Pain. Harrel's.
Paint. Davis's, Ritchie's.
Paper / Paperwork. Grubnick's,
Hale's, Karl's, Kington's.
Parachuting. Brown's.
Paradox. Gudeman's.
Parenting. Alt's, Joliffe's,
Rippetoe's, Toner's.
Parking. Evans's, Farkus's,
Fereire's, Hansen's, Peter's,
Seeberg's, Soika's, Weber's.
Parkinson's. Parkinson's.
Parties. Collins's, Salak's.
Passion. Comer's.
Pencil. Humphrey's, Tom's,
Yearwood's.

Pens / Penmanship. Bailey's,
Depuy's, Dykema's, McKenna's.
Pentagon. (p. 10), Ferreire's.
People. People's.
Perfection. Chamfort's,
Mendenhall's, Randall's,
Rosengren's.
Pessimism. Caron's, Cohen's,
Dickson's, Foley's, Nathan's,
Pidduck's, Skole's, Story's.
Pets. Addis's, Clay's, Goldthwait's,
Koolman's.
Philosophy. C.J.'s, John's, Klutz,
Lichtenberg's.
Phonies. Randall's.
Photocopiers. Driscoll's, Joe's.
Photography. Briggs's, Harber's,
McCormick's.
Physics. ACW's, Briggs's,
Davidson's.
Pi. Throckmorton's.
Pickles. Soudriette's.
Pigeons. Addis's.
Pimples. Briggs's.
Pins. Dwyer's.
Pizza. Cockrell's, Hancock's,
Leavitt's, Ozmon's, Pepperoni.
Plagiarism. Kass's.
Planning. Hackett's, McDougal's.
Poker. BB's, Buffett's, Hauser's.
Police. Badger's.
Policy. Klutz.
Politics. Ackley's, Anderson's,
Beck's, Byrd's, Carson's,
Celine's, Chaplin's, Cooper's,
Coucheron–Aamot's, Crenna's,
Dart's, Davis's, Dugger's,
Duverger's, Hall's, Hart's,
Herold's, McAdoo's, Maddock's,
Mann's, Ottinger's, Perot's,
Peter's, Unruh's, Plato's,

Reynold's, Smith's, Smolik's,
Stapley's, Todd's, West's,
White's, Wilson's.
Pollution. Broome's.
Popularity. Allen's.
Population. Murray's.
Postal Service. Cooper's, Gill's,
Louw's.
Potential. Sawhill's.
Potluck. Welch's.
Poultry. Achilles', Brewster's,
Butler's, Doctor, Grant's,
Krotky's.
Poverty. Fast, Graziano's,
Haldane's.
Power. Quigley's, Truman's.
Presentation. Holton's.
President of the United States.
Ackley's, Boren's, Kenworthy's,
Murphy's, Pole's, Reagan's,
Willis.
Principle. Cooper's, Slevin's.
Priorities. Priorities.
Probability. Dunning's,
Lichtenberg's, Mason's,
Murray's.
Problems / Problem Solving.
Aman's, Brady's, Hewitt's,
Indiana, Mills's, Ottinger's,
Rickover's, Ryder's, Shephard's,
Seymour's, Stine's, Zmuda's.
Procrastination. Armitage's,
Hoffnagle's, Malik's.
Products / Product Development.
Beste's, Frand's.
Production / Productivity.
Doherty's, Gregory, Randall's.
Profanity. Andrea's.
Profession. Bastl's, Horton's,
Svaglic's.
Programming. Basham's.

Progress. Austin's, Ryder's, Tilp's,
van der Byl's.
Projects. Evans's.
Promotion. Jacobson's.
Proofreading. Barker's.
Propaganda. Brown's.
Proverbs. Banacek's, Feldman's,
Gramm's, Proverbs.
Public Relations. Kroeger's.
Public Service. Backhouse's.
Public Speaking. Batt's, Gren's,
Joany's, Johnson's, Kastor's,
Publishing. (p. 1), Bakalar's,
Barker's, Garreau's,
Kirshbaum's, Plimpton's,
Rothman's, Twain's, Vincent's,
West's.
Punctuation. Humphrey's.

Questions. Bishop's, Elway's,
Harrel's, Rucker's, Weed's,
White's.
Quotations. Anonymity.

Radicals. Carver's, Rolark's.
Radio. Hall's.
Rain. Hackett's, Jacobson's,
Riberdy's.
Rake. Tammeus's.
Reading. James's.
Real Estate. (p. 6), Guy's.
Reality. Hammer's, Nevin's,
Thomas's.
Reason. Naden's.
Receipt. Boehm's.
Records / Recording. Blay's,
Gurney's, Recording.
Refrigerators. Kazurinsky's,
Malik's.
Regulation. Pratt's.

Relativity. Emery's, Gannon's, Inlander's, McCabe's, McEwen's, Quisinberry's.

Religion. Allen's, Bangs!'s, Bishop's, Brogan's, Christmas, Morley's, Evans's, Gallup's, Louis's, Whatley's.

Rent. Jim's.

Repair. (p. 7), "Automatic," Pratley's, Raymie's.

Reporting. Bagdikian's.

Research. (p. 5), Alkula's, First, Heisey's, James's, Katz's, Muzik's.

Responsibility. Hoff's, Seckel's.

Rest. Hassell's.

Retaliation. Mayes's.

Restaurant's. Briggs's, Findsen's, Lopez, McGuire's, Means's, Murray's, Quinn's, Reiss's, Robert's, Robinson's, Stine's.

Restrooms. Dunning's, Long's, Nanna's, Prince, Shoe's.

Return. Andrea's.

Revolution. Issawi's, Rolark's.

Rights. Alinsky's.

Risk. Carvlin's.

Roads. Hoffman's, King's, Schmidt's, Sherekis's.

Roller Skating. Ackley's.

Rough Rider. Rough Rider.

Rules. Corvin's, Dobson's, Scoville's, Smith's.

Sailing. Jobson's.

Salary. Backhouse's.

Sales. Boswell's.

San Juan Capistrano. (p. 9).

Scandals. TRB's.

Satire. Lehrer's.

School. Brattman's, Thomas's.

Science. Bernstein's, Laithwaite's, Ming's, Racker's, Tammeus.

Scold. Addis's.

Scoreboard. (p. 4).

Seat. Borkon's, Cannon's, Fowler's.

Secretarial. Campbell's, Diane's, Koolman's.

Secrecy. Beville's, Helms's.

Sequels. Douskey's.

Self. Amis's.

Self-Employment. Ames's, Moran's, Rathbun's.

Self-Help. Suplee's.

Self-Praise. Scharringhausen's.

Self-Service. Bodine's.

Selling out. Marlin.

Sense. Bishop's.

Sensitivity. Jan's.

Sewing. Feldman's, Smythe's, Teaford's.

Sex. (p. 5), Ackley's, Baird's, Crinklaw's, Dickson's, Eyberg's, Gold's, Gooden's, Issawi's, Nolan's, Paulson's.

Shoes. Blackwell's, Brock's, Burns's, Carson's, Holleran's, Levey's, Lindvig's, Mendonca's, Shoe.

Shopping. Kraver's, McSpiritt's, MacPherson's, Rosen's.

Showing Up. Allen's.

Silence. Logan's.

Simplicity. Dottie's.

Sin. Campbell's.

Sincerity. Dr. J.'s.

Sitting. Alden's.

Sleep. Harkness's, Honcho's, Hynes's, LeGuin's, Leterman's, Ruby's.

Slogans. Beck's.

Small Stuff. Inskip's.

Smell. Epps', Spring's.
Smile. Fields's, Rabinowitz's.
Smoking. Elsner's, Hanlon's,
  Hewitt's.
Snobs. Verplanke's.
Social Security. Regan's.
Sociology. (p. 3), Chuck's, Gunn's,
  Leavitt's.
Solitude. Hepburn's.
Solution. Fenwick's, Graziano's,
  Humphrey's, Lathrop's.
Sophistication. Corrales's.
Soup. Dillon's.
Speech. Bangs!'s, Batt's, Bear's,
  Brother, Martin's, Stine's.
Spelling. Fuchs's, Kesulab's.
Spills. Briggs's, Stoebner's.
Sports. Cannon's, Kelley's,
  Oldfield's, Plimpton's, Stones's,
  Thomas's, Woolridge's,
  XXcellent.
Squirrel. Cosnow's.
Stairs. Italian.
Standards. Boyle's.
Staples. Critchfield's, Hitchcock's.
Statistics. Burgy's, Gallup's, Jack,
  Martinez's, Moynihan's,
  Prince's, Skole's.
Stereo. Beste's, Blay's, Lloyd.
Stories. Dolan's.
Stubbornness. Bunn's.
Study. Pajari's.
Stupidity. Ellison's, John's, Slay's.
Subway. Carmel's.
Success. Allen's, Ames's, Banks',
  Beville's, Canfield's, Douskey's,
  Evans's, Leterman's,
  Lichtenberg's, Louw's, Nichol's,
  Russell's, Sacremento, Sutton's.
Suicide. Peterson's.
Surprises. Rosenau's, Rosendahl's.

Survival. Putt's.
Swallows. (p. 8).
Sweepstakes. January's.
Swimming. King's.
Switchboard Operators.
  Balliew's.
System. Parkins's.

Table Tennis. Reisman's.
Talent. Allen's, Hinshaw's.
Tape. Gill's.
Tax. Buchwald's, Jones's, Mix's,
  White's.
Taxis. Taylor's.
Teacher / Teaching. Brattman's,
  Grice's, Harrison's, Old,
  Peacock's, Pfister's, Principal's,
  Teacher.
Technology. Stine's.
Teenagers. Anjard's, Burns's,
  Immutability.
Teeth. Brinnick's, Burno's,
  Meuse's, Missinne's, Vlachos.
Telephone. Bailey's, Balliew's,
  Batt's, Brady's, Dunn's,
  Ferguson's, Fullner's,
  Grewenfield's, Gustafson's,
  Helen's, Huddleston's, Irving's,
  Maller's, Ozmon's, Radcliffe's,
  Royko's, Tom's, Wilson's.
Television. (p. 9), Bailey's,
  Barbour's, Bianculli's, Boliska's,
  Collin's, Confusion, Eling's,
  Hagman's, Hellinger's,
  Kitman's, Markgraf's,
  Roddenberry's, Royko's,
  Schmitz's, Shales's, Staedler's.
Temptation. Humpert.
Tennis. Agel's.
Termite. Hilldrup's.
Tests. Alex's, Rippetoe's.

Texas. Brotman's, Dolan's, Dugger's, Henderson's.
Theater. Borkon's, Corrales's, Lunt's.
Theory. Huygen's, Macfarlane's.
Thermodynamics.
Thermodynamics.
Thought. Cuomo's, Evans's, Silverman's.
Throwing. Salier's.
Tickets. McBain's.
Time. Allcock's, Born, Chism's, Elliott, Flory's, Hanson's, Harvey's, Hewitt's, Mel's, Munro's, Pratt's, Tobin's, West's.
Toys. Jolliffe's, Raub's.
Toes. Corrales's, Hofstadter's.
Tools. Clark's, Hagan's, Main's, Saul's.
Track. Stones's.
Traffic. Belcher's, Carmel's, Critchfield's, Davis's, Jeff's, Just's, McCabe's, Peterson's, Poer's, Rinzler's, Schumer's, Szadokierski's, Tobin's, Willis.
Trains. Carrington's, Gramm's.
Travel / Transportation. Andrea's, Badger's, Belcher's, Ben's, Beton's, Byron's, Carrington's, Connolly's, Crescimbeni's, Fraser's, Galbraith's, Geist's, Gordon's, Gramm's, Gunter's, Kernan's, Ladwig's, Lawson's, Lewis's, Miss, Saki's, Tobin's, Travelers.
Trash. Hinson's.
Trees. Ensminger's, McPherson's.
Trouble. Nobel's.
Trust. Amis's.
Truth. (p. 4), Dabney's, Hoover's, Hoskin's, J's, Jan's, Korologo's,

Louw's, Pfeifer's, Rizzo, Whatley's.
Typing. Campbell's, Clark's.

Ukulele. Bagdikian's.
Undergarments. Quick's.
Unexpected. Doctor.
United States. (p. 3), Trudeau's.
Universe. DeVries's.

Vacations. Ann's, Haas's, Hale's, Vacation.
Vacuum-tube. Albrecht's.
Value. ACW's, Ritchie's.
Vices. Pugh's.
Victory. Amundsen's.
Virtue. Hynes's.
Vision. Depuy's, Evans's, Fraknoi's, Payack's.
Volkswagen. Ancient.
Volunteers. Holliday's.

War. Jones's.
Warnings. Broder's, Davis's, Leonard's, McCarthy's, McGorty's.
Warranties. Dick's, Shea's.
Washington, Broder's, Dabney's, Krauthammer's, Washington.
Waste. Issawi's.
Water. Culkin's, Horowitz, Italian, Lament, Robert's.
Waves. Sailor's.
Weakness. Addis's.
Wealth. Fast.
Weather. Carl's, Davidson's, DeLaney's, Durocher's, Hackett's, Harwitz's, Magary's, Moore's, Muir's, Rosendahl's.
Wheels. Corrales's, Wheel.
Wierdos. Ragucci's.